WARRIOR

WARRIOR

A Life of War in Anglo-Saxon Britain

EDOARDO ALBERT

with

PAUL GETHING

GRANTA

Granta Publications, 12 Addison Avenue, London W11 4QR

First published in Great Britain by Granta Books, 2019

A CIP catalogue record for this book is available from the British Library.

1 3 5 7 9 10 8 6 4 2

ISBN 978 1 78378 442 4
eISBN 978 1 78378 444 8

Typeset by Avon DataSet Limited, Bidford on Avon, B50 4JH

Printed and bound by CPI Group (UK) Ltd, Croydon, CR0 4YY

www.granta.com

In memory of David Whitbread
(1936–2018)

Contents

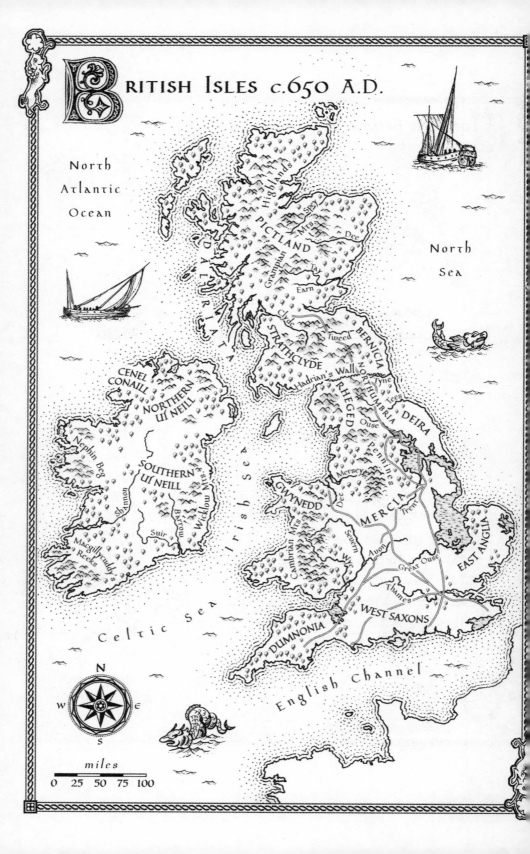

British Isles c.650 A.D.

North
Atlantic
Ocean

North
Sea

Highlands

Spey

Grampian Mts.

Dee

PICTLAND

Tay

Earn

DAL RIATA

Clyde

STRATHCLYDE

Tweed

BERNICIA

Hadrian's Wall

NORTHUMBRIA

Tyne

Tees

CENEL
CONAILL

NORTHERN
UÍ NEILL

RHEGED

DEIRA

Ouse

Pennines

Nephin Beg

SOUTHERN
UÍ NEILL

Wicklow Mts.

Mersey

Shannon

Barrow

Dee

MERCIA

Suir

GWYNEDD

Irish Sea

Trent

Macgillycuddy
Reeks

Cambrian Mts.

Severn

EAST ANGLIA

Wye

Avon

Great Ouse

Celtic Sea

Thames

WEST SAXONS

DUMNONIA

English Channel

N

W   E

S

miles

0   25 50 75 100

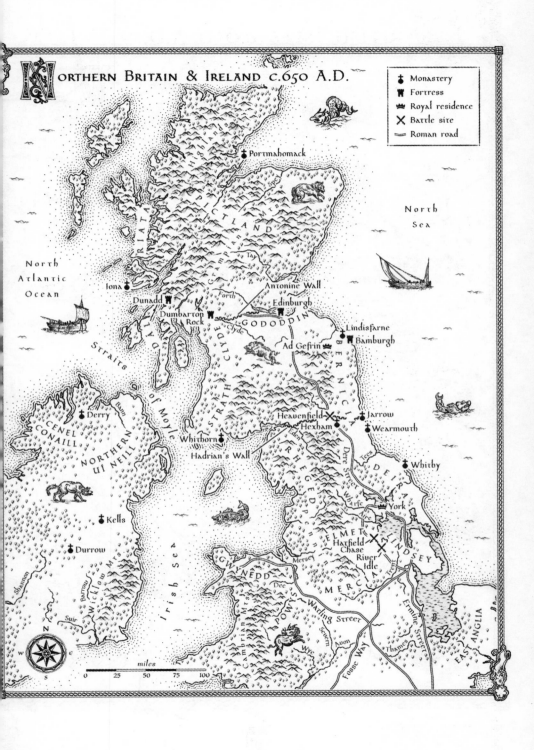

Northern Britain & Ireland c.650 A.D.

Legend:
- † Monastery
- ♜ Fortress
- ♔ Royal residence
- ✕ Battle site
- ⚊ Roman road

North Sea

North Atlantic Ocean

Portmahomack

PICTLAND

GRAMPIAN MTS

Spey

Tay

Iona

Dunadd

Dumbarton Rock

Forth

Antonine Wall

Edinburgh

GODODDIN

Clyde

STRATH CLYDE

Lindisfarne

Bamburgh

Ad Gefrin

BERNICIA

DAL RIATA

Straits of Moyle

Derry

Bann

CENEL CONAILL

NORTHERN UI NEILL

Whithorn

Hadrian's Wall

Heavenfield ✕

Hexham

Jarrow

Wearmouth

RHEGED

Eden

Derwent

Tees

Whitby

DEIRA

Dere Street

Wharfe

York

Kells

Irish Sea

Wicklow Mts

Barrow

Durrow

R. Shannon

Suir

GWYNEDD

Dee

Mersey

ELMET

Hatfield Chase

River Idle

LINDSEY

Cambrian Mts

POWYS

Watling Street

MERCIA

Trent

Severn

Wye

Avon

Fosse Way

Ermine Street

Thames Street

EAST ANGLIA

miles

0   25   50   75   100

N W S E

North Sea

HOLY ISLAND

1.

St Aidan's Church

Pilgrim's Causeway · Lindisfarne Monastery

BERNICIA

Low Tide

Bamburgh·

BAMBURGH CASTLE c.650 A.D.

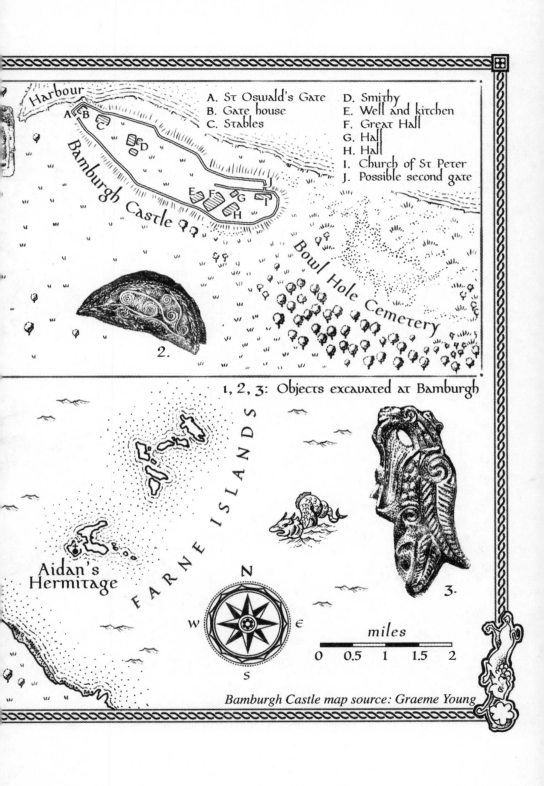

Harbour

A. St Oswald's Gate
B. Gate house
C. Stables
D. Smithy
E. Well and kitchen
F. Great Hall
G. Hall
H. Hall
I. Church of St Peter
J. Possible second gate

Bamburgh Castle

Bowl Hole Cemetery

2.

1, 2, 3: Objects excavated at Bamburgh

FARNE ISLANDS

Aidan's Hermitage

3.

N
W   E
S

miles
0   0.5   1   1.5   2

Bamburgh Castle map source: Graeme Young

I

A Warrior . . .

People stop when they see an excavation. They stop and look and then, mostly, they move on. Some ask a few questions before going about their business. But there are those who stop and look without saying anything, then walk past only to return ten minutes later. These are the people who have something to say. Some theory of their own as to what might be found, some idea they would like the archaeologists to investigate. Or sometimes they have a memory.

The lady was old with alert and penetrating eyes. She'd walked past with her dog and stopped to look, silently, at the small team of diggers arranged across the bottom of the trench, a series of hump-backed mounds sifting sand and earth. But then she returned when they stopped for tea and paused beside the trench.

'I used to come here when I was a little girl,' she said.

She looked down at the archaeologists with the upright deportment of an Edwardian lady and a voice that could have polished the glass after cutting it. She told the archaeologists that her family had lived in the village for generations before moving away, but she had come back to visit a cousin.

'We would picnic on the beach and my grandfather, an antiquarian, would go off and dig.' She patted the dog sitting beside her. 'He found something. A skeleton.'

The archaeologists were used to this sort of comment. While the rest of the team rested, the lead archaeologist put on his interested face.

'It was curled up like a baby, lying on its side. Only the strange thing was, it had no head. Where the skull should have been there was a stone, a big stone. Do you think the stone was a memorial that was put there to commemorate the dead man?'

'Maybe.' It was one of those precious hot summer days in Northumberland, when the sun beats down endlessly from a huge sky. Digging is thirsty work on days like that. 'What did he do with the skeleton?'

The old lady gestured off into the distance: the gesture of a northerner indicating and dismissing the south in the same movement.

'When my grandfather finished excavating the skeleton, he sent it off to one of the museums in London, but he didn't hear anything back. I don't know what happened to it after that.'

The lead archaeologist thanked her for the information. 'If you ever find out anything more, please tell us.' He put down his mug of tea. 'Time I got back to work.'

The old lady walked away, the dog at her side, but her words lingered, nudging a memory at the back of the archaeologist's mind of what had first brought him here: a hand smoothing out the first edition (1865) of the Ordnance Survey map on the kitchen table and tapping an area just south-east of the castle.

Old Danish Burying Grd.

The lady's antiquarian grandfather might have consulted that very map. The archaeologist stepped out of the trench, looking in the direction the old lady had gone, but she and her dog had disappeared.

The archaeologist shading his eyes and peering into the distance was Paul Gething. A Yorkshireman, he had come up to Northumberland to dig at Bamburgh Castle at the invitation of an old friend and fellow archaeologist, Graeme Young, who had secured permission from Lady Armstrong, chatelaine of the castle, to open a couple of test pits in the area.

This was the second time Bamburgh Castle had been excavated. The first was in the 1960s and early 1970s when Brian Hope-Taylor, one of the almost legendary first generation of professional archaeologists, had dug at the castle. But Hope-Taylor had never published his findings, although the report of his excavations at Ad Gefrin, the royal hall of the kings of Northumbria in the shadow of the Cheviot Hills, had become one of the seminal foundation texts of archaeology as a science. Graeme Young had grown up in Blyth, a few miles south of Bamburgh, and the castle, squatting on a huge outcrop of granite commanding land and sea and sky, had filled his childhood dreams and school holidays. Having obtained permission from Lady Armstrong to dig on the site, Graeme had invited Paul Gething to join him to see how much Hope-Taylor had excavated and if there was anything that he had missed.

The Danish Burial Ground was one possibility. There was no mention in published or unpublished sources of Hope-Taylor having found anything like this. Later editions of the Ordnance Survey map omitted any mention of a burial ground, but there must have been something there for those first cartographers to label it on their map. Only it couldn't be Danish – even when the Norsemen conquered York and established the Danelaw, the old Anglo-Saxon kingdom based at Bamburgh Castle had remained unconquered and independent.

Visit Bamburgh Castle today and you will see the castle squatting atop the great extrusion of dolerite that provides it with such a commanding position over land and sea. Holiday-makers tend to be more attracted by the vast expanse of beach that opens out in front of the castle. At low tide, the gently shelving sand stretches for three or four hundred yards out to sea, while at high tide the grey waves wash up to the bottom of the extensive system of sand dunes that surround the castle and stretch away to the south, most of the way to Seahous-es, the next settlement on the Northumberland coast. The dunes around the castle are huge, their shifting slopes stitched together by the questing roots of marram grass, sand couch, red fescue and lyme grass, and they have been designated a Site of Special Scientific Interest by English Nature. Hollows amid the dunes become sweltering suntraps in the summer, while children practise sand-skiing and dune-running down the slopes on to the beach. But all of this is new. Two centuries ago, there was just beach and castle: no dune field. Then, in the early part of the nineteenth century, in 1817, one sweep of the weather pencil dumped thousands of tons of sand on the coast during an apocalyptic storm, creating overnight the dune fields around Bamburgh Castle.

The memory of the burial ground endured long enough for it to be included in the first edition of the Ordnance Survey map but the later editions no longer mark it. It was buried under twenty or thirty feet of sand. But, in 1996, when the founders of the Bamburgh Research Project (BRP) gathered at Graeme Young's house to discuss where to excavate, the burial ground marked on the old Ordnance Survey map was a strong contender.

There were four of them then: Graeme Young, Phil Wood, Rosie Whitbread and Paul Gething. Having learned more about the site, the archaeologists now knew why the burial ground had been lost. But could they find it again? If it was under the dunes, then it was lost; they couldn't dig down that far even if English Nature gave their blessing to disturb an SSSI. But there was another possibility. A ridge led down from the castle towards a depression, named rather accurately the Bowl Hole. Before the great storm, the ridge would have been the first raised ground beyond the beach. Although they knew the burial ground was not Danish, the archaeologists still thought the people buried there would have been seafarers. What better place for the dead to rest than somewhere in sight of the sea and the rising sun?

So, armed with spades, shovels, trowels, sieves and 30-metre tapes they set off along the ridge. Graeme and Phil stopped at various points along the way, convinced that the burial ground would be on the ridge itself, but Paul continued downwards with Rosie Whitbread and Ellie Hambleton. Rosie had been instrumental in getting the funding for the Bamburgh Research Project; Ellie was a university friend doing her PhD on animal bones. She is now a lecturer in archaeology at Bournemouth University, still specialising in animal bones.

The past is buried all around us, interred beneath the earth, but by that very fact the past is diffuse because it's spread so widely. The great skill in archaeology is identifying the locations where the past is concentrated. When starting a test excavation, archaeologists normally start with a one-metre square pit to see if they have found one of those places. But a one-metre square, out in the open countryside, is a very small area; finding something interesting by this method is like trying to put the 'x' in the right place in the old spot-the-ball competitions. So what tells the archaeologist where to first push the shovel into the ground? Sometimes it's clear: a map location, a landscape feature, local records and reports. Sometimes it's a dig in the face of development, looking to see if there is anything in a particular spot that has been earmarked for building. A landscape, however, is different. The best archaeologists, Paul among them, have a skill that lets them see through the multi-layered landscape to the parts where the past might be concentrated. Paul can look at a place and paint a picture of what it used to look like. He compares it to turning the pages of a big sketchbook. Each leaf has an earlier version of the site. He looks at the site and mentally turns the pages of the past until he is at the time he wants to investigate.

Walking down the ridge from the castle with Rosie and Ellie, Paul turned the pages in his mind.

'Stop. We'll dig here.'

After setting up a one-metre grid line and marking out the square, they started digging, taking off the top soil, which was more sand than humus, until they reached the subsoil, a layer of red clay that sits under the sand and grass. This wasn't deep, only 30 centimetres or so. Then they started hitting small fragments of bone mixed with the sand and clay clumps. They had only been digging for an hour or so. Ellie was able to say immediately that the bones were not animal but human. What they had found were tiny pieces of human bone in a circle, a small, tight-packed circle about the diameter of a dinner plate. They learned later that these bones had been dug up long before when the burial ground was still in use. The bones had been uncovered when digging a new grave and the gravediggers had carefully gathered them together, put them in a bag and then reinterred them on top of the new burial. Centuries ago gravediggers treated human remains they encountered with the same respect as the newly dead they were about to bury, while unwittingly setting interpretive traps for future archaeologists. But, on that day, seeing this collection of bone pieces, Paul, Rosie and Ellie assumed they were the remnants of a cremation that had been collected and then buried.

But a bag of bones does not a burial ground make. It was a beautiful July day. They kept on digging, isolating the finds and clearing the area. As they cleared away the marram grass, they began to find stones laid on edge. The shaped dolerite immediately suggested a cist. These are stone-built ossuaries, usually made with four stone retaining walls and often with a capstone. They began cleaning off the stone, working on the assumption that the cist had been sunk to hold the bag of bones. Finding the cist suggested they were close to finding the 'Danish Burying Grd' marked on the first OS map. Paul passed word to Graeme and Phil of what they had found and the three archaeologists kept on digging through the long light of a July day.

It was 1997.

Although they didn't know it, their lives had changed. Any archaeologist worth his trowel will have excavated skeletons. But it was the suspicion that they had found the burial ground that made the day stand out. Even so, they had begun the excavation on the final weekend of the season. To investigate it properly they would have to return next year.

In the meantime they had established that the bones were human but they did not have a date for them. What they did have was a lot of tantalising but contradictory evidence. The OS map labelling the burial ground as 'Danish' argued against it being an Anglo-Saxon burial ground, although Bamburgh had remained in the control of Anglian lords throughout the two centuries of Norse control of York and the Five Boroughs (and, indeed, the earls there had played a key role in bringing down one of the most famous Viking kings of York, Eric Bloodaxe). The cist was not oriented directly east–west, so that could mean it predated the conversion to Christianity, as Christian graves are generally aligned towards the rising of the sun. So the burial ground might even predate the conversion to Christianity in the seventh century.

When they returned the following season they had a larger team and were able to widen the area of excavation from the metre square to three metres by two – large enough for any grave. They had left the bones in situ over winter, having covered them over to protect against the rigours of a Northumbrian winter. This was for two reasons: they did not want to remove the bones until they were ready to examine the area around them and they did not have a full burial licence. The law, specifically section 25 of the Burial Act 1857 and the Disused Burial Grounds Act 1884 (amended 1981), requires anyone wanting to move human remains to apply for a licence before doing so. There are licences for relatives who want to move a body to a new burial ground and licences dealing with remains that have been buried for more than a century. Today, applications are made to the Ministry of Justice but that only came into existence in 2007. Back then the Bamburgh Research Project had to apply to the coroner for a burial licence, including in their application details as to what would happen to the remains they found.

The project also informed the police, who said they were sending out an officer to determine that the bones were actually ancient. In reality, two coppers turned up, had a look about and asked Paul if the bones were old. Paul told them they were Anglo-Saxon. The two policemen had a cup of tea with the archaeologists and then went away again, calling in from time to time over the years to see how the dig was getting on.

Excavating human remains is the most dislocating piece of archaeology you can do. While the archaeological principles are the same, every so often, as you're kneeling down, brushing subsoil from bone, the realisation hits you: this was a person, a living, breathing person with his own hopes, fears, loves and dreams. But human remains also present technical challenges. When excavating a body, the first step is to remove the fill, the admixture of soil and surface material that the grave diggers shovelled back in to the ground to cover the body. However, there are particular difficulties with interpreting human remains because a body does not behave like a piece of pottery when buried under ground. Pottery, the most commonplace of all archaeological finds, remains where it was deposited, an honest if passive piece of the past. But a human body is not like that. The corpse putrefies, expands, sometimes it explodes; it is active, almost alive, under the ground.

The fear of revenants, of the unquiet dead returning to plague the living, is almost universal among human cultures. Indeed, a key aspect of funerary rites is to stop the dead person becoming a revenant. Perhaps one contributory factor towards this universal fear is the dance of decay that can cause the ground over the dead person to shift, settle, bubble and even, occasionally, erupt. This underground shifting creates unique problems when excavating a body. The fill, the soil and surface material, which was put in on top of the corpse and even layers of earth laid down later can be mixed and disrupted by the movements of the corpse layer. When the cavities of the body collapse the earth falls into the vacant space, mixing the layers above.

Once the skeleton is uncovered, it has to be cleaned down to the bone level. The archaeologist can't get underneath the bones – not until they have been lifted from the ground – and the bone itself is often in a very fragile condition. Since it's not possible to remove all the soil the archaeologist has to create a mental three-dimensional map as it is being excavated. On top of this a three-dimensional model of the human body has to be held in the mind, one adjusted for the changes that occur in bodies when they are buried. The different burial positions – crouched, foetal, supine or prone – also have to be considered. Sometimes the mental picture has to be flipped when a bone turns up in an unexpected place. So the process of excavating a grave involves the archaeologist comparing a three-dimensional model of the grave against a three-dimensional model of the human body, and rotating these until the two match.

A typical result of decomposition is that the head tilts and the jaw drops open, producing what are called 'screaming skulls'. Paul prefers to block-lift skulls – that is to lift a cube of earth containing the skull, as one whole, since this allows post-excavation examination for teeth and other remains that might be lost or misplaced if the skull is removed without its encasing soil.

Once the skeleton is completely exposed and ready to be excavated the archaeologist mentally divides it into four so that different bones, such as the fingers of the left and right hands, do not become confused. All the long limbs are bagged up individually. Fingers and toes are put into smaller bags, carefully labelled. Before this, of course, the site has been carefully photographed and mapped, and the excavating tools noted down, since tools made from different materials can notch and mark the remains. To minimise this there has been a big drive in archaeology to use bamboo tools when excavating skeletons: Paul uses either unsharpened trowels, or plastic or bamboo tools. If he is working on anything that might potentially be carbon-dated in later analysis he uses a demagnetised trowel.

Using a theodolite the remains are marked precisely on an Ordnance Survey map. As well as being photographed, drawings are made of the dig to bring out significant details in a way a photograph cannot. After everything has been bagged up the remains are put into a box and taken off site. Then the grave is excavated downwards to see if there is anything below the body, with any finds recorded and lifted. It's a complicated process, one needing sensitivity. When the Bamburgh project put in the application for a burial licence they undertook to treat the remains excavated with the utmost respect and then, when the investigation was over, to rebury them where they had found them, but deeper, so that they would be protected from any future erosion or disturbance.

Burial licence in place, the BRP reopened the dig and carefully removed the bones they had found last year before digging down further. Working on the assumption that these bones were the remains of a cremation that had been interred in a cist, they expected to find the bottom, base layer of the cist. What they actually found was more bones: a complete skeleton. This told them that they had discovered the burial ground they were looking for: one set of bones might be a solitary burial but another in the same place tells you that the site is home to the dead.

They excavated this second set of remains but left them in place while they uncovered the full extent of the grave. It was not a cist at all but a lintel grave. A proper cist has stone sides, base and lid. It is more or less a buried stone box. But this grave had the lintel without the stone sides: the grave had been dug and the lintel placed to commemorate the dead man but without the normal reinforcement of stone sides. Lintel graves are a good indicator of an Anglo-Saxon date. Pieces of the jigsaw were beginning to fall into place.

Having reached the layer of red clay where the bodies were buried, the archaeologists realised that this represented the subsoil level before the great storm. With this knowledge in place, they set about reconstructing the landscape as it had existed before the storm.

The following season, 1999, the BRP really began the broad excavations of the site, with the aid of a grant from the Society of Antiquaries. During this year and the following decade they found a number of skeletons that matched those the old lady walking her dog had described to Paul: bodies buried on their side, in a foetal or semi-foetal position, and some with no head but a stone. The stone, they realised, was put into the grave as a pillow for the dead person but by raising the head it exposed the skull to different erosion rates, leaving them to find some apparently headless bodies. The old lady and her dog never returned, so Paul could not tell her what he had found. He made enquiries with the London museums as to whether they had ever received a skeleton excavated at Bamburgh and there was some indication in the records that this was the case. But if so, the body had been lost or remains deep in storage.

It was at the end of the digging season, with only another day to go, that Paul uncovered the remains of the warrior who is the subject of this book. The season for archaeology is usually short. This is because of the climate: not only is it no fun to be sloshing around in a trench ankle deep in water but a waterlogged trench makes archaeology impossible. So apart from emergency and rescue digs, most research archaeology in Britain runs in the summer. But the other reason for the short digging season is that you need the rest of the year to evaluate what you have found and, using that information, formulate the questions you want to ask the site. The archaeologists of the BRP also needed to make a living.

While archaeology is a scientific discipline, applying some of the most cutting-edge analytical techniques as well as some very old ones, it cannot meet some of the criteria that philosophers of science require of a science. Unlike with experimental science its evidence cannot be repeated. A dig cannot be redug with a different dependent variable. This is why modern archaeology is fastidious about mapping and recording excavations: while a dig is not replicable, proper record-keeping should allow any interested archaeologist to follow the progress of an excavation.

The team had been hard at work since early in the morning, uncovering and recording a grave. Apart from a skeleton, the grave also contained a seax, the short knife (relatively speaking – anyone toting a seax today would be rapidly pulled over for carrying an offensive weapon) that was so ubiquitous among the Saxons that it gave them their name. It was possible that the grave predated the conversion of the Anglians to Christianity in the seventh century, since the general practice was for Christians to be buried unadorned for their journey into the afterlife, whereas pagans were generally sent on their way with as many grave goods as their family could afford – think of the extraordinary burial of wealth that accompanied the king buried at Sutton Hoo.

As the day warmed up, the Bowl Hole began to live up to its name, concentrating the heat and stopping all but the

merest zephyr of breeze. By mid afternoon the team was wilt-
ing. With students on the brink of expiring, Graeme and Phil
loaded them into the back of the Land Rover and juddered off
down the track and back to Seahouses for some refreshments,
leaving Paul alone in a hole in the ground. Not that Paul was
disappointed. He'd volunteered to stay behind because he
valued these times when he could work alone.

Left alone in the place of the dead, Paul began to feel a sense
of isolation unusual nowadays. Yes, over the dunes there were
many families on the beach. But few of these ever came deep
into the dune field, and fewer yet reached the area around the
Bowl Hole. He was alone in a landscape that appeared all but
untouched by the centuries that had passed since these people
were laid in the ground. Hunched over, brushing sand and grit
away, it was the sudden trickle of sand back into the trench
that pulled Paul's attention back up and out of the ground. He
sat up. The wind, a wind that had not stirred all that day, lashed
at his face. Looking to the east he saw that where before there
had been the prospect of unbroken sky, now clouds as thick
and dark as anvils piled high. To the west, the sky still showed
blue, but the storm was coming in fast. Really fast.

Of course, in this part of the world, summer storms can spring
up suddenly, but Paul had never seen anything to match this.
Even as he watched, the clear sky was blacked out. Faint and
far away came the cries of a British summer: holidaymakers on
the beach, running for cover. Day was becoming night.

Then the storm spoke. From its depths, thunder rumbled.
Sheets of light split the pressing darkness but the darkness
pressed in tighter between the lightning flashes. Standing in
the trench, Paul looked around for something to protect the
skeleton from the coming deluge and, as he did so, a thought
came to him. It was Thursday. Thor's day. He was excavating

the skeleton of a man buried when people still worshipped the God of Thunder in these islands, though for them his name was Thunor. The seax sitting upon the bones shone dull.

The thunder struck, so loud it was as if the world had cracked. The branches of the trees lashed in the sudden wind. Paul looked up to the dark thunderhead above him.

'I'll look after him.' He had made these compacts with the dead before, but always silently in his mind. This time he spoke it to the storm.

And the storm passed. It passed without a drop of rain.

When Graeme and Phil and the rest got back later, they found Paul sitting by the trench. He pointed down into the trench.

'We've got to find out about this one,' he said.

And so they did.

As archaeology has developed as a science and a technique, the questions it can ask of the dead, and expect them to answer, have grown wider (and more expensive). The first question that can be asked is, 'When did you die?'

When the result came back of the man uncovered in thunder, it was significant – AD 635. This put his death very close to the historically attested Battle of Heavenfield. However, there was no proof that he had died in this battle. It was a possibility but Paul and the team were faced with the great difficulty of archaeology: the dead have no names. The remains archaeologists excavate with such care are mute. After so many centuries, there are no headboards to tell who they were and what they did. Only dry bones.

Today archaeologists can ask the dead further questions. In addition to carbon-14 dating the project also had funding for a small number of more detailed isotopic, DNA and RNA analyses of the remains they had excavated. They sent the selection, which included the 'son of Thunder', off for analysis and got on with their work – this sort of stuff does not happen quickly.

When the results came back, two stood out. One was a young woman, in her early twenties, who had died right at the earliest reach of this burial ground, somewhere around 550. She was from Norway. Quite what a Norwegian, presumably a high-status Norwegian, was doing in Northumbria at this period, a good hundred years before there were any reported contacts between Britain and Norway, is a mystery. Had she sailed across the North Sea to cement some sort of alliance, unreported in the historical sources, between the kings in Bamburgh and one of the royal families in Norway? We don't know and, in this case, probably never will – but she served as a reminder that some people in the early medieval period travelled surprising distances. Although the possible Norwegian princess was fascinating, she raised so many unanswerable questions that she remains a frustrating enigma.

The other person who came from far away was the son of Thunder.

When an archaeologist receives a report on an isotopic analysis, it normally gives an arc of possibility, laid over geographic areas, indicating where that person might have come from. But the arc of possibility for this person mostly curved over sea, only touching land in one place. Since there was nothing to suggest that he was a merman, it meant it was possible to say with an unusual degree of certainty where he had been born.

Iona.

It's a small island lying off the long peninsula of the island of Mull that points like a finger into the Atlantic Ocean. Standing today in the port of Oban, the entry point to the Western Isles, you see a prospect of blue and green (if the sun is shining!), of mountains and hills rising from the sea, and long ridges marching to the south-west, interspersed by sea lochs. It is a landscape very different from the straight up and down coast of the eastern side of Britain between the great bights of the Humber and the Forth. And, like Norway, it is a long way from the burial ground at Bamburgh. But while Paul and the other archaeologists had no idea how a woman from Norway might have ended up buried in the north-east of England, they had a clearer idea of how a man from Iona might be buried at the capital of the kings of Northumbria. For one of these kings, the greatest of them, Oswald, had returned from exile in the kingdom that contained Iona to meet his enemies at the Battle of Heavenfield and, victorious, reclaimed the throne and changed the course of history.

Suddenly, the bones were speaking.

A leitmotif of archaeology is someone holding up their find and saying, 'This is the first time anyone's touched this for (however many) years.' It is the physical, tangible connection with the deep past. But this was the first time in his career that Paul could tie the person he had excavated to particular events and places: the bones were telling a story.

The Bamburgh Research Project has trained hundreds of young archaeologists over its history and if there's one thing these students have taken away with them it's 'The Talk'. The one Paul gives where he stands the students on the edge of a trench where they've been digging. First they stand looking down into it, and then he gets them to turn round, so they've got their backs to the excavation and they're looking out at the world.

'You don't stand on the edge of the excavation looking in. You stand on the edge of your excavation looking out.'

That's what they've all had drummed into them. Usually, Paul has given this lecture while his students have been excavating a post hole. After pottery, post holes are the most ubiquitous of archaeological finds. A post hole is exactly what it says it is: a hole where a post was. Posts, being made of wood, decay, but the holes that were dug to hold them remain. There's never any shortage of post holes, so the techniques required to excavate them are among the first things a student learns. That's often when they get 'The Talk'. It usually comes at the end of an exhausting day. Their backs are aching from being hunched over. If the day was sunny, then there's the possible spreading heat of sunburn where they forgot to put sun cream on the lower back where the T-shirt rides up as a result of being bent over. If the day was cold, their fingers are numb and there's no feeling left in their toes. And if it was wet, then their misery has gone past words.

'Your post hole is part of a building. That building is part of a village. That village is part of a locale. That locale is part of a kingdom and that kingdom is part of a polity. That polity is part of a country and that country is part of the world.'

That's when Paul stops and looks at his group of tired, hungry and thirsty young archaeologists and says: 'You should be able to follow all those steps, from post hole to the whole world, by extrapolation, interpolation or analogy. This hole in the ground is the hole out of which the world tree grows and it's your job to scale this hole up to the whole kingdom and, ultimately, the world at the time it was dug because, if you've done your homework, you know what the people were like, you know the culture they were living in, how they were living, their technologies. All this should be locked in your head already through having read the archaeological reports and historical documents for the surrounding period. That's why I am an expert in this field and that's why you will be: because you'll have all this information in your head.'

Excavating a post hole is a straightforward process with a particular technique. Paul has written a manual telling his students how to do it, how it's half sectioned, which sections to take out, what depth to dig to, what tools to use and so on. The elements are all prescribed. During this mechanical and frankly repetitive process, the archaeologist should be thinking of the context in which the hole sits. If there is a post hole here, where would the rest of the building have gone? Potentially a building could be either rectangular or round – those two options were the only possibilities in this period – so looking at this post hole where could the other post holes be to define and shape the building? If the corners or the arc of the building lie here, then how does that connect to the rest of the site? And if I was putting a building here, why would I do so? Does it lie in the lee of the hill? Is it near water or sheltered from the prevailing wind? All these questions should flow through the mind of the archaeologist and be answered as he or she digs deeper, because answering them is what allows us to dig deeper.

However, the conclusions archaeologists come to are dependent upon a chain of inferences that resembles nothing so much as a house of cards. The conclusion will stand as long as the cards supporting it are stable, but take any one of them away and the whole structure collapses. For instance, Paul excavated a piece of fifteenth-century green glaze pottery from the castle. He knew it was from the fifteenth century because another piece of pottery, similar to that found at Bamburgh, was excavated in Coventry in a layer that had a silver coin dated 1450. Another excavation in Nuneaton had shown that this green-glaze pottery was made there. So in theory a piece of pottery, made in Nuneaton around the middle of the fifteenth century was brought north to Bamburgh, where it did what pottery always does in the end: it broke and was thrown away. It's clear, though, that this conclusion depends on the conclusions made by the other two excavations; if either is incorrect, then what we think about that sherd of green-glaze pottery found at Bamburgh will be wrong.

So the conclusions derived from archaeology are only secure if the legs they stand on are solid, and the higher the house of cards a particular conclusion is based on, the greater the likelihood that it is wrong.

'Sometimes, you are right, and you know you're right.' Paul looks at the circle of tired young archaeologists, their faces turned up to him, wondering if they will ever know that moment. 'All the ducks line up and everything falls into place. These moments are why we do archaeology and why it's worth getting bad backs and sore knees and no money.'

The ducks were beginning to line up for the son of Thunder, the man excavated in the Bowl Hole amid the storm that did not break. His grave shows that this man was not a king. Rulers, being the dispensers of wealth and power, are memorialised in a way that other people are not. Through the historical blanks of the fifth and sixth centuries in British history, more or less the only names we have are the names of kings, recorded in king lists that were written to give legitimacy to their later descendants and that reach so far back into the past that, in the case of the Anglo-Saxons, they terminate at the gods.

This man was a foot soldier, one of the vast majority of people who, having died, are forgotten, vanishing into the past as those who remembered them are in turn swallowed by death. Yes, he had taken part in significant events, as did the 19,000 British soldiers who died during the first day of the Battle of the Somme. They at least are remembered in war graves; their names are inscribed on the memorials all over the country.

There are also war dead who are still being found, particularly in the old battlefields of the First World War. The Commonwealth War Graves Commission deals with an average of eighteen newly found bodies each year. Most of these are uncovered during work for new developments or by farmers ploughing their fields and, in many cases, it is impossible to know who the man was. It is up to the armed forces of the country that the soldier was serving to identify the body. Although many remain unidentified, it has been possible in some cases to name the individual. Occasionally, identification discs can reveal the name of the soldier but in recent years DNA tests have helped, particularly when other factors allow the authorities to narrow down the number of possibilities beforehand. In all cases, the relatives have been eager to provide the DNA samples necessary – even though these relatives never knew the man.

With our skeleton there was a chance of establishing the same sort of connection. He was a man born and brought up in a particular place, who sailed to a different land on a desperate venture and there fell. We can begin to write the biography of the man with no name. And the story of this man provides a new and fresh foundation for a well-known story of the return of the king, but one where the focus is not on the doings of kings and princes, but on one of the ordinary people, one of those forgotten by history.

This book is about his story and the other quiet dead. We have written it to tell their story as far as possible and to affirm through these lives, long forgotten, that none of us are anonymous.

2

The Sword and the Archaeologist

It doesn't look like much. A strip of rusty metal, with the tang tapering nearly to a point, and the blade snapped off halfway down. It was a sword, once. It's in a display case in Bamburgh Castle. About eighteen inches long. The iron looks dark brown, almost black under the glass. If it wasn't for the information card beneath it, the casual visitor would not guess what it was. There's another complete sword at 45 degrees to it in the cabinet. The information cards tell the facts but convey nothing of the wonder. For these two blades, and particularly the one snapped in half, are among the most astonishing artefacts to have ever been made by human hands. And the story of their finding is almost as extraordinary as the swords themselves.

The archaeologists of the Bamburgh Research Project did not excavate just the 'Danish Burying Grd'. There was a castle next door, with a history stretching back to the early medieval period at least. Given the commanding situation of the extrusion of the Great Whin Sill on which the castle sits, the human history of the site almost certainly stretches much

further back. But in turning their trowels and tape measures to
the castle, the archaeologists of the BRP knew they would be
cutting into the trenches of a previous archaeologist, one of the
most eminent in the twentieth century.

Brian Hope-Taylor's excavations of Ad Gefrin by the great
hill of Yeavering Bell in the Cheviots are among the most
important digs in Britain during the last century. Looking at
aerial photographs of the area, Hope-Taylor made what proved
to be an inspired identification. The photographs revealed
field markings to the north of the hill, near the River Glen.
Hope-Taylor guessed that these markings showed the site of
an Anglo-Saxon royal palace, and a very specific one at that:
Ad Gefrin, the great hall of King Edwin of Northumbria. This
was where the Christian missionary Paulinus, who had come to
England as part of the second wave of the Augustinian mission
that Pope Gregory the Great sent to attempt the conversion
of the pagan Angles and Saxons, preached the message of
new life to the Northumbrians. According to Bede, Paulinus
accompanied Edwin and his wife, Queen Æthelburh, north
from York and spent thirty-six days preaching at Ad Gefrin,
baptising the newly converted in the nearby river. This took
place in the year AD 627.

If the excavations proved Hope-Taylor's identification
accurate, then this empty field in the shadow of Yeavering
Bell would provide one of the very few places in Britain able
to corroborate and fix, in place, Bede's account. Hope-Taylor,
under the auspices of the Ministry of Works, began digging
in 1952 when plans for the expansion of a nearby quarry put
the site under threat. The ministry only paid out money to
archaeologists in the field – there were no funds for writing
up reports or doing further analysis after the excavation was
over. So Hope-Taylor spent most of the 1950s digging two

sites: Yeavering Bell in the winter and Old Windsor (another Anglo-Saxon royal site) in the summer.

However, despite the hardships of winter archaeology, the dig proved Hope-Taylor's identification correct and made his name. The story is that when Hope-Taylor presented his findings to the Society of Antiquaries in London they gave him a standing ovation. On the back of his PhD thesis on Ad Gefrin, Cambridge University appointed Hope-Taylor assistant lecturer in archaeology in 1961, promoting him to full lecturer in 1967 despite his never having done an under-graduate degree. Always a perfectionist in his work, it took a thorough dressing down from Sir Mortimer Wheeler, the most high-profile archaeologist of the day, to finally make him send his write-up of the excavations at Ad Gefrin for publication. When it eventually came out – the publication date is 1977 but for various reasons the book did not actually appear until 1979 – *Yeavering: An Anglo-British Centre of Early Northumbria* immediately became a classic of archaeological possibility: this was what all that sifting of dirt could accomplish.

So it was with some trepidation that one of the BRP's on-site directors, Graeme Young, tried to get in contact with Hope-Taylor in 1998. Graeme wanted to find out where and how much of the castle the great archaeologist had excavated. Hope-Taylor told Graeme that he had excavated all the West Ward of the castle. Graeme tried to find out what had been done at what level of detail and what had been found. But Hope-Taylor, by this time in his late seventies, was cagey in his replies. He still expected to publish the results of his excavations, despite the length of time – twenty-five years – since those excavations had ceased.

There may have been another factor at work. Archaeologists can become protective, even paranoid, about the sites

they have excavated. It is their site – trowels off! On a more
prosaic level, reputations are made by excavations in the same
way that physicists are tied to explanatory theories: Heinrich
Schliemann and Howard Carter are tied to Troy and Tut-
ankhamun as tightly as Albert Einstein and Isaac Newton are
synonymous with the theories of relativity and the laws of
motion. Finding, excavating and publishing a great site will
make an archaeologist's name, or raise it much higher. Strangely, it's often the publishing that proves the stumbling block.
Brian Hope-Taylor was by no means alone in having excavated
many more sites than he ever published reports for. It seemed
that he was not keen on a bunch of young whippersnappers
crashing in on the site he'd dug; so much so that, at best, he
misled the BRP as to what he had already excavated, telling
them he had dug all the West Ward when in fact he had covered much less than 10 per cent of the area. Nor would he
let the BRP look at any of his archives, or pass on any of his
findings.

So the BRP put out enquiries to people who worked at
the castle, asking if anyone remembered Hope-Taylor's excavations, or knew someone who did. It turned out that one
of the castle's tour guides had worked, as a schoolboy, on
Hope-Taylor's dig, and he pointed out where they had excavated. Once word got out that the BRP was interested in what
Hope-Taylor had started and never finished, people began to
bring them mementoes, artefacts and photos. One local lady
gave them a collection of site photographs that Hope-Taylor
had given her for safe keeping and then never went back for.
The castle's custodian also showed the BRP staff some storerooms near where Hope-Taylor had excavated. These had not
been opened since Hope-Taylor had left the site and, opening
them for the first time in decades, they found that the store-

rooms had doubled as Hope-Taylor's site office: in them were his desk, tools, soil samples, boxes of bones and some finds.

As a result of news of the dig spreading through the archaeological community, the phone rang. It was the Royal Commission on the Ancient and Historical Monuments of Scotland (RCAHMS). Did the BRP know that Brian Hope-Taylor had died on 12 January 2001?

They did.

Did they also know that a large part of Hope-Taylor's archive had been rescued from his house in Cambridge? The Royal Commission had it, and would they like to have a look at it? They most certainly did want to look at it. But why on earth did Hope-Taylor's archive need rescuing in the first place? Something so significant should surely have been committed to the safe keeping of Cambridge University or the Institute of Archaeology. But, it turned out, the archive of Hope-Taylor's digs and finds had only just been saved in time, through the action of two of his ex-students.

When Brian Hope-Taylor died, there were no near relatives to claim his effects. Nor had Hope-Taylor given his archive to any of the institutions that would have been glad to receive it because he had become increasingly withdrawn and secretive in his later years, charming if met on the street by old friends and acquaintances but unwilling to allow anyone into his life. If this makes Hope-Taylor seem like a socially withdrawn misfit, nothing could be further from the truth. Those who knew him at his peak remember a man of great energy and vivacity, who seemed to have friends in every corner of the country. But Hope-Taylor lived in a culture that deemed it appropriate to separate one's life into different compartments and to keep them separate. In the end, Hope-Taylor's life became as boxed up as the accumulated finds of his archaeological career.

Following Hope-Taylor's death, his lawyers contacted Professor Ian Ralston, Abercromby Professor of Prehistoric Archaeology at the University of Edinburgh, a colleague who had known and worked with Hope-Taylor since boyhood. Quite literally. As a boy growing up in Haddington in Scotland, Ian Ralston heard from his father, the local vet, about a man who had brought his black poodle into the surgery for treatment. It turned out the man was an archaeologist, in the area because he was digging on Doon Hill, and would Ian like to do some digging with him? Would he ever! The young Ian Ralston was already fascinated with archaeology, and he immediately signed up to be part of Hope-Taylor's team, working on the Doon Hill dig for the summers of 1965 and 1966. Doon Hill was the site of another wooden hall and Hope-Taylor soon determined that it was Northumbrian: evidence for his theory of the wide reach of the Northumbrian kingdom in the early medieval period. However, in one of the great ironies of archaeology, the boy who had done his first digging on Doon Hill would grow up to be the archaeologist who re-evaluated and reinterpreted much of Hope-Taylor's work.

Despite Hope-Taylor's withdrawal from most human contact, Ian Ralston had continued to send him Christmas cards as well as making the occasional phone call. However, his attempts to meet in person had been rebuffed: there had been a couple of occasions when, in Cambridge, he had gone to visit Hope-Taylor with a hopeful bottle of wine in hand, only for there to be no answer to the doorbell despite his old boss clearly being at home. So when Hope-Taylor's lawyers informed Ralston of the archaeologist's death, Ralston arranged with them that he be given access to the house to assess the state of Hope-Taylor's work.

Entering the house, it was all too apparent where Hope-Taylor's work was stored. It was everywhere. The whole flat was covered in his career. Maps, books, papers, boxes, finds, plans spread over every surface apart from a single chair. Even the bed was covered over, so he could not have slept in it. It was the home of a man who had hoarded his knowledge until it had overwhelmed him. There was far too much there for Ralston to go through in half a day and, with Hope-Taylor's estate having to be settled, Ralston needed to find an organisation with the time and resources to store and sort out everything. Fortunately, another of Hope-Taylor's old students, Diana Murray, was now with RCAHMS and an expert in the care and preservation of archaeological archives. Ralston phoned Murray to ask if she would be willing to come to Cambridge to assess what needed to be done.

When Diana Murray arrived she immediately saw the value of all the stuff in the house and in a leaking garage, but, since most of Hope-Taylor's excavations were in England, she contacted English Heritage to see if they wanted to take over. But when English Heritage got back saying they could not take responsibility for it, Murray decided to take the archive back to Scotland for sorting, cataloguing and preservation. Arriving back at Hope-Taylor's house with the van to transport the archive to Scotland, Murray found the clearers already there, throwing Hope-Taylor's effects into boxes to be sold at auction.

'Stop!' Murray told the workmen. 'What are you doing?'

'Oh, some old guy died. We're just clearing the house,' said a workman.

'We're here to look at the archaeological archive. It's very important and that "old guy" who died was a very important man.'

'Don't worry, love. It's just boxes. He was a hoarder. Seen it loads of times. It'll all be rubbish.'

'He was a professor of the university and this is not rubbish.' She then pulled out her Royal Commission ID card and brandished it. (The card gave her absolutely no jurisdiction over anything in England, nor in Scotland for that matter. But the workmen did not know that.) While the house clearers retired in confusion, Murray and her colleagues started sorting through Hope-Taylor's effects, loading everything salvageable into the van before driving it up to Edinburgh.

The remainder of Hope-Taylor's effects went up for auction. Before he became an archaeologist, he had been an artist, and a good one, with a range spanning from natural history illustrations to vivid landscapes in a style reminiscent of but predating by three decades Maurice Sendak (*Where the Wild Things Are*). Two of his best works, *Enchanted Pond* and *Enchanted Forest*, are at Wolfson College, Cambridge. Hearing of the sale, Paul went down to Cambridge to see if there was anything connected to Bamburgh, or York, where Paul lives. He bought all he could afford. (He couldn't afford very much. Archaeology is not a discipline you enter to make money, the reason why so many of the early archaeologists were independently wealthy.) One of the books Paul bought that day did provide a vivid insight into Hope-Taylor's personality: *Fabric Rolls and Documents of York Minster, or a Defence of 'the History of the Metropolitan Church of St Peter, York'* by John Browne (1862) was meticulously annotated by Hope-Taylor, the margins littered with comments like 'Foolish statement' and 'The man knows nothing'.

Having taken everything they could salvage of Hope-Taylor's archive to Edinburgh, the first step for the Royal Commission was emergency preservation. Much of the archive, particularly that part of it retrieved from Hope-Taylor's garage, was water damaged. To stop it deteriorating further, the Royal Commission did the only thing possible for the emergency preservation of wet documents and artefacts: they froze them. That at least stabilised the part of the archive that was most at risk, allowing further work to be done on it once the material had been sorted and categorised. The fact that the Royal Commission was willing to put so much time and effort into saving Hope-Taylor's archive showed both its efficiency in dealing with decaying materials and the intrinsic value of the material.

With the most vulnerable part of the archive stabilised, the Royal Commission made an initial sort through of what they had found before putting out calls to any parties who might be interested in the Hope-Taylor archive.

The Bamburgh Research Project was among the organisations they called. Paul, Graeme Young and a couple of other people went to Edinburgh to see what was there. Walking into a conference room they realised that it must have been a very big van that brought the archive. The Royal Commission asked the archaeologists if there was anything relevant to Bamburgh. Paul had already dug some test pits in the West Ward of the castle, so he knew what the stratigraphy looked like and he could quickly say, looking at the contents of a box, whether it belonged to Bamburgh, the layers of deposition in a site being as unique a signature as DNA. The BRP archaeologists found some boxes with the Bamburgh signature stratigraphy, which were labelled, and then they investigated those nearby to see if they were related. They slowly realised that Hope-Taylor had used an idiosyncratic grid system when labelling his finds, with L in the west and S in the east, and numerals from 6 to minus 1. So any box containing finds labelled, for instance, L1.5 came from Bamburgh.

Over the day the team went through many, many boxes. But not just boxes. The Royal Commission archivists also brought Paul a suitcase to look at. Inside was some acid-free tissue paper used to wrap up the contents of the suitcase, which had just been loose inside.

'You might want to take a look at this,' they said.

Paul unwound the tissue paper to reveal what looked at first glance like three swords and, according to the quick classification by the Royal Commission, an unidentified piece of metal. A closer look revealed that the three swords were in fact two, and the unidentified piece of metal was the blade of a broadaxe.

A short time later the BRP archaeologists found one of Hope-Taylor's Bamburgh site reports, where he records finding a blacksmith's cache including two swords, one broken, and an axe blade. This had to refer to the swords and axe head they had found in the suitcase, which meant that they came from Bamburgh, from the castle.

But this brought to a head the question of what would happen to Hope-Taylor's archive and its finds. There was some thought that the entire archive should go, intact, to a single institution. While this was discussed, the Royal Commission was more than happy to copy any documents related to Bamburgh and send them to the BRP, but until the question of the fate of the Hope-Taylor archive was settled they were not prepared to release the swords and axe blade to anyone's keeping. This, though, was not a case of institutional annexation but rather an illustration of the work the Royal Commission did to preserve the archive. Until matters were properly resolved and the fate of the archive settled, they wanted to keep as much of it together as possible.

At this point, Bamburgh Castle got involved. They assured the Royal Commission that they would safeguard the swords and axe and put them on display and if later investigation should prove that they actually came from somewhere else, then they would be happy to return them. After the requisite legalese was written and signed, Paul went up to Edinburgh to collect the swords and the axe. This was his first chance to have a proper look at them. On first inspection, he had thought the swords were pattern-welded. But further reports from the Royal Commission had said that the blades were plain welded, so he had put the thought from his mind. But now, holding the blades and examining them close up, he became convinced that they were pattern-welded.

What does this mean?

It means that these swords were extraordinary. Pattern-welded swords bear as much relation to ordinary swords as the Koh-i-Noor diamond does to a lump of coal. But in their corroded state, it was hard to tell. Hope-Taylor appeared not to have thought that there was anything unusual about these finds.

But it was one thing to suspect the swords were pattern-welded, and another to prove it. For that, specialist equipment was necessary, far beyond the means of a team of archaeologists. However, Paul knew a man . . . To be precise, he knew a man at an institution that specialises in the conservation of arms and armour: the Royal Armouries Museum at Leeds.

'We've got two swords, excavated from a tenth-century context but possibly much older, that I think are pattern-welded. What tests would you be prepared to do on them?' (with the implication that these tests would be done for free).

It turned out that the Armouries would scan, photograph, X-ray and resonance-test them. Not bad at all. Particularly the scan, which would be done with a scanning electron microscope. Such an instrument would reveal the structure of the sword in detail.

Dr David Starley, archaeometallurgist, from the Royal Armouries rang Paul with the results.

'Yes, they're pattern-welded. They're incredible.'

One of the swords, the complete one although broken in two, was four-stranded and very similar to the sword excavated from mound 1 at Sutton Hoo, the burial place of a seventh-century king of the East Angles, most probably King Rædwald, whom Bede writes about at length in his *Ecclesiastical History*. Swords in the early medieval period were uncommon weapons, being wielded by kings and the highest echelons of warrior society. So any sword would have stood out, but this one, bearing comparison with the sword buried beside the king over all other kings in Britain at the time, was truly out of the ordinary.

As David Starley said, 'It's an amazing sword. It's in two parts but they're very clearly from the same blade. It's one of the best swords we've seen.' Then he added, 'However, the other sword is infinitely better.'

The making of a sword is perhaps the most difficult task a blacksmith was called upon to undertake. The two fundamental qualities necessary to make a good sword are contradictory: a sword must be flexible, so that it will flex rather than break in battle, but it must be hard, so that it can be sharpened to an edge that will cut through leather and muscle and bone. Iron is flexible, and will bend, but it is not particularly hard – an iron sword, subject to the impacts of battle, will quickly become little more than a metal club. Steel, which is iron alloyed with carbon, can be made extraordinarily hard but this comes at the price of brittleness. As an example, the katana, the sword of the Japanese samurai, was made to be extremely hard so that it could be honed to the sharpest edge possible – stories of katanas slicing the wind and water stem from this extraordinary sharpness – but as a weapon it only worked when facing other samurai similarly armed. When the social hierarchy that put samurai, as a class, beyond the reach of ordinary peasants began to break down, the peasants quickly realised that administering a solid thwack to the flat of the katana with a stout wooden staff could often shatter the blade. Pattern-welding is the method that smiths in the early medieval period developed to make a sword that overcomes this contradiction: hard enough to hold a cutting edge, flexible enough not to break in battle. To do this, they took two or more billets of iron, heated them and then forge-welded them together. The welded stacks were then twisted to force out any imperfections and impurities. The twisted billets were then hammer-welded together, side by side, to create the intricately patterned core of the blade. Although the smiths of the time did not have the metallurgical knowledge to describe the effect of what they were doing, the essential function of this repeated heating and beating out of the iron was to disaggregate the impurities in the metal. The best pattern-welded swords took hundreds of hours to make.

Often, in this period, iron ore came in the form of bog ore. That is iron that is produced in swamps or bogs by the oxidation of iron that has dissolved into the water seeping down into the bog. The water of the bog will have a characteristic rusty red brown colour. The bog ore itself is muddy red in colour; a hard, irregular clump. Bog ore was the principal source of iron throughout the early medieval period in northern Europe, and continued as an important source of iron in medieval times, particularly in Russia and Scandinavia. The great advantage of bog ore is that it renews itself. A good bog can be harvested at regular intervals, say every decade. This knowledge would have been conserved and guarded jealously, either by the smith himself or traders in iron ore. Traders in bog ore processed the lumps into iron ore, melting it down into more easily portable shapes: flat, long and thin rods of iron, like a blunt, crude sword blade. In this form, the processed bog ore was traded across great distances.

Holding a lump of bog ore in your hands, it's a marvel that anyone ever thought that this could be turned into something useful, still less that it could, through heat, turn into the yellow/red flow of liquid iron.

The iron, naturally enough given its source, contains many impurities. If enough of these impurities aggregate in the final implement, then they create a weakness, a fault rather like a knot in a tree branch, which can make the implement fail when it is placed under stress. The difficulty is made worse by the molecular structure of the impurities being 'sticky' or 'jagged', whereas iron atoms flow easily in the molten state, making the impurities more likely to coalesce. In the case of a horseshoe, this does not matter so much. With a sword, failure is likely to be fatal. By the lacing together of different cores, and the repeated heating and beating out of the metal, the impurities in the iron are evened out, ensuring that they do not gather together and produce a fault.

An effect of pattern welding is to create intricate, irregular patterns on the finished surface, which can be further highlighted by the smith through polishing and etching. These patterns look something like the irregular growth lines in wood, or the spread patterns of lichen: the overall effect is to give a strangely organic feel to a length of iron.

Pattern-welded swords were truly lethal weapons. Firstly, they were far beyond the capabilities of the average spear or shield deployed against them: a pattern-welded sword could cut open a shield or slice through a spear haft. The Norse sagas describe formal duels between warriors, and these often feature each warrior having three shields, which shows just how much damage a good sword and an experienced warrior could do to a thick piece of wood. Secondly, if you were a peasant or small landholder of the time, called out to add your weight to the forces of your lord, and you saw that the man facing you in the enemy shieldwall was holding a pattern-welded sword, then you'd know that death was staring you in the face. For the only men who carried pattern-welded swords were those whose lives were dedicated to warfare and who trained every day for it. The quaking peasant would have as much chance of beating a warrior with such a sword as a recreational tennis player would have of beating Roger Federer.

The Romans did not widely use pattern-welded swords because these are weapons that require many man hours to produce, whereas they required weapon-making on an industrial scale to arm their legions. But in Britain, in the fifth, sixth and even seventh centuries, an army could consist of a few dozen men. Indeed, the law code of Ine, King of Wessex, that was promulgated around 694 is quite specific about this: 'By "thieves" (*peofas*) we mean men up to the number seven; by "a band" (*hloo*) from seven to thirty-five; by "an army" (*here*) above thirty-five.'[1]

It is likely that the small kingdoms carved out of Roman Britain in the fifth and sixth centuries were created by men leading warbands of less than a hundred warriors; in many cases a warband of fifty or so men might have been enough to win a crown. With such small armies, individual warriors would play a crucial role – and particular weapons would be vital too. This was the age when a well-made sword wielded by a skilled warrior could swing a battle and either bring down a kingdom or create one. It was a time when favourite weapons were named and praised; the scops, the poets, singers and tale tell-ers, the PR men of kings and the memory makers of peoples, hymned the most renowned weapons and their wielders, the two linked together as firmly as Arthur and Excalibur, Aragorn and Andúril, Elric and Stormbringer.

The two swords that Hope-Taylor had found at Bamburgh would have been such blades. But while the first, the intact but broken blade, would have inspired tales, the second would have been the subject of epics. The second sword, which has become known as the Bamburgh sword, was composed of six billets, six strands of iron pattern-welded together. That is exceptional in itself: it's extraordinarily rare for even the best pattern-welded weapons to have cores made with four billets. So far as we know, this is the only sword yet found to be composed of six billets of iron. For David Starley, it was the most complex pattern-welded sword that he had ever seen.

As to when the swords were forged, Starley was of the opinion that they were made in the early to mid-seventh century, that is somewhere between AD 620 and AD 650. Looking at the archaeological context in which the swords were found dates their deposition to the mid-tenth century. So they were probably in use for four hundred years. The dating of a sword is the result of a century and more of painstaking study by dedicated, not to say obsessive, sword collectors, enthusiasts and scholars. To the casual observer, a sword is pretty much a sword, a pointy thing for cutting up people. But for these collectors and armourers, swords are objects that have been put under the fiercest evolutionary pressure possible: their success or failure was a matter of life and death. The response to this pressure has been, through generations of painstaking work, catalogued into a developmental sequence tied closely to the calendar. Think of it like this. A layman, looking at photos of a Model-T Ford, a Ford Cortina and a Ford Focus could put them in sequence.

An enthusiast would be able to add the models in between. An expert could differentiate every variation of the Model-T and date them. It's like that with swords. The subtle changes in blade length, breadth and depth, the scoop of the fuller and the angle to the point, all changing through the years of sword evolution, allow the accurate dating of a sword.

The forging and breaking of the Bamburgh sword tie in rather neatly, possibly too neatly, with hugely significant periods in British history. Its making puts it in the time of our warrior, the son of Thunder. Not that the sword was forged for him. Such a weapon must have been commissioned by a king. Only the king would have attached to his household a smith capable of both making such a weapon and able to devote the amount of time it required. In the whole of the country there would have been no more than a handful of men able to make a weapon like the Bamburgh sword. Given the weapon's uniqueness, perhaps there was only one.

These master sword smiths guarded their knowledge jealously and they were guarded jealously in turn. This was a time when a king demonstrated his power by the giving of gifts but, notably, kings did not give away knowledge, and neither did the smiths who carried that knowledge. A smith capable of making such a sword would elicit awe and trepidation and he and all his clients would have known the stories surrounding Wayland, the smith god of the Angles and the Saxons. Indeed, some elements of the stories around Wayland typify the fear towards and the restraints placed upon master blacksmiths. One story of Wayland appears in the *Völundarkviða*, one of the poems collected in the *Poetic Edda*, which was written in Iceland in the thirteenth century but originates from a much older oral tradition. A carved relief on the front panel of the Franks Casket, an eighth-century casket made of whale's bone, shows the story of Wayland was known to the Anglo-Saxons of Britain. The relief is next to the Adoration of the Magi, as incongruous a juxtaposition as is possible to imagine. In the ninth century, Wayland is mentioned by Alfred the Great in a note of his translation of Boethius's *Consolation of Philosophy*. So the master smith figured large in Anglo-Saxon imagination and culture for many centuries.

In the story in the *Völundarkviða*, Nidud, king of the Swedes, hearing of Wayland's skill, inveigled the smith to come to work for him with promises of riches and a royal bride. But when Wayland arrived, Nidud reneged on his promise and, to ensure that the captive smith did not escape from his enforced royal employment, Nidud hamstrung him – rendering Wayland lame – before imprisoning the smith on a small island. (There is an obvious parallel here to Hephaestus (Vulcan), the lame smith of classical mythology. Although smithing is difficult and dangerous work, the dangers are usually more to the hands and eyes than the legs. Maybe it was more common than we think for kings to ensure the retention of smiths by removing their ability to walk away.) Wayland appeared to accept his fate, crafting marvellous trinkets for the king's children and winning their trust. But that was just a prelude to the terrible revenge Wayland had planned. First, when Nidud's two sons came secretly to his smithy to ask Wayland to forge weapons for them, Wayland killed and dismembered the youths. He then turned their skulls into drinking bowls, embossed with jewels, and gave these as a gift to Nidud, who appears to have been an inattentive father as he had failed to notice his sons' disappearance. Wayland turned the young men's eyes into jewels, which were fixed into jewellery and given to the queen, who similarly hadn't missed her sons. As for their teeth, Wayland made them into a particularly beautiful brooch: a gift for Nidud's daughter, Bodvildr. Charmed, Bodvildr visited Wayland, only for the smith to drug the girl, rape and impregnate her. That done, Wayland needed to make his escape before Nidud discovered what had happened to his sons and daughter. But he'd planned for that too. In the weeks before, Wayland had limped the shores of his island, collecting feathers. Now, he riveted the feathers into two metal wings he had forged and, taking wing, flew from his island. But just to make sure that Nidud got the message, Wayland circled over the king's stronghold and yelled down to him the news that the drinking bowls he had been drinking from were fashioned from the skulls of his dead sons, and that his only remaining child, Princess Bodvildr, was pregnant and he, Wayland, was the father. Wayland then flew away, leaving the bereft king to contemplate the fact that his only surviving heir would be Wayland's son. Not the most obvious companion piece to the Adoration of the Magi.

The message from the story of Wayland and King Nidud seems to be not to mess with smiths. In early Medieval Europe, a master smith was important but also feared. Smiths were outsiders. This was, in part, for practical reasons: a forge was a major fire risk and it was best kept away from other wooden buildings. Smiths also needed to be near sources of iron and wood, which often led to them siting their smithy away from settlements but near bogs and woods. There was something deeply mysterious about the work of the smith, a mystery deepened by the reluctance of smiths to share their knowledge. This outsider status of smiths has continued into the present day in some societies. For instance, in northern Cameroon, smiths are segregated from the rest of society, the reasons given being the usual litany of complaints against outsiders: smiths are dirty, dangerous and their furnaces can give you a bad cough.

The renown of the Bamburgh blade accompanied it through the centuries, a tale told in whispers or chanted in the alliterative metre of Old English verse, a tale stretching far longer than any of the individual kings and warriors who owned it. Imbued with such mystique, the weapon acquired what was virtually a personality of its own: wielding it, a warrior wielded its history and its life, its soul. They were objects of great power. The Norse sagas recount tales of heroes breaking into burial mounds to recover famous swords interred with a fallen warrior. More often, they would be passed on to a son or favoured retainer, to add fresh battle honours to the sword's legend.

So how could such a legendary sword, even if broken, be in the ground for archaeologists to find centuries later? Further work on the Hope-Taylor archive has allowed the BRP to fix, reasonably exactly, the location where the swords and axe head were excavated. They've got the horizontal position down to within a half metre, and a very accurate vertical location. The vertical location gives the time when the swords and axe were deposited: the tenth century, during a period in the castle's history when, as Hope-Taylor said in his excavation notes, there was a 'catastrophic burning event'. He thought that event coincided with a Viking incursion when raiders burned the castle. Paul disagrees. Yes, there is evidence of a serious fire, but he interprets the evidence as showing that the swords and the axe head were part of the inventory of the castle's resident blacksmith and the forge experienced the perennial danger for forges throughout history: it burned down.

In Paul's own forge – as part of his work as an experimental archaeologist he has learned the skills of the blacksmith and makes weapons and implements – he has stacks of scrap metal piled up wherever there's space. If the place ever burned down, all these bits of metal would end up lost under the ashes of his smithy. So he thinks that the 'catastrophic burning event', rather than being a result of a Viking raid, was a more localised affair, sparked when the smithy caught fire. The blades waiting repair or reuse were simply lost in the ashes of the fire. Any blacksmith losing his inventory to a fire would not bother going through the ashes afterwards to retrieve the metal, since it would have lost its temper – such a marvellous phrase, it means that it would have lost the properties that make iron useful. The burned down forge was then built over and the swords and axe head sank progressively lower under ground until Brian Hope-Taylor dug them up.

The archaeologists of the Bamburgh Research Project began to look into how the Anglo-Saxons could forge weapons of this quality. They also began to re-excavate the area that Brian Hope-Taylor had dug so they could fit his findings into the stratigraphy of the castle, while also expanding the dig to cover new areas. When they got down to the level that Hope-Taylor had reached, they found that the dig had been back-filled. Hope-Taylor had left the site with every sign that he intended to return. He had left his section grids, nails and occasional marker tags in place, and simply covered them over with tarpaulins and plastic sacking before backfilling – normal practice when an archaeologist is expecting to return. But Hope-Taylor never came back. Not wanting to waste what they had found, and as a tribute to Hope-Taylor, the archaeologists of the BRP reused some of this material: the section string nails Paul now uses are those he salvaged from Hope-Taylor's dig and his trowel – there is no more personal tool for an archaeologist –

was once Hope-Taylor's too. Paul found it in the lock-up that had been closed for thirty years.

So why didn't Hope-Taylor return? Firstly, he was called away to do emergency work. He had completed three years at Bamburgh in this second phase, 1969–1972, when word came that York Minster was in danger of collapse. Hope-Taylor was called in to do the emergency archaeology as underpinning was done to save the Minster.

After that, though, Hope-Taylor's life entered an obscure phase. He was teaching at Cambridge, continuing his association with the university that had begun in 1958 when he was registered by St John's College to write his PhD on the excavations at Ad Gefrin. Not only was he highly regarded by his peers, but he became something of a TV personality as a result of two television series he made for ATV in the 1960s, *Who Were the British?* and *The Lost Centuries*. Hope-Taylor had been a child actor and he took to the medium as much as it took to him. With a mane of swept-back blond hair, he looked something like the Michael Heseltine of 1990. He was on the brink of becoming a major cultural and intellectual figure in Britain. But then, he disappeared. Or, rather, he receded.

For someone who had cut such a dashing figure – Cambridge professor, TV star, artist, top-flight archaeologist, pilot – Hope-Taylor's obscurity from the mid-1970s onwards is strange. The assumption made by those who knew him was that drink took an increasing toll. Alcohol plays a large but unacknowledged part in archaeology, having fuelled and warmed many a dig, and loosened tongues in campfire discussions. Hope-Taylor was part of that culture and thought nothing of digging when worse for wear after the night before. Those who knew him often described him as a force of nature, a hurricane of charm, words and verve who rarely stayed at a hotel because he always knew somebody in the area he could stay with. After the death of his fiancée, he began to drink. The tale of drunk days is indicated in the site reference from Bamburgh. There are days where every single thing is recorded in meticulous detail and there are days when there is nothing. If the whole dig had been recorded on good days it would have been the perfect archive but, as it is, there are big gaps in it. Hope-Taylor also cared for his parents into their old age. He lived a compartmentalised life: Diana Murray remembers going to the house that he shared with his parents, but she was never asked inside to meet them. But it is clear that he was deeply affected by their deaths.

In 1976, Hope-Taylor resigned his post at Cambridge and moved to Wooler in Northumberland. There, two old friends, Vera and Lionel Rutherford, helped him recover his health, so much so that he returned to Cambridge with the intention of finishing the site report on his excavations at Old Windsor. These excavations had run concurrently with his dig at Ad Gefrin and probably would have provided as great an insight into the history of the early medieval period as his report on Ad Gefrin. There was also the work on Doon Hill that formed part of his thesis on the spread of Northumbrian hegemony into Scotland.

But none of this work was ever completed. By the 1980s it was clear that Hope-Taylor had turned his back on his previous work: he spent the last decades of his life investigating the churches of Essex. A clue as to why he abandoned his life work might be found in his last written work: a defence of his interpretation of the timber building that he'd excavated at Doon Hill as being Northumbrian in origin. His schoolboy protégé Ian Ralston excavated a building in Aberdeenshire very similar to the one at the Doon Hill site, but Ralston dated this building to the early Neolithic period rather than the early historic period to which Hope-Taylor had assigned Doon Hill. Yes, Hope-Taylor had reported finding plenty of Neolithic stone and flint, but he had interpreted these finds as evidence of previous habitation of a prominent site. In the mid-1960s, when Hope-Taylor had excavated Doon Hill, there had been little thought given to the possibility of Stone Age people building in wood, but by the time Ralston was excavating, many examples of wooden Neolithic buildings had been found, particularly in Europe. However, Hope-Taylor mounted a vigorous defence of his findings, in effect calling Ralston and his collaborators fools, but he ignored all requests for the samples that would have settled the argument. He had wooden samples from his excavations of the foundations of the buildings that he had interpreted as being Northumbrian. With the advance in carbon-14 testing, it would have been straightforward to test these samples and date them, settling the argument once and for all. But Hope-Taylor simply ignored these requests.

Some of his colleagues had long suspected that Hope-Taylor had a tendency to fabulism. One of his heroes was T. E. Lawrence – Lawrence of Arabia. Lawrence famously left the manuscript for *Seven Pillars of Wisdom* at Reading railway station and then had to rewrite it all from memory. Hope-Taylor lost the only copy of his PhD thesis at Berlin railway station and had to rewrite that. The parallel is telling.

Hope-Taylor had also always been self-conscious about his lack of formal qualifications. Perhaps to compensate, he affected great confidence in his views but with the new findings about Doon Hill steadily undermining the archaeological edifice he had constructed, it seems that rather than admit he had made a mistake, he turned his back on his work, obstructing the requests of other archaeologists for the context of his findings, and withdrawing into a different world. He knew that his life's work was slowly unravelling, but he would not help those doing the unravelling, and nor would he engage further with his previous life. It was dead to him. His tragedy – and tragedy is not too strong a word – was that though he had turned his back on his life's work, he could not let it go. It filled his house until his death. He could not bring himself to dispose of it himself, but perhaps he hoped that it would be found after his death. Whatever the answer, it remained, mouldering in boxes and files, slowly rotting in a leaking garage: the finds of a life, denied.

In trying to understand the swords, the BRP were greatly helped by one member of staff at Bamburgh Castle: the armourer. It's not something generally known, but a castle, such as Bamburgh, with a large collection of arms and armour usually has an armourer to look after the collection. The armourer of Bamburgh Castle at this time was David Oliver, who had previously been an armourer at the Tower of London. He had also doubled his duties by dealing with the Hope-Taylor archive as it applied to the castle. His speciality was swords, and in particular Anglo-Saxon swords; his personal collection of swords is among the best in the country. As a sword specialist, David Oliver had a particular interest in the two blades that Hope-Taylor had excavated. So Paul could compare the two swords with other examples, David brought some of his collection of ancient swords and laid them out in front of him and told Paul to pick one up. At the invitation, Paul looked for the white latex gloves – on the face of it, these were weapons that fell in the see-but-only-touch-with-extreme-care category. But

David grabbed a sword and handed it to Paul. 'Here,' he said, 'try it. It's a sword. It's meant for killing people. It won't break if you wave it around.'

Being able to hold and wield an authentic Anglo-Saxon sword for the first time was a revelation for Paul. He had always imagined them as heavy, battering weapons that owed most of their effectiveness to strength and momentum: essentially clubs with a cutting edge. But holding an actual sword put the lie to that idea. These were weapons of balance and fluidity. Fencing masters often say that the sword should be an extension of the arm. But their weapons are the foil, epée and sabre, the light, flexible swords designed for duelling. Anglo-Saxon broadswords were forged for the brutal melée of the shieldwall, where men stood shoulder to shoulder, shield overlapping shield, and strength and weight counted much more than finesse. The idea of a sword as an extension of the arm surely did not apply in such a context? But, holding one of these blades for the first time, Paul realised what fencing masters mean. The smallest movement produced a huge arc in the tip of the sword. Holding the sword out in front of him, Paul saw the tip bounce at the slightest movement of his fingers. It told its wielder what it was doing. It felt alive.

As a sword, it exemplified how those old smiths had managed to marry contradictory demands in creating the ideal weapon: it was flexible and felt in the hand as light and responsive as your fingers, yet it retained a cutting edge sharp enough to slice through muscle and bone. Holding that sword, Paul believed, for the first time, the tales he had read in ancient Norse sagas of swords that were so flexible that the tip could be bent back to the pommel, without breaking, before springing straight.

Paul stood with sword in hand, cutting arcs through the air, a grin of seeing and understanding, and the sheer joy of swinging a sword, upon his face.

David nodded. 'That there sword is good, but the sword you found, that would have been as good again. Maybe even better.'

Paul looked at the sword, holding it up before him, turning it so that the light caught in the swirls of the pattern upon the blade.

The Britain of the early medieval period was a fractured society. The imposed unity of Rome had shattered. The land had shivered apart into a thousand competing, fighting, warring polities. In such circumstances, it is little surprise that the medieval conception of, not to say obsession with, unity had its beginning then. By the high medieval period, society had been hammered into the most complete unity it would probably ever know: one king, one faith, one nation. The body as metaphor for the state. But its beginnings lie in these early, obscure centuries, when small kingdoms were hammered together into larger ones, when a warrior from a small Scottish island would follow an Anglian prince across sea and land to retake a crown, and sword smiths took rods of iron and forged them into one.

3

Iona

The boy stood in the bow of the currach, the salt spray breaking over his face, white gulls wheeling overhead, riding the wind and racing the boat.

'Go faster, go faster!' he cried, turning back to his father. Joining his son in laughter, the father trimmed the sail tauter until it hummed like a bowstring in the wind. The boy could feel the tarred hide that skinned the boat flexing as it moved through the water. Sometimes the boat seemed like a thing alive, a sea-going companion to the white mares of the king's herd. Now it was running with the wind, the good south-westerly that brought rain for the crops, skimming across the wave-tossed, tide-ripped Straits of Moyle.

The father was taking his son to the Isle of the Blessed to see God and his holy one, Colm Cille. Ahead of them, the cliffs of the Mull of Kintyre rose from the sea, their skirts white-washed by the waves. They had made the trip to Iona many times through the boy's young life, but the excitement did not lessen. There was the exhilaration of the sea journey. His father's string of jokes. The joy of arrival on Holy Island. They were making swift progress up the west coast of Kintyre, the long peninsula of land that pointed like a finger to the boy's own home in Ireland. Islay lay to their left, in the west, Jura lay north, its three mountains thrusting to the sky.

'Two breasts are good,' said his father, pointing, 'but three are better.' The boy laughed.

The isles of Islay and Jura protected the currach from the full force of the ocean, creating a channel between the islands and the Kintyre peninsula that allowed a relatively easy passage from Ireland up to the king's stronghold at Dunadd. They had been to Dunadd too, to pay homage to their king and to see the holy stone. But this trip they were going to sail past Dunadd and on through the maze of small islands, past Scarba and Lunga west of long Luing, before striking out across the Firth of Lorne for the Isle of Mull and Iona. With the long westward arm of the Ross of Mull continuing to provide shelter from the Atlantic waves, they would run along its coast until they saw the Holy Isle and then across the Sound of Iona, listening for the sound of voices, for the monks were always singing.

'Do you think they'll sing this, Papa?' asked the boy, and he began singing, in his high unbroken voice, one of the chants they had heard before on Iona. He did not know the language the monks sang, but with an ear tuned to song and a memory trained to recall, the boy had fixed the first verse in his mind and now, returning, he was determined to learn the rest.

'Altus prosator vetustus . . .' he began, the song joining the music of wind and sea and wave.

'We've got to get there first,' said his father. 'Weather's drawing in. Mayhap we'll need to take shelter with our kin at Dun Mhuilig. I should not want to be near the Gulf of Corryvreckan when the tide is running and a westerly blowing.'

The boy gestured ahead to Achanarnich, another of the spits of land pointing south-west towards the homeland of the Gaels. Rising above the low, wind-battered trees, was the tall, blind broch: the home and fort of their kin at Dun Mhuilig.

'We're nearly there,' the boy said.

'None too soon,' said his father, steering the currach into the calmer waters of Loch Beag. The seashore shelved gently up into a sandy bay and, as the sand started rubbing against the bottom of the boat, the boy jumped out and, together with his father, drove the currach up onto the beach. They made their way towards the stone tower rising from the top of the hill.

The remains of the tower are still there. The experience of sailing in a small boat from Northern Ireland across the thirteen miles of the Straits of Moyle to Scotland has hardly changed. The boy who grew to manhood and was laid to rest in sight of Bamburgh Castle was born and brought up either on Iona or the northern tip of Ireland. That he would have sailed frequently across the Straits of Moyle is all but certain, for he was born into a new, sea-spanning culture for which the sea was not a barrier but a highway: the kingdom of Dál Riata.

In such a place, where a natural geography of peninsulas jutting south-west into the sea and long islands following the same declination imposes itself upon all human intercourse and the sea and the wind are master, human life changes only slowly. The tall tower of Dun Mhuilig is one of those changes that has left a tumbledown mark. It is a broch, one of the Iron Age skyscrapers built mainly in the first century BC which are among the most extraordinary structures to be found in Iron Age Europe. They were round, conical dry-stone buildings, probably with a thatched roof, no windows and a single, defensible door. Think of an upside-down plant pot, but with the irregular stone exterior characteristic of a dry-stone building, and with a thatch hat on top. There were two walls, an inner and outer wall, with a spiral staircase in the gap between the two walls, and probably galleries at various floors of the broch. The most intact broch today is the Broch of Mousa on the island of Mousa in the Shetlands. It stands nearly 44 feet (13.4 metres) high, with a diameter of 50 feet (15.24 metres), which actually makes it one of the smaller brochs in terms of width, and massive 15-foot-thick internal walls at the base. Standing overlooking the sea, the Broch of Mousa gives a striking impression of what the fringes of Scotland would have looked like when these brochs jutted from a headland and stood upon cliffs, looking blindly out to sea. As to what they were for, the obvious first theory was defence: early strongholds, perhaps built in response to the Roman incursions into northern Britain; Pictish defiance expressed in cold straight stone giving the finger to imperial might.

But without any historical attestation as to their purpose, other theories have been proposed to explain their peculiarities and in particular the lack of windows, which would appear to make their defence much more difficult. So for a while, brochs were thought to be in the nature of Norman castles, structures designed to overawe and intimidate the local population and let them know, firmly, who was in charge. Then, in the 1980s, archaeologists suggested that they might have functioned as visible centres of prestige and wealth, again establishing control over the surrounding area but more by a conspicuous display of wealth than by force. However, given that brochs are frequently sited in strategic locations and many have further defences like ramparts and ditches, or are placed to take advantage of the local terrain at the ends of peninsulas, on cliffs or atop hills, it is difficult to escape the conclusion that many were built as some sort of refuge and stronghold.

The signal fact about brochs is their extraordinary height. That suggests a further purpose. Brochs were generally built within sight of another broch. They took advantage of high points, stood alone on promontories, and were built higher than the surrounding trees. The great Caledonian Forest, which had covered northern Britain following the retreat of the glaciers, was much more extensive then – only relicts survive today, covering some 44,000 acres where once it covered 3.7 million acres – and the height to which brochs were built would have allowed signals to be passed from one broch to another. Given their locations, brochs may also have served as a form of early warning and signal system, allowing local people to see the sails of raiders and invaders from afar, and then to alert other members of the clan to the arrival of enemies. But any further insight into the purpose of brochs will require further investigation: surprisingly few brochs have been properly excavated.

Brochs represent the pinnacle of the developments that had proceeded from the most momentous change in human history: when people stopped moving and stayed put. Previously human beings had lived as travelling family and tribal groups, moving from one location to another to reap seasonal harvests and to avoid the most inclement weather. Communities existed, certainly, but they existed in space as well as time. Then, sometime around the late Neolithic and early Bronze Age, people stopped. They built houses and settled down. The change to settled populations occurred at different times in different places around the world: in northern Britain, it took place around 3000 BC. It also happened first around what is now considered Britain's periphery: the islands of northern Scotland. Excavations at the Tomb of the Eagles on Orkney show that many of the culture-changing innovations in

tomb-building and agriculture began in the northern reaches of Scotland and its islands, spreading south from there to
inform the creation of such better-known prehistoric monuments as Stonehenge. Even though this was the Stone Age,
people moved long distances and ideas moved with them. Of
these, the most foundational was the claim that people made
upon the land. That claim drew its power from the dead.

It was through the preservation of the dead, by a northern
version of mummification that involved smoking and drying
the corpse, that the living put their stamp upon the land, interring the honoured dead in their own homes, thereby sealing
the bond holding living, dead and place together. The dead
were very present to the living: they remained with them, preserved, and were probably brought out at important times to
participate in rituals. By their witness, the dead proved that
the family or tribe had indeed been here, in this place, for generations and that their claim was hallowed by the ancestors
who still dwelt there alongside the living.

The islands and peninsulas that start from Orkney and run
anti-clockwise round the north-west of Scotland were good
places to live in these centuries. These early people made use
of the sea to provide for their needs. Through the centuries
before the Roman invasion of southern Britain the prehistoric inhabitants of northern Britain had slowly developed their
living quarters, changing from circular wooden houses to more
elaborate stone structures. The oldest house in Britain is in
Scotland, in South Queensferry, dating to 8240 BC. This was
long before even the start of the Neolithic Age in Scotland,
which is dated to around 6000 BC (the last part of the Stone
Age, when agriculture was invented). As for the Bronze and
Iron ages, northern Britain entered them respectively in 2000
BC and 700 BC. The successive ages of prehistory are defined

by developments in the technologies available to people, but not surprisingly these changes were accompanied by profound cultural reshaping. This is exemplified in northern Britain by *where* people lived. The first – indeed some of the oldest found anywhere – stone dwellings are on Orkney. The Knap of Howar, the oldest stone building still standing in northern Europe, is on Papa Westray and consists of two rather cosy semi-sunk stone buildings, linked by a covered passageway. The house was occupied for five hundred years, from 3600 BC to 3100 BC, and the remains found on site indicate that the people who lived there farmed barley and wheat, reared sheep, cattle and pigs, and were very fond of oysters – huge middens of discarded shells have been found on the site. The oyster shells are also evidence for how the landscape must have changed since the site's occupation, for oysters require quiet, sheltered water to flourish. The sea that is now, in its wilder moments, sending spray spumes over the Knap of Howar was then sequestered behind sand dunes and, probably, half tamed by a sand bridge connecting Papa Westray to Westray, providing the sheltered conditions that allowed the oysters to thrive in such large quantities.

To go with their stone houses, these people started building stone monuments too: houses for the dead that consisted of a stone chamber, sometimes with a passage leading to it, over which a cairn was raised. Then, roughly when the Knap of Howar was abandoned, they started to erect the stone circles and standing stones that march across the northern sky.

With the coming of metal weapons in the Bronze Age, people began to band together for protection and strength, building forts on top of hills protected by stone ramparts, and crannogs, wooden dwellings built on artificial islands in lakes and estuaries.

The Iron Age brought new homes, in particular Atlantic roundhouses, whose name tells their shape and general location. These were large, dry-stone dwellings, the precursors of brochs. By the dawning of the Christian era, the first wheelhouses had also started to appear. These were circular buildings, the largest of which were substantial affairs, with a circular outer wall and inner piers: from above they look like a spoked wheel.

However, the most widespread remains of the Iron Age, and ones that continued right through the Roman era and on into the early Medieval, were the hill forts. Northern Britain is so rich with these that it seems you can barely climb a hill without stumbling over a ring of tumbledown stones making a necklace round its summit. Oxford University's online database of the hill forts of Britain and Ireland lists 1,694 in Scotland, with 408 in the Scottish Borders region alone, and 271 over the border in Northumberland.

The changes marked in the northern landscape tell the transformation of a people who had lived in a landscape in much the same way that migrating herds of reindeer do, to a people who laid claim to a landscape, in their own names and by right of their dead. It was the dead who granted legitimacy to the claim of the living on the land: they made it a place that the clan and the family could call their own. And if anyone should doubt the claim then all the living had to do was point at the burial mound and say, 'See, that's my father, and my father's father, and they are still here: this land is their land, so this land is my land.'

But by the time our young boy and his father were taking refuge in the broch at Dun Mhuilig – it is called a 'dun' because it represents a type of prototype broch, with one flat side, making for a 'D'-shaped structure – there had been other profound cultural changes among the people of north-west Britain and Ireland for which we have, at last, some historical evidence. We have historical evidence because one of the profound cultural changes was writing. Writing came to northern Britain with the monks who were the prime vector of the greatest agent of cultural change at this time: Christianity. And writing and Christianity came together in the form of the man the boy and his father were going to see on Iona: Colm Cille, the 'Blessed One of God'. No matter that Colm Cille had been dead for a century: his presence lay over the island as thickly as the Atlantic rain and like the rain, ran in streams over the surrounding lands. His influence would later stream over north-western Europe, where his name, which means 'Church Dove', was Latinised to Columba, and then worldwide.

Colm Cille was born in c.521 in Donegal. He hailed from the Cenel Conaill, who were related to the northern branch of the Uí Neill clan, and was thus of, potentially, royal lineage. Sixth-century Ireland was even more of a patchwork land than sixth-century Britain, with hundreds of kings, some ruling over little more than a bay and a bog, but the northern Uí Neill were, very slowly, expanding the area under their control. According to later tradition, which might be spurious but nevertheless perhaps sums up the man, Colm Cille went into exile as the result of a battle over a book.

The story is that the young Colm Cille, already a monk, went to St Finnian of Movilla Monastery in order to copy his psalter. Finnian allowed Colm Cille to copy the psalter but, work done and psalter complete (and remember, this would have been a task that involved preparing the necessary vellum, mixing inks and carving styli, not to mention the actual copying of the text), when Colm Cille went to leave with the psalter Finnian would not let the book go. In effect, he was claiming copyright. The dispute went to King Diarmait mac Cerbaill, king of Tara and thus high king of Ireland, who ruled for Finnian, saying, 'To every cow belongs her calf, therefore to every book belongs its copy.' Not prepared to forgo his book, Colm Cille called in his relatives, the Uí Neills, and the matter was settled at the Battle of Cúl Dreimhne which, for obvious reasons, is also known as the Battle of the Book. There were said to be 3,000 casualties during the battle and, as a result, Colm Cille was condemned by a council of his fellow religious. To expiate for the bloodshed, Colm Cille agreed to go into exile. In a society where ties of family and clan were all-encompassing, this was almost to cut yourself off from life itself – but it had many precursors in the courageous asceticism of Irish monasticism. The Irish had embraced Christianity with a fervour that suggested it must have struck the deepest of cultural and spiritual chords with them; it had sunk its deepest roots into the monastic tradition that had originated with Anthony and the other desert fathers. There was one problem with this identification: there was a lack of deserts in Ireland. In seeking to emulate their spiritual heroes, Irish monks and anchorites took to withdrawing to the nearest temperate equivalents: the mountains and solitary wooded valleys, the strange islands where they might hear God's silent music. Given the peaceful nature of the conversion to Christianity, enthusiastic Irish monks had no chance to claim the red crown of martyrdom. Many had already taken the green crown of solitude. What was left to Colm Cille, scion of the royal house of Cenel Conaill, was the white crown of exile.

So, in 563, Colm Cille sailed away from his native land. However, being of such high birth, Colm Cille did not go alone, but took twelve companions with him. Given the biblical warrant for twelve companions, both in the number of Jesus's disciples and the tribes of Israel, the choice of twelve suggests either that Colm Cille was conscious of writing a new chapter in Christian history and would begin with the appropriate number of companions to place himself as an *alter Christus*, or that his later hagiographers massaged the numbers to fit the eminence they were claiming for their Blessed One.

If Colm Cille was cheating a little by going into exile with his relatives, he was also pushing at the edges of meaningful exile by where he went. Tradition says that he rejected his first landing, Kintyre, for being in sight of Ireland but his final resting place on Iona did not exactly render him a stranger in a strange land. In the connected world of sixth-century Irish nobility, everyone was related to everyone else and they could work out their degree of connection with relative ease, the tale of a king's forbears being among the staples of court bards. The lords of the land where Colm Cille settled were closer to him than most: cousins of a reasonably close degree.

It is to the inhabitants of the kingdom of Dál Riata that we owe the name Scotland but at that time they weren't even Scottish. In the south and east of Britain, Angles, Saxons, Jutes and other Germanic-speaking peoples were slowly establishing the kingdoms that became the basis for many English counties; the Britons, the inhabitants of the country during the Roman centuries, had been pushed from political control, and possibly displaced entirely from the east. But they had regrouped under a legendary war leader, Ambrosius Aurelianus, and were secure in the more mountainous regions of the country in the west, and to the north-west of the Pennines. In the north of Britain, the Picts, never conquered by the Romans, remained in control of the Highlands; while from out of the myriad of small Irish kingdoms, a group of Gaelic-speaking settlers, called *Scoti* by the Britons from the Latin word for 'pirates', were slowly colonising Argyll. So, in the sixth century, the Irish were Scots, the English were Germans, the Welsh were British and the Scots were Picts. Which is why contemporary terms are misleading in the context of early Medieval Britain.

As for those 'pirates', they had been crossing the Straits of Moyle from about the start of the sixth century, settling on the peninsulas and islands of Argyll. They brought their language – Gaelic – and customs with them. Quite what happened to the Pictish tribe, the Epidii, that the Roman geographer Ptolemy recorded as living in Argyll before the arrival of the Gaels is not clear: they disappear from the historical record. They may have been displaced by or merged with the incoming Gaels, or the distinction between the Epidii and the Gaels may be an artefact of Ptolemy's information rather than a historical reality. Whatever the truth of the obscure fate of the Epidii, by the time Colm Cille and his companions were sailing up the coast of Kintyre, a Gaelic-speaking kingdom, Dál Riata, had been established in Argyll with its stronghold on the rock of Dunadd.

So Colm Cille was going into exile in the kingdom of his cousins – somewhat removed, but related nonetheless. With Colm Cille's own royal connections, it made perfect sense for the king of Dál Riata, Conall mac Comgaill, to settle such a high-born relative on a prime piece of accessible land. What's more, he put Colm Cille within easy reach: it's forty miles as the crow flies from Dunadd to Iona. Dunadd means stronghold on the River Add – the rock rising from the flat plain is in a loop of the river – so it would have been a straightforward matter for royal messengers to take a boat, row down the river and then sail across to Iona, although the most direct route would have taken them through the Gulf of Corryvreckan, with its dangerous currents and notorious whirlpool. Even so, when the quickest and, in fair weather, the easiest mode of

travel was by boat, this arrangement allowed for straightforward coordination between the secular and spiritual lords of
Dál Riata. It would be an arrangement later repeated when an
exiled Northumbrian prince returned to Bamburgh to claim
his kingdom and established a daughter house of Iona within
easy sailing distance of his stronghold.

We don't know whether Conall mac Comgaill, king of Dál
Riata, was expecting a visit from his high-born cousin. As Colm
Cille and his companions made their way north, there must
have been some nerves about the sort of welcome they might
face, albeit tempered with the absolute faith in God's provi-
dence for which Irish monks were famed: it was not unknown
for the most fervent to cast themselves adrift in currachs,
allowing the wind and waves, as agents of God's will, to take
them where they might. For their foundering would be no
less God's will than their finding safe harbour. The very way
currachs sailed reinforced this sense of dependence on God's
mercy: they flex and bend, sitting as lightly on the sea's surface
as a seabird, following the swell and dip of the waves down,
down, down into the green cave of the trough and then up, up,
up onto the crest.

But for Conall mac Comgaill it was a straightforward decision to grant Colm Cille land for his monastery. The land he
granted was not big: Iona is 3.4 square miles (8.8 square kilo-
metres). It is possible that Colm Cille asked for a small island
so that his community might meet the eremitic ideal of Irish
monasticism, cutting themselves off from anything other than
the minimum of human intercourse. If so, Colm Cille had not
reckoned on the spread of his reputation for holiness and the
constant stream of visitors – pilgrims, aspiring monks, miracle
seekers – that followed.

In one of the many telling details that pepper Adomnán's

Vita Columbae, we learn that Colm Cille left Ireland in early June. The seas are calmer with less chance of storms and everything about travelling long distances in a small boat is more pleasant in good weather. But this also means that, in their first year on Iona, the monks would have needed support, for there would not have been enough time to sow, grow and reap a harvest before winter. The *Vita* also includes remarks of monks bringing timber and other building materials to Iona by boat. All this indicates that, while the original intention of the settlement may have been eremitic, a combination of Iona's strategic position, which allowed the monks there to have good water-born communication over a wide area, Colm Cille's lineage as a member of the high nobility and his relationship with Conall mac Comgaill, meant that the community became a key hub in the network of relationships that made up the kingdoms around the Irish Sea and north-west Britain. Iona's monks also quickly garnered a reputation for scholarship, based on Colm Cille's own commitment to the importance of carefully copying and transmitting books. While the story of his banishment being the result of the Battle of the Book is relatively late it is of a piece with Colm Cille's dedication to this monastic function. He himself dedicated much time to copying manuscripts and, when thus engaged, was reluctant to stop:

> Once, one of the brethren, Molua Ua Briúin by name, came to the saint while he was engaged in copying a manuscript and asked him: 'Please bless this implement which I have in my hand.' St Columba did not look up, but continued to keep his eyes on the book from which he was copying. However, he reached his hand out a little way and, still holding his pen, made the sign of the cross.[1]

The community's commitment to the accurate transmission of texts is apparent in the final words of the *Vita Columbae*, where Adomnán enjoins future copyists:

I beseech any who wish to copy these books, nay rather I call on them in the name of Christ, the judge of the ages, that when the copying has been done with care, they should then diligently compare what they have written with the exemplar and correct it, and they should add this injunction here at the end of what they have written.[2]

Much of the detail of Colm Cille's life and that of the early Ionan community comes from Adomnán's account, written between 697 and 700. Normally a text that old has to be reconstructed from copies of the original made centuries later, the various scribal errors compared against each other by diligent editors to produce a critical edition of what the author originally wrote. But that is not the case with the *Vita Columbae*. For after the colophon, quoted above, there's another sentence: 'Whoever may read these books about St Columba's miraculous powers, pray to God for me Dorbbéne that after death I may have life eternal.'[3] This Dorbbéne we know, from the monastery's annals, was a senior member of the community on Iona when he died in 713. The sentence asking for prayer for his soul was found in 1621 in a copy of the *Vita Columbae* in the library of the monastery of Reichenau, which is on an island in Lake Constance in southern Germany. Its finder was Stephen White, professor of theology at the University of Dillingen, a Jesuit and an Irishman, who made it his practice to search the libraries of the monasteries within reach for ancient manuscripts. With this small book, he hit the book-detecting bullseye.

Adomnán died in 704 and it's likely that this simple and plain copy of his work would have been scribed by Dorbbéne when he was still a young monk: the natural conclusion is that Adomnán himself oversaw its copying and signed it off as an accurate copy of his original work. At some point, a monk from Iona must have taken Dorbbéne's little book with him when travelling so that it ended up at Reichenau. This is not unlikely, as the monastery there was a popular stop for Irish monks going to study in Germany, France and Switzerland.

The history of ancient manuscripts is never straightforward, however. The monks of Reichenau allowed Professor White to make a copy of the *Vita Columbae*, through which the text became known to the scholarly community, but then the book was returned to the monastery. It then went wandering again, although we don't know who took it, until it eventually turned up in a town not far away from the monastery in the eighteenth century. Dorbbéne's copy – and it was, literally, his copy – has been kept at the library in Schaffhausen ever since and a facsimile has been published online.[4] It's fascinating to 'leaf' through: the pages are 28cm high, the cover is plain cream leather with metal book clasps and there are 136 pages of text between the covers; the text itself is written in a clear minuscule script, with occasional slight adornments to initial capital letters, such as dotting, or colouring the interior of the letter in red or yellow. Some passages are written in red ink, but mostly it's black. Reading the book is to be taken back to the time when small groups of monks, hunched over their copying slates in monasteries strewn around the fringes of Europe, were all that stood between the continent and a collapse back into prehistory. It is a testament to long labour and even longer, patient study; it is a statement of learning as a heroic activity.

Colm Cille was fortunate in being presented with Iona as

his base, for its near neighbour, the king's stronghold at Dunadd, was the centre of a major trading network, with links to the Bordeaux and Loire regions of France, and the Mediterranean, from where it received imports of exotic foodstuffs and other wares. Excavations at Dunadd have unearthed more imported storage vessels, called E ware, than anywhere else in Britain or Ireland. These storage vessels probably contained high-value goods such as spices and honey, as well as wine and salt. Further finds within the power radius of Dunadd indicate that the kings of Dál Riata then distributed these goods, as gifts, to their retainers and local lords. Unusually, the Gaels did not make pottery themselves, nor make much use of it except to receive traded goods, preferring wood or metal containers. The pottery and glass that has been excavated from Gaelic sites all comes from overseas.

Colm Cille's new community could follow these networks and, as Colm Cille's fame and influence grew, he began to set up other houses of monks on the islands and mainland of Dál Riata and beyond. In the course of his *Vita*, Adomnán writes of thirty monasteries founded by Colm Cille. Eventually Colm Cille returned to Ireland and founded monasteries at Derry and Durrow; the latter would endure after Iona declined in importance following the Viking attacks of the tenth century: in 986, the abbot and fifteen monks were killed on Christmas Eve.

Colm Cille's power grew rapidly after Iona's foundation, so much so that in 575, twelve years after he had left Ireland, Colm Cille returned to take part in a meeting between the king of Dál Riata, Áedán mac Gabráin (the previous king, Conall mac Comgaill, had died in 574), and Áed mac Ainmirech, king of the northern Uí Néill. There is some suggestion that Colm Cille may have even called the meeting. The outcome

was an alliance between the two kings – one Colm Cille's kinsman, the other his landlord – and a secure environment for
Colm Cille and his community to continue their work.

That work was prayer. We write much today of the role
of early medieval monastic communities in preserving and
transmitting the cultural heritage of the ancient world, how
monasteries became centres of agricultural innovation and the
hubs from which later towns and trading networks grew, but
first and foremost monasteries were prayer factories. Adomnán does not give us much detail about the liturgy used on
Iona and its daughter houses, but the community observed the
standard canonical hours, with the monks being summoned to
the church by the ringing of a handbell so that they could join
with the prayers, chants and hymns. Although prayer leaves
no mark on the historical record, it was this life of prayer that
was the heartblood of Colm Cille and his community, drawing
people to its regular rhythm with the insistence of gravity.

In writing how Colm Cille passed his time, Adomnán tells
the tale of how the community Colm Cille founded spent its
day: '[he] could not let even an hour pass without giving himself to praying or reading or writing or some other task'.[5] This
commitment to writing and study would bear fruit in the exquisite design and workmanship of Insular art that combined Irish
and Anglo-Saxon styles of decoration to produce the *Book of
Kells* and the *Lindisfarne Gospels*, among other masterpieces.

Learning, careful painstaking learning, was a necessary cor-
ollary of copying books. First, the monks had to learn Latin;
there is some evidence that Colm Cille also studied Greek.
Then they had to study the calendar and the movement of the
moon in order to date various church feasts, most importantly
Easter, correctly. This, combined with the necessary labour to
feed and support themselves, was the daily work of the monks

and Colm Cille was still engaged upon it the day he died. He was at work copying the psalms, and had reached psalm 33 and the words 'But they that seek the Lord shall not want for anything that is good.' The bell summoning the monks to prayer was rung and Colm Cille, now seventy-six, made his way to the church but there collapsed and died. The abbot of Iona had not wanted his funeral to turn into a scrum of mourning visitors and in that the weather came to his aid: for three days there were storms, preventing any visitors getting to the island, and by the end of that time the monks had laid their abbot to rest in a grave marked by the stone that, in life, Colm Cille had used as his pillow.

The way Colm Cille was buried, in an unsealed grave, is evidence that the later cult of physical relics had not yet taken firm hold. The community on Iona did keep relics of Colm Cille, but these were the things he had used, such as his books and psalter, rather than his bones and dried flesh, as would become customary within a century.

The power of Áedán mac Gabráin had increased after Colm Cille had anointed him as ruler of Dál Riata and it continued to wax after Colm Cille's death, expanding to include control of the west coast of Scotland and the islands up to and including Skye. However, Dál Riatan expansion was checked at the Battle of Degsastan in 603 when Áedán's army was defeated by an apparently smaller force led by another rising power in north Britain: Æthelfrith, king of Bernicia, the northern portion of Northumbria centred on Bamburgh. Degsastan was a brutal battle in which most of Áedán's men were killed and the king only just escaped with his life, while Æthelfrith lost his brother. But the battle put a permanent stop to Dál Riatan expansion southwards. The defeat gave the Dál Riatans reason to pause and consider, for not only was Æthelfrith an

Angle, one of the Germanic peoples that had been gradually taking control of southern Britain from the Britons, but he was a pagan too. This was a time when God was expected to take sides on the battlefield, and reveal his favour through victory or show his displeasure in defeat. If the pagan king of Bernicia had defeated the Christian army of Áedán mac Gabráin then there must be a reason for the defeat: in some way or other the Dál Riatans had broken their covenant with God.

As for Æthelfrith, with the pressure from Dál Riata removed he was able to turn his attention to Deira, the southern Northumbrian kingdom centred on York. In 604 he took control of Deira; this appears to have been done through removing the incumbent king rather than by battle. Not long after removing the king of Deira, Æthelfrith's new wife, Acha, produced their first son together. Æthelfrith named him Oswald. They had further children, a daughter called Æbbe and a son named Oswiu, while Æthelfrith's power continued to grow, pulling more and more of the kingdoms of Britain under his overlordship.

Meanwhile, in Iona, a new generation of monks under the abbacy of Fergnae (abbot from 605 to 623) was continuing their work. And a baby was born to reasonably well-off parents around the year 607, possibly on the island itself, and was brought up amid the islands and peninsulas of Dál Riata. We know the boy's parents were well off for there are none of the stress marks on the warrior's skeleton and teeth that are the physical signature of childhood deprivation. Growing up, he had enough to eat, even in the inevitable thin years when the harvest was poor and storms made fishing and the gathering of shellfish difficult. The family made frequent trips to Iona as the baby grew into boyhood. From the monks on Holy Island he heard the tales of the miracles of Colm Cille; from them he learned the new faith. Now he and his father were returning to the Holy Island.

After dragging the boat out into the calm waters of Loch Beag, they rowed round the headland before setting sail. There were many ways of making the final crossing to Mull, but the boy's father decided to steer for the Sound of Luing, between craggy Scarba and little Lunga to the west and long Luing to the east.

'Is the Grey Dog running, Papa?' the boy asked as they neared the narrow channel between Scarba and Lunga.

'I'll not take us near enough to find out,' said his father. He was steering the boat as close as he could to the more gentle shores of long Luing, riding the wind blowing from the south while feeling always lest it should shift to a southwesterly and push them on the rocks. They sailed past Lunga and into the maze of rock stacks that separated the islands from the broad expanse of the Firth of Lorn.

'Nearly there, Papa,' said the boy.

Across the Firth, which spread blue and broad under a clear sky, rose Mull, so big that it hardly seemed it could be an island. Clear of the stacks, the boat skimmed across the Firth as lightly as a bird. The boy pointed. There were other boats sailing across the Firth, heading west along the long arm of the Ross of Mull.

'Papa, they must be going to the Holy Island too,' he said.

His father nodded but looked thoughtfully at the boats. They did not look like war boats, but squinting his eyes he could see the glint of steel and metal. Certainly some of the men aboard them were armed.

While not war boats, they might be the boats of men who were going to war, coming to the Holy Island to seek the blessing of the Blessed One before setting forth.

The boy pointed to the lead boat. 'It is flying a banner.'

'Can you see what it is?'

The boy screwed up his face and shaded his eyes from the sun though he could not block out the water glitter.

'It is purple and gold,' he said, eventually. 'Do you know who that is, Papa?'

His father nodded. 'It is the young prince of Northumbria who has been fighting with the king, Eochaid Buide. His name is Oswald Iding, and they have given him the name *Lamnguin*, the White Blade.'

In the bows, the boy stared ahead with bright eyes.

'The White Blade,' he said.

Oswald, prince of Northumbria, was a prince in exile. As a twelve-year-old boy he had fled with his mother, brother and sister, and those retainers willing to join them in their desperate flight. The man they were running from, the man who had killed their father and taken the throne of Northumbria and the stronghold at Bamburgh, was their uncle, their mother's brother, Edwin.

The story of their flight began twenty-five years earlier, when an Italian fetched up on the Isle of Thanet and asked to see the king.

4

Italians Abroad

The boats had pulled up onto the shingle at the southern end of the channel, the Wantsum, that separated the island of Thanet from Kent. It was a broad channel, two miles wide in places, its bed scoured clean of sand and shingle by the twice daily tides and the outflow of the River Stour. Centuries of silt deposition and the dams and drainages of medieval monks and farmers slowly reconnected Thanet to the rest of the country so that by the latter part of the eighteenth century it had ceased to be an island. But during the centuries it spent detached from the rest of the country, the island saw more genuinely historic moments than anywhere else in Britain.

The early inhabitants of Britain made their homes on the island and filled it with their burial mounds. The Romans, when they returned during the reign of Emperor Claudius, landed on Thanet. According to tradition, Hengist and Horsa, the Saxon mercenaries who came to Britain on contract and stayed on as freelancers, landed on the island in 449. And then, in 597, a group of some forty Italians gathered on that shore;

it must have seemed to them as if they had passed beyond the edge of the world. Indeed, the reality of what they were about to face must have become clear on the final stage of their journey as they sailed across the rough waters of an ocean very different from the quiet sea that bathed Italy. The Mediterranean was a sea embraced by land. But rowing over the cold grey waves towards the distant line of white cliffs, they entered the domain of the encircling ocean, water without end.

Although they did not know it, they were stepping out of history. Many of them would have known the old Greek tales that made Ynys Thanatos the island of the dead. The dead were rowed across the sea to the island during the night in boats with no crew and then, the dead consigned to their place of waiting, the empty boat returned again before the dawn. They had also heard tell of the barbarians who lived in this land, of their practice of painting their skins and their fierceness in battle, of the shortness of the days in winter and the length of the nights, and of the cold and the wet.

And, like all decent Italians presented with such a prospect, they really, really didn't want to be there. The leader of the group of Italians was named Augustine and he was as reluctant as his men. Standing on the slopes of Cliffsend, looking down into the estuary of the Wantsum, Augustine and his fellows could see the broken-down remains of a link to the world they had left behind: Richborough Castle, the old Roman naval fort of Rutupiae. Through the nearly four centuries of Roman rule, Rutupiae had been the main embarkation point linking Britannia to the Empire. Built upon a platform of compacted sand, it guarded the eastern entrance to the Wantsum. Through the long defeat of the western Empire, Rutupiae had been one of the key bases of the military commander given the task of protecting the coastlines on both sides of the Channel from the raids of Germanic barbarians. But the command had failed, the barbarians had overwhelmed the empire and now, to the men squinting into the distance, the ruins of the old fort told its tale. The walls were higher then, so Augustine and his men would not have been able to see the remains of the old triumphal arch, the four-gated quadrifons that had been the ceremonial doorway to Britain. Once it had stood, clad in gleaming imported marble and visible to all approaching boats as a symbol and sign of Roman power. But as the power declined, and the need for defensive walls grew more pressing than the preservation of monuments, it was pulled down and its stone employed in building the Saxon Shore fort. But, behind the walls, the foundations for the gate still stood.

Now the ruins of Rutupiae stood as mute memorial to the passing of the old Roman order. But for Augustine and his men, Rome was more than a memory, it was home. By the end of the sixth century, even Rome had become a memorial to its past glory. At the height of the empire, the population was over one and a half million. When Augustine and his forty fellow travellers set off from Rome in AD 595, the population had dropped to some eighty thousand. But despite its low ebb, Rome remained a bustling metropolis compared with what Augustine saw. For, as the sun set, Augustine and his men slowly realised that Rutupiae had not been abandoned. Flickering fires told of inhabitants; people lived in the ruins. Augustine had met some of them earlier.

The king of this land, Æthelberht, styled himself 'High King' over the other petty kingdoms that fought amid the ruins of Britannia. Æthelberht was High King through force of arms but also by reason of the wealth he could command raising taxes upon those merchants willing to cross the Channel. The king's official, his port reeve, had come skimming over the waves to meet the boats creaking towards land, hailing them from his own vessel.

The words had sounded harsh to Augustine's ear, the language uncouth. The Italian did not understand, yet, what the reeve shouted to them across the waves, but the ship's master knew the language well. For his part, Augustine had found interpreters among the Franks, slaves born among the Angles and Saxons who knew the language. He had brought them with him to translate while he and his men learned the new tongue. But even without knowledge of the language, the reeve's pointing was clear. The reeve wanted them to land on the shingle beach that stretched south from where the chalk cliffs ended. With Augustine's men taking turns on the oars, the ship master drove the boats towards the land, sail cracking overhead. But for the final stage, the ship master put his own men on the oars while he stood, holding the steering oar and peering through the breakers.

The master drove his boat up onto the beach, the shingle grinding against the hull, and the other boat made landfall nearby. The reeve came ashore too, his own men beside him, and he approached the large group of men with all the caution necessary for such a meeting, while still retaining the dignity of his position as the king's man. He looked askance at the group of bedraggled Italians. He had not seen men dressed like these before. But though their clothes were strange, their hair was stranger, for it was cut in a ring around their heads, so that above and below the circle of hair they were shaved.

Augustine stepped forward, with his interpreter beside him, that he might speak to the reeve. With the slave telling his words, the Italian spoke the message he had rehearsed in his mind during the long journey north. He told the reeve that they had come from far-off Rome, with gifts and messages for the king of this land. He told the reeve that they came with the friendship and support of the king of the Franks, and his dukes, through whose land they had travelled. He told him that they wished to see the king and speak with him, that they might give him a gift beyond any other.

When the reeve had asked what this gift beyond any other might be, Augustine told him, 'Life.' And when the reeve asked what manner of man he was, and his companions, for by their dress and hair they revealed themselves as standing outside the categories of folk that he knew, Augustine told him that they were monks.

Monks.

The translator struggled to find a word in the language of the reeve to match what Augustine had said. In the end, he explained as best he could. These were men who had offered themselves to the gods – although they praised only one god. They made sacrifices, and called down favour from heaven to this middle-earth. At the mention of sacrifice, the reeve's eyes glowed with the gold lust, for he had seen the sacrifices offered to the gods when a king or great man died: the rich bowls and hangings, pattern-welded swords, their hilts studded with the blood tears of garnets. But the translator had to disabuse him. The sacrifices these monks offered were chiefly prayer and song, although they also, he thought, did something mysterious with bread and wine.

Wine. This was something the reeve knew. Merchants sometimes brought it across the sea. The king had left instructions with him that all wine landed was reserved to him and his retinue. But what was the mystery accomplished through bread and wine?

There the translator found the limit beyond which his words would not go. In the end, he fell back on a single word.

'Drý.' Sorcery. Magic.

At that, the reeve stepped back.

Augustine, not knowing what his translator said, saw the strange, warding gestures the reeve made against him and his men. Later, when the Italians were in the hall waiting upon the king he asked after the meaning of the gestures. The translator told him the reeve made the gestures for protection against magic.

When Augustine protested that they were not sorcerers, the translator told him that to the reeve and the people of this land they were. And there, in the hall at Cliffsend, within sight of the old Roman fort of Rutupiae, Augustine and his monks waited for the king to come to them.

Nearly twenty years later, the mission was in crisis and near to failing. After initial success – Æthelberht had converted and used his influence to convince tribute kings to accept the new religion too – the next generation of kings had largely returned to the old tribal gods. Although the plan envisaged by Augustine's sponsor, Pope Gregory, was for Augustine to be the archbishop of Britain from an episcopal see based in London, the powers of the land had required otherwise. Under the protection and patronage of Æthelberht, Augustine had made Canterbury his base – hence the archbishop of Canterbury, fourteen centuries later, remaining the highest-ranking cleric in the country – but in the first years of successful evangelisation, he had installed bishops in London and Rochester. However, with Æthelberht's death, the mission had been forced into retreat. His son, Eadbald, if he had been Christian before, abjured his faith.

At about the same time, the king of the East Saxons, who had also converted to Christianity under Æthelberht's influence, also died, bringing the bishopric of London under the rule of his three sons, all curious but unswerving pagans. Fascinated by the claims of the new religion, the brothers demanded of Mellitus, the bishop of London, a taste of the 'food' with which he had fed their father and his flock. When Mellitus said that they could have the food, that is the Eucharist, after they had been baptised, the brothers refused the water but continued to ask for the food. Mellitus continued to insist that they could only eat after they had been washed but the brothers would have none of that and they expelled Mellitus from his somewhat rickety seat – London was at the time a tumbledown shell of its imperial glory. Bede refers to it as 'a trading centre for many nations who visit it by land and sea'.[1] This statement long puzzled archaeologists as there was very little trace of Anglo-Saxon activity in Roman London. However, excavations in the 1980s revealed the answer: Anglo-Saxon remains showing a settlement about a mile upriver from Roman London, running roughly from the National Gallery to Aldwych. Furthermore, as dating techniques have improved, it's becoming clear that there was Saxon occupation of Roman London too. It had been impossible to prove this before for the simple reason that the people living in London after 410, when the legions left, were the same as the people living in London before 410. With much the same people living much the same lives in the same place, it is very difficult to distinguish between Roman and post-Roman layers of occupation.

When Æthelberht's son, Eadbald, having already abjured the new religion, made to cement his rule by marrying his father's wife – a move that shocked clerical sensibilities but also revealed to the priests that had survived from the original mission that they had lost all powers of influence over the young king and his court – the remaining clerics decided to cut their losses, scrape Britain's mud from their sandals, and return to the continent. According to Bede the bishops of London and Rochester had already sailed for the kingdom of the Franks, leaving only Lawrence, the archbishop in succession to Augustine, to shut up ecclesiastical shop in Canterbury before following them back to a land of drier weather and better wine.

Only St Peter had other ideas. In a dream, he berated Lawrence for his faithlessness and then proceeded to beat him, whipping the bleating cleric until his back was marked enough for the lash marks to endure after his waking. Lawrence, both chastised and emboldened, showed his stripes to King Eadbald who, fearing similar punishment, apparently reconverted on the spot. Lawrence summoned his brother bishops back to Britain, sending word that they had better hurry lest they also fall foul of Peter's wrath.

There the mission stood, confined impotently to a corner of Britain. Of course, there was already a church in Britain and a well-established one at that: the Christian church that ministered to the Britons. However, Augustine had fluffed the chance to co-opt them into his mission when they had first met and he had remained sitting when the bishops and priests of the Britons had come to see him. By choosing to remain seated, he had shown, at least to the Brythonic clergy, that he sought to impose himself upon them with no regard for their local customs, nor the many years of struggle they had endured in the face of the pagan invaders of their land. Augustine had come armed with the authority of a man that the Britons recognised in theory – the pope – but who in practice had had very little communion with them during the years of their struggle.

One of the kings who had, under the influence of Æthelberht, flirted with the new religion was Rædwald, king of the East Angles. Although there is no headstone, the common view

is that Rædwald was the king buried, in splendour and gold, at
Sutton Hoo. A pragmatist, politically and religiously, Rædwald
evidently thought it best not to cut off one god to compliment
another, and maintained shrines to the old gods alongside one
to the new god (an insurance policy for the afterlife reflected
in the mixture of pagan and Christian goods that accompanied
him to the grave).

King Æthelberht had died on 24 February 616. He had ruled
Kent for twenty-seven years and he died in his late sixties
from natural causes. But his death meant that the balance of
power between the other kingdoms was gone: with no enduring institutions or power structures other than the king's own
warband, the death of a mighty king threw all the other power
relationships into question. And there was a new power rising
in the north.

The warbands of Germanic incomers who started arriving in Britain in the fifth century (and possibly before) had
used the rivers, islands and littoral regions of the east as their
roads and initial bases. It was a slow-motion conquest, spread
over centuries, with the Britons successfully holding the line
and regaining territory for long periods of time. But the Britons had, gradually, been pushed back, with first the eastern
counties and then the midlands coming under the control of
Anglo-Saxon warlords. However, Brythonic kingdoms endured
longer in the north. An Anglian warband had seized the stronghold of Bamburgh around the middle of the sixth century but
the Brythonic kingdoms of the Old North – Yr Hen Ogledd –
were powerful in their own right and the sway of the Anglian
rulers of Bamburgh did not extend far beyond their stronghold
for the next few decades. Indeed, the kings of the Old North
joined forces to besiege these pagan, Anglian warriors, eventually forcing them to retreat to Lindisfarne.

But while they had their enemies trapped on Lindisfarne, the internal enmities that were always a key weakness of the Brythonic kingdoms emerged. According to the sixth-century poet bard Taliesin, from whose work most of the details of these obscure conflicts come, the foremost of the Brythonic kings besieging the Anglians on Lindisfarne was Urien, king of Rheged. But jealous of his power and fame, one of the kings allied to him arranged for Urien's assassination before the siege was completed. In the anger and recriminations following the assassination, the siege was ended, and fighting broke out between the sons of Urien and the men responsible for their father's death.

The pressure relieved, the Anglians returned to Bamburgh and slowly expanded their control. The ruling kin group traced their lineage back to a roving adventurer named Ida, so his descendants and heirs were called Idings. Although the Idings were Anglian and pagan, there are indications that they sometimes formed alliances with the other kings and warlords of north Britain, be they Britons, Picts or Dál Riatans. Urien's assassination revealed that an apparent friend might be more an enemy than your declared foes. In such a context of shifting alliances and short, violent reigns – if the Bernician king list can be trusted, among the first seven kings, the longest reign was twelve years and the average just under seven years – then it made sense to ally with whoever commanded the most trust, be he Anglian or Briton. However, by failing to finish off the Idings when they had the chance, the kings of the Old North opened the way for the man who would prove to be their nemesis and one of the most influential men in British history.

Æthelfrith is listed as the eighth king of Bernicia, and the first king of Northumbria. For during his reign, from c.593 to 616, the two northern Anglian realms of Bernicia, centred on

Bamburgh, and Deira, the southern Anglian realm with its chief seat in York, were forcibly united to create a single kingdom, Northumbria. It was Æthelfrith who did the forcing, albeit with careful planning. He married Acha, the daughter of the previous king of Deira. Æthelfrith had been married before. The original name of Bamburgh, legend has it, was Bebban-burgh, that is the stronghold of Bebba. Æthelfrith had given the fortress and its associated lands to his first wife, Bebba, as her portion. However, Bebba had either died or Æthelfrith, spotting a better-connected bride, put her aside to marry Acha. Once this second marriage was consummated and secure, Æthelfrith moved on Deira. We don't know how he gained control of the kingdom, whether by outright conquest or polit-ical manoeuvring, but by AD 604 he was king of Deira too.

There was, however, one inconvenient in-law. Acha's broth-er, Edwin. For his part, Edwin did not wait around. By 604, Æthelfrith's reputation as a ruthless and effective leader was well established. It was probably Æthelfrith who had defeated the men of the Old North at the Battle of Catraeth around 600, a battle commemorated in the poem 'Y Gododdin', that sings elegy for the slain warriors; it was definitely Æthelfrith who defeated Áedán mac Gabráin, king of Dál Riata, at the Battle of Degsastan in 603, ensuring the Northumbrian kingdom would not be attacked from that direction for a generation. Such was Æthelfrith's reputation for trickery that his Brythonic enemies gave him the name *flesaur*, which means 'twister'.

With a man like Æthelfrith in control, Edwin had little choice but to go into exile. He spent the next twelve years on the run while Æthelfrith's power grew. And as his power grew, so did his reach. Some later stories suggest that Edwin's first stop was the Brythonic kingdom of Gwynedd, where he was a youthful friend and rival of another young prince, Cadwallon. If true, this would lend a poignant layer of tragedy to later events but the story is probably too good to be true. However, we do know that Edwin was given sanctuary in the kingdom of Mercia, for he married the king's daughter, Coenburh by whom he had two sons.

As an exile with a claim to the throne of Deira, Edwin was a useful card in the power plays of sixth-century Britain. While the image of the lonely wandering exile is romantic, Edwin did not go into exile alone. As a prince, he had a retinue of warriors attached to him by oaths of loyalty, friendship and, probably, blood. But if Edwin was a card that the king of Mercia hoped to play against his neighbour and rival, Æthelfrith trumped him. Through threat and intimidation, Æthelfrith forced Cearl, the king of Mercia, to ask Edwin to leave. Æthelfrith would have preferred Edwin delivered to him, in whole or in part, but the ties of blood Edwin had forged through marrying Coenburh were too tight for Cearl to betray him outright. However, by 616, Edwin had left Mercia to seek protection from Rædwald, king of East Anglia. Which was when Æthelberht, fatefully, died.

The death of the high king pushed reset on the power balances between the different kingdoms. Æthelberht had been Rædwald's patron and ally. With Æthelberht dead, Æthelfrith was free to exert maximum pressure on Rædwald. So he did. Three times Æthelfrith sent messengers, mixing threats and promises, telling Rædwald to give up Edwin. Under the pressure, Rædwald cracked.

Then, the story goes, one of Edwin's retainers, learning that the king of the East Angles proposed to deliver Edwin into Æthelfrith's hands, came to Edwin at night and warned him of the threat he faced, while offering to find a way to get him to safety. Such was Æthelfrith's reach that that meant taking the grey sea road and going into exile abroad. The scene, as Bede writes it, highlights his gifts as a storyteller and, as such, rouses the suspicion of the historian. Did Bede telescope events to heighten the tension?

In despair, Edwin remained outside Rædwald's hall into the night, conflicting thoughts and emotions roiling in his mind and heart. Then, as Edwin was sitting on a stone, he saw a man, a stranger approaching. Although mindful that it might be an assassin, Edwin did not run: indeed, at this point he was all but paralysed by indecision. But the stranger spoke to him, asking why he was sitting alone outside when everyone else was asleep in the king's hall. Edwin replied that where he spent the night was his own concern. At which the stranger told him that he knew well the troubles that afflicted him, and then asked what reward he might give to someone who could relieve him of his troubles. Not surprisingly Edwin said he would give any reward in his power for such service. Then the stranger foretold that Edwin would become king. But not just any king: rather he would be a king whose power surpassed that of any of his ancestors. Finally, the stranger asked if Edwin would follow the guidance of a man who, as well as foretelling his earthly future, could also guide him to fortune and salvation. With such promises suddenly, mysteriously given to him, Edwin said that of course he would follow the counsel of whoever provided such blessings. Then the stranger put his right hand on Edwin's head and admonished him to remember the sign, and his promise. And, with that, the stranger disappeared.

Shortly afterwards, Edwin's retainer came to find him. Rædwald had changed his mind. Under the urging, not to say taunting, of his wife, Rædwald had decided that he could not betray the laws of hospitality and his own honour by handing Edwin over to Æthelfrith. It's likely too, that Rædwald, with his wife's prompting, saw an opportunity. Æthelberht was dead: everything was up for grabs. In the short-lived world of sixth-century kings, sometimes it was worth risking everything on the thrust of a sword.

Rædwald was going to fight.

Battles in the early medieval period were very different from those of high and late medieval times. The combatants were up close and on foot, rather than the mounted armoured charge that defined later medieval battles. Ranged weapons – bows, javelins, throwing axes – were certainly used but rarely seem to have had a decisive impact on the battle. And most importantly of all, the kings took part. In the early medieval period the king led and centred the line, surrounded by his household retainers. As the anchor and lynchpin of the line, the king was also the main target: kill the king and the battle was won. Rædwald knew that he was staking his life on the outcome of a battle with the most feared warrior in Britain.

Bede tells us a little about the ensuing battle: '[it] was fought in Mercian territory on the east bank of the river Idle'.[2] The consensus is that this was near the town of Bawtry, which lies on the west bank of the Idle: the town was a Roman settlement, situated to take advantage of the bridge carrying Ermine Street over the river. The Idle was navigable down to Bawtry, allowing easy access to the River Trent and then the Humber estuary and the North Sea. But Bawtry is a good twenty miles south of the Humber and the border of Northumbria: what was Æthelfrith doing there, so far from home?

It was not unknown for kings to campaign far from their core lands. Æthelfrith himself had won his most notorious victory at the Battle of Chester, more than ninety miles from York, when he defeated a Brythonic army from the kingdoms of Powys and Gwynedd. The notoriety of the victory resulted from the number of non-combatants Æthelfrith killed: before the battle began, Æthelfrith saw that the Christian Britons were accompanied by monks who were praying for victory for their brethren. Determined to even the battlefield of prayer before turning to the battlefield of armies, Æthelfrith directed his first attack against the assembled monks, saying, 'If they are crying to their God against us, they are fighting against us even if they do not bear arms.'[3] The men entrusted with guarding the monks turned tail at the approach of Æthelfrith's warriors, leaving the unarmed monks, who had come from the monastery at Bangor, to be slaughtered. Few returned. With their prayer shield removed, the Brythonic army was destroyed in turn. There are other examples of far-flung military expeditions so it was not unprecedented. But what was strange is that he had come so far with relatively few men. For Bede writes: 'As soon as the envoys had gone home, he [Rædwald] raised a great army to make war on Ethelfrid and allowing him no time to summon his full strength, encountered him with a great preponderance of force.'[4]

The place where the armies met and fought was on the borders of Mercia and the somewhat obscure kingdom of Lindsey (which roughly maps to modern-day Lincolnshire). This was a waterland, where the headwaters of the Humber flow together, and the Roman road marched on a causeway through the low floodplain. The outline of Britain, so familiar to us from maps nowadays, was different then. In particular, the east of the country was indented with meres, salt marshes and tidal reaches. East Anglia was only connected to the rest of the country via the relatively narrow strip of land running south from Cambridge; north of there the vast expanse of the Fens and the tidal plains of the Wash were unnavigable except for locals. North of the Wash and south of the Humber, the kingdom of Lindsey was also all but an island, the marshes at its northern and southern borders reaching long arms round towards each other and almost meeting. These geographical barriers had the effect of funnelling armies along particular arteries. Roman military engineers, with their usual surveying genius, had built roads that traversed the low eastern plains, suitable for carrying long columns of marching legionaries. Two centuries after the last legionary had marched upon them, the Roman roads were still the main inland routes used by the much smaller armies of the Anglo-Saxon kings.

Except when they went by water.

Bede is quite specific: Æthelfrith made his stand on the east bank of the River Idle. But seeing that he was beset by much greater forces, why didn't he make a run for it? It's likely that Æthelfrith fought because he had no choice: he was caught, taken unawares. At this distance of time, we don't know how Rædwald gathered the intelligence telling him where to find Æthelfrith, but experience would have told him that a king's warrior band, travelling from Northumbria, must go by one of the old roads. If Æthelfrith had been able to cross the River Idle, he would have been able to ride north to safety. So Rædwald, with his son Rægenhere's retinue and Edwin's retainers filling out his warband, somehow managed to pin Æthelfrith and his men back against the river. Their most likely avenue of approach, given the surprise Rædwald achieved, was from the north: Æthelfrith would not have expected attackers to come from the direction of home. But there was a way for Rædwald to attack from the north using a tactic that Edwin would later exploit: amphibious assault. If Rædwald had embarked his men on boats and sailed up the coast to the Humber, then it would have been a matter of hard rowing upstream of the Trent and the Idle to catch Æthelfrith unawares. Cut off and surrounded, the Twister, the greatest warlord of his time, had no choice but to draw his men up into the shieldwall and fight.

There are no military manuals from early Medieval Britain. The few written sources we have for the time were written by monks who had no interest in recording the tactics of kings and warriors. The better recorded history of the latter part of Anglo-Saxon England suggests shieldwalls were composed of levies of peasant farmers, poorly armed and worse trained, who were told to hold fast in line, shield to shield, poking with spears and trying not to get stabbed. It was an unsubtle and unsophisticated battle plan where simple weight of numbers would generally prevail.

Such might have been the case in the latter part of the Anglo-Saxon era, but in the sixth century, armies consisted of, at most, a few hundred men, and these spent the major part of their lives training for battle. There is every reason to suppose that such men would have deployed all their thoughts and resources for the developing of battle-winning tactics. So to think that these battles were won or lost solely by the push and shove of a spear-filled scrum is unlikely. However, the shieldwall was still the basic formation and when Æthelfrith saw the banners of Rædwald and Edwin and knew that he must give battle, he would have formed his men into line. Then came the dry mouths and whispered prayers, the invocations and rubbing of charms: the age-old preparations for men in battle.

Battle in the early medieval period was up close, personal. Killing, you saw the life light extinguished in the man you'd killed; you smelled the iron tang of spilled blood and the stench of voided bowels. Before battle was joined, men hurled insults, boasted, drummed on the sides of their shields with their spears. Seeing himself outnumbered, Æthelfrith probably tried to goad Rædwald into facing him one on one. It was useless, of course: Rædwald had the numbers and would bring them to bear, but showing his enemy unwilling to meet him face to face was one way for Æthelfrith to give heart to his surrounded men.

Then the missiles started flying. Javelins, arrows, throwing axes, stones even. The javelins were meant to strike and stick into shields, weighing them down so that eventually the man carrying what was becoming a hedgehog would have to lower it, leaving himself open to a swift spear thrust. It's likely the ranged weapons were directed at particular parts of the enemy's line: where the king had his banner, the flanks, or any areas made weaker by difficult ground underfoot.

Then, the advance. In line, or perhaps in a staggered formation known as the boar's head that was intended to break through the enemy's shieldwall by concentration of weight and force. Æthelfrith must have attempted to anchor his line so that it could not be turned, putting at least one wing against the river and using whatever other landscape feature he could find to protect the other. But looking at the number of men advancing upon him, their battle mettle proved by the glint of garnet on sword hilts and buckles, the Twister knew that the time for twisting was done. Now it was time to fight.

The shieldwalls met. And Æthelfrith's line broke. In the vicious melée, men were cut down, bodies stripped of their armour and weapons, and the dead mutilated. There was no quarter: among the dead was Rædwald's own son, Rægenhere. Having inflicted such a casualty, Æthelfrith and his men would have expected no mercy.

For a king's man, a bondsman held by oaths of loyalty, to survive his lord's fall was a matter of disgrace. It's likely that none of Æthelfrith's men suffered such a disgrace for, according to a later chronicler, Henry of Huntingdon, 'The river Idle was foul with the blood of Englishmen' (you can tell it was a later chronicler as no contemporary would have called the dead 'Englishmen': they were East Angles, men of Deira, Bernicians). By the banks of the River Idle, Æthelfrith Iding, the greatest warrior king of his time, was cut down and died. And his kingdom died with him.

With Æthelfrith's death, there was nothing and no one to go on: no institutions, no independent secular powers, no spiritual powers able to continue without the Twister. The kingdom he had carved out in northern Britain dissolved almost immediately. For the victors, Rædwald and Edwin, it was vindication and exaltation. Although victory had cost the life of his son, the defeat of Æthelfrith, coming soon after the death of Æthelberht, transformed the king of the East Angles from a vassal of Kent to the power in the land. He installed Edwin as king of Northumbria, who was obligated to Rædwald for life and position.

The battle of the River Idle was fought in 616. Rædwald's imperium lasted for another ten or so years and the wealth it brought him is shown by the riches buried alongside him at Sutton Hoo. Bede and the *Anglo-Saxon Chronicle* list him as the fourth high king, or *bretwalda*, a much written-about term indicating some sort of overlordship of the other kingdoms of Britain.

That such a turnaround should follow a single defeat highlights the brittle nature of power at this time. And none felt its breaking more keenly than Æthelfrith's wife and children. Despite being sister to Edwin, Queen Acha fled, taking her children with her. Edwin had spent most of his life in exile, being hunted by the father of her children: she evidently did not wish to risk their lives upon his mercy.

For his part, Edwin rode north. He was of the royal family

of Deira, a lineage that had been expelled during Æthelfrith's takeover of the kingdom, so it is likely that he received a warm if nervous welcome along the way of his royal progress up Ermine Street to York. The news must have spread before him, whispered in wonder and fear: the king is dead.

With Æthelfrith's passing, all the power relationships, all the patronages and gifts devolving from the king were up for grabs. To cement his position, Edwin must have confirmed some in their positions as he went north, recalling some shared memory of his childhood. Others he would have supplanted with men who had followed him in his long exile and whose faithfulness he knew to be absolute: now was the time for their reward. Land was the chief gift a king might give. This was land rendered in return for service, the king's gift that returned to the king upon the recipient's death. The king might choose to bestow it afresh upon the dead man's heirs, but there was no obligation upon him to do so: in many cases, the land had to be earned anew.

As Edwin made his way north, passing through Deira, he was in familiar and relatively safe territory. But on entering Bernicia, he was passing into the land of the Idings. There was no surety of a welcome there, and Edwin must have ridden with caution, surrounded by a warband of nervous warriors. But such was the shock of Æthelfrith's defeat and the complete-ness of his losses that there seems to have been no resistance to the new king on his progress.

However, there was one stronghold that might hold against him. Bamburgh.

The Anglo-Saxons, the Britons, the Picts and the Gaels were not builders in stone as the Romans had been: while they dug ditches and dykes, there was very little in the way of buildings in any way comparable to the castles of the Norman period and afterwards. Most royal centres were wooden halls, exquisitely made from wood, but protected mainly by the strength of arms of the men guarding it. As a result, the small armies of this time had very little in the way of siegecraft. If an initial assault did not take a stronghold – there were a few, such as those at Dunadd, Dumbarton Rock and Edinburgh – then there was little prospect of capturing it since small armies did not provide enough men for the thorough interdiction required for a successful siege and nor did they have later castle-breaking technologies such as trebuchets and siege towers. So, if Bamburgh was held against Edwin, there would have been little he could do except wait for its defenders to come out.

As the ancestral stronghold of the Idings, Bamburgh was where Edwin might have expected to find his sister. But when he arrived there with his men, Acha and her children were gone. Although her children were still young – Oswald was twelve, Oswiu was four and Æbbe, her daughter, even younger – they were dangerous as the potential future focus of revolt. Edwin also had to consider their obligation to revenge: he had killed the boys' father. Unless he paid them the blood money, the *weregild*, due for the killing of a king, they would be bound to avenge their father's death. In a time without courts, police or any form of redress other than calling curses down from the gods, the only sanction available for the murder of a relative was the bloodfeud. Such feuds would come to haunt Northumbrian politics in future centuries, bleeding out its strength. It would have made a hard, bleak sense for Edwin to find and kill the sons of the Twister, and to marry Edwin's daughter to one of his own sons. Maybe he had counted on his blood ties with his sister persuading her to remain and trust in his restraint.

But Acha was gone.

Edwin, through the many years of his exile, had always tended south: possibly Gwynedd, certainly Mercia and East Anglia. His outlook and his contacts all faced south. So Acha went north. Sometime later in 616, a small group of refugees, protected by the handful of men who had remained to guard the queen, made their weary way up to the gates of Dunadd, chief stronghold of the kingdom of Dál Riata. Acha was about to put herself and her children at the mercy of the people whom her husband had defeated thirteen years before at the Battle of Degsastan. If it was a hope, it was a desperate hope.

5

Stories of Who We Are

Keys can come in all sorts of shapes and materials. Sometimes they're iron and key shaped. On this occasion, the key was bone, about four inches long and an inch wide, with a hole at one end and twin tines at the other. It was found in one of the trenches at Bamburgh Castle and when the student excavating first brought it to the archaeologists of the BRP, nobody knew what it was. So, being archaeologists, they researched it.

Turned out the bone was a lucet, a tool that is used for making cord, edging or belt material. The product is about one centimetre wide although it can be made narrower or broader depending on what kind of twine is used. The cord a lucet produces is generally multicoloured and patterned, with a huge array of patterns possible.

As Paul researched modern lucets – the craft has been revived recently after falling into abeyance for many centuries – and compared them to the excavated example from Bamburgh, he realised that he was looking through a bone-shaped window into the culture of the time. For the lucet was intricately carved with the angular knotwork typical of the time. Originally, it might even have been painted, bringing out the detail of the carving. The edging that the anonymous woman made with her lucet was brightly coloured and patterned as well, as has been demonstrated by the fragments of Anglo-Saxon clothing that have been excavated.

The lucet had been made by a people who loved colour and intricate patterns. Think on the surviving art of the time and shortly afterwards, such as the *Lindisfarne Gospels*: it would be hard to imagine anything more richly decorated than the *Gospels*, yet the decorative borders and carpet pages that dazzle us today were not out of the ordinary for the time: people really dressed like that. Their tunics and cloaks were edged with interlocking, intricate patterns that paralleled the carpet pages of the *Gospels*.

A generation of films have schooled us into seeing the medieval world in a palette of greys and browns – a washed-out, wintry world. It was not like that. Strange to say, but the Technicolor Hollywood epics of the 1950s were a more accurate representation of the colour of Medieval Europe than more recent efforts. Even those glories of high medieval civilisation, the cathedrals, we see today drained of the colour that once covered them, their frescoes and murals and paint-ed statues having been whitewashed or destroyed during the Reformation. Think of a Hindu temple, with its painted stat-ues of the gods and coloured walls and ceilings. That was what the cathedrals would have looked like.

In the seventh century, churches in Britain were few and simply decorated, the austerity of the Ionan monks carrying over into the paucity of decoration. But the people, at least those who could afford it, were colourful. Given the general love of bright colours, even the poor probably tried to brighten their clothing and their homes, using local, easily produced dyes, and flowers. The rich, of course, flaunted it, wearing their wealth. Of these, the most ostentatious was the king.

However, becoming the king of an Anglo-Saxon kingdom in early Medieval Britain was not a straightforward matter of being first-born to the ruling monarch. While being the son of a king was preferred, it was not essential. More distant relationships could suffice, which meant that there were a range of men who could be called *ætheling*, that is throne worthy. The king was, in the end, the man who could command the loyalty and the fighting skills of enough warriors to bolster his rule. He was the boss of the local bosses, the man who went around with his retinue of killers and imposed peace by leading a gang that was bigger and scarier than anyone else's. If that sounds like a racket, in many ways it was. The warrior aristocracy imposed themselves upon the food-producing peasantry as 'protection': you feed us and we'll defend you from other men like us.

However, at the start of this period, the social hierarchy was relatively narrow. At the bottom were the slaves. Raiding and warfare was endemic, with slave-taking one of its principal aims. Slaves from Britain were valuable and traded over long distances; Gregory had seen a party of fair-haired Anglo-Saxon youths for sale in Rome at the end of the fifth century. In times of famine a family might sell itself into slavery as an alternative to starvation, a master being obliged to feed his slaves. Unlike under Roman law, slaves weren't entirely without rights. Later Anglo-Saxon law codes stipulated *weregild*, blood payment, for the injury or killing of a slave, although these would be paid to the slave's master rather than his relatives.

The mark of a free man was the right to carry a spear. The great majority of the population in this early period belonged to the class known as *ceorls*, from which 'churl' derives. However, Anglo-Saxon ceorls had none of the negative connotations of the later churl. These were free men who worked the land, although there was a wide range of wealth among the ceorls, from those who scraped a living on a small plot of land and were bound to work their lord's land, to others who owned considerable acreage and paid their lord for his protection by rent, in this period paid in kind rather than in cash.

Above the ceorls was the warrior class, the class into which the son of Thunder was born. Among the Anglo-Saxons, these men were called *gesiths* in the earliest texts and *thegns* in later writings. A gesith was a companion to the king, which suggests how a man might ascend the social classes at this time: by being useful with sword and spear and becoming part of the king's squad of warriors. The reward for faithful service to the king was land. Once granted land, the thegn became the king's man on that particular piece of ground, enforcing peace and taxing the population, passing on the spoils to the king while taking a cut for himself. The highest-ranking companions to the king would have had several parcels of land, with a number of associated halls, allowing for a more local variation on the peripatetic life of the king and his household.

However, almost all the records for this social organisation come from the seventh century and later, when the hierarchy had formed and promulgated laws to protect itself. The way this organisation, very different from that of Roman Britain, emerged is still mysterious, for it took place during the fifth and sixth centuries, two hundred years that deserve, at least in one respect, to be called Dark Ages.

The written sources for these two centuries are extraordinarily meagre. Apart from the two that we will go on to examine in more detail, there are the *Senchus fer n-Alban* (The history of the men of Scotland), a tenth-century document written in Old Irish believed to contain material that is much older and which deals with the military obligations of the constituent clans of Dál Riata; the Welsh *Triads*, found in books dating between the late-thirteenth and late-fourteenth centuries, which contain much of the folklore of Wales, references to King Arthur and collections of sayings about the history of the Britons grouped in triplets (hence Triads); and the poem *Y Gododdin. Y Gododdin* survives in one manuscript, the *Book of Aneirin*, written in the second half of the thirteenth century. *Y Gododdin* is ascribed to the poet Aneirin, and probably contains material first sung and chanted soon after the Battle of Catraeth around 600.

As poems, and poems written down much later than the events they deal with, the *Triads* and *Y Gododdin* provide much valuable information about the culture in which they were formed, but they are difficult to mine for historical facts. For these, the most obvious sources are the two contemporary writings that we have for the fifth and sixth centuries: Patrick (*fl.*fifth century), erstwhile Brythonic slave, latterly saint of Ireland, and his short defence of his life and work commonly called the *Confession* and an even shorter *Letter to Coroticus*, denouncing that king for taking some of Patrick's people as slaves during a raid into Ireland, and Gildas (*fl.*fifth–sixth centuries), a Brythonic priest and monk, who wrote a lament and jeremiad *De excidio et conquestu Britanniae* (*On the Ruin and Conquest of Britain*); parts of some of his letters also survive, as well as a penitential but it's the *De excidio* that is the most important, and most frustrating, work to survive from the obscure centuries when the country was utterly changed. The *De excidio* is a full-on jeremiad against the rulers of the Britons, written by a cleric convinced that God's wrath waxed against the cruelty and injustice of the men who had taken on the rule of the Britons and, as a result, had visited upon their people the alien Saxons as scourge and punishment. For this there was much biblical warrant, as the story of the Jews, in Gildas's reading, was the story of an erring, errant people hauled back from their wanderings from the true path by the barbed whips of an angered God. He set his hooks into the flesh of his wandering people and hauled them back to His worship. For Gildas, the lesson was clear: God had set Nebuchadnezzar as the whip of his anger against the Jews' failure to uphold their covenant, destroying the Temple and transporting them into captivity. Now, He was doing the same to the Britons, with the Saxons as the instruments of his wrath.

De excidio makes for an intensely frustrating historical document. It's the only contemporary account of the arrivals of the Germanic barbarians in Britain, but there are barely any named figures in it, and no dates. But what is clear, from the text itself, is that Gildas was a highly educated man. *De excidio* is written in excellent Latin by a man who was steeped in biblical texts but who also had a thorough grounding in classical literature. So a century after the end of Roman Britain, a Briton was still able to benefit from a thorough Roman education, combined with the Judeo-Christian elements proper to a monk. This indicates that a certain amount of the old Roman Britain had survived through the first century of the *adventus Saxonum*, at least in some parts of the British Isles.

The story told by Gildas was accepted by historians through the nineteenth and on into the twentieth century – there wasn't much in the way of an alternative. The standard text for students of Anglo-Saxon history through most of the twentieth century was Sir Frank Merry Stenton's *Anglo-Saxon England* – a book for which the word 'magisterial' might have been coined – and in it Stenton concludes that the Anglo-Saxons did conquer a kingdom, although its extent was limited to the south and east, their advance being checked by military victories of the Britons in the middle of the sixth century. This view, although more nuanced than the popular history of Victorian times, saw the history of Britain as one of the conquest and displacement of the Britons westwards until they became the Welsh and could be safely ignored by the incoming ancestors of the English.

With no other sources of information forthcoming from historical sources, this view might have remained cemented in places. But by the twentieth century, a new scientific discipline was beginning to find its place and its confidence. Archaeology is young, among the most youthful of the sciences, which lends a certain appropriateness to its close relationship with history, the oldest of the humanities. It began to develop as a discipline in its own right when various servants of the British Empire, who had administered vast colonial possessions during their time abroad, developing a deep interest in foreign cultures and histories, started coming home. A number of these Imperial officers started to look at England's green and pleasant land with eyes trained under the unflinching glare of the tropical sun: and they saw it differently. To them, it was as strange and foreign as Hindustan or Ceylon.

Of these Imperial servants, the most important in the history of archaeology was Augustus Lane Fox Pitt-Rivers (1827–1900). An officer in the Grenadier Guards, Pitt-Rivers was appointed to the commission overseeing the introduction of rifles to the British Army (soldiers had used muskets before). While working for the commission, Pitt-Rivers developed a deep interest in the evolution of firearms and began collecting weapons, slowly constructing a typology of their development. He then extended this interest in collection and classification to show the development of other aspects of human culture, amassing large collections of artefacts, tools and weapons from all over the world. In response to Darwin's theory of natural selection, Pitt-Rivers developed a theory of the evolution of culture, using his collection to illustrate this. Pitt-Rivers's insight that he could devise a chronological sequence based on slight changes in the design of weapons and tools was crucial for the key archaeological concept of typology that allows sequences to be worked out.

Pitt-Rivers also developed many of the techniques of field archaeology. In this he was blessed by the inheritance that gave him his name. Originally christened Augustus Henry Lane Fox, in 1880 he inherited the estate of his cousin, Horace Pitt, the sixth Baron Rivers, and changed his name to Augustus Henry Lane Fox Pitt-Rivers. While still Lane Fox, Pitt-Rivers had begun doing archaeology when posted to Ireland, then continued after his return to England in 1867, excavating in Yorkshire, Sussex and the Thames Valley. But with his inheritance of Cranborne Chase, Pitt-Rivers was gifted a huge area of land straddling Wiltshire and Dorset that had been left largely untouched since prehistoric times. With the inheritance from Horace Pitt, Pitt-Rivers had become an extremely wealthy man and he used that wealth to finance the team of excavators, draughtsmen and labourers he employed for his excavations. He had a unique set of skills and experience from his army career and he applied these skills and the most up-to-date scientific methods, such as mapping and stratigraphy, in his investigations of Cranborne Chase. He also started developing some new archaeological techniques such as drawing sections, cutting straight edges and making models of what he had found, as well as retaining all the artefacts that had been excavated rather than just the obviously interesting items. It was Pitt-

Rivers's insistence on retaining everything dug up that marked out his approach as different from what had gone before. There had been many prior excavations by antiquarians and treasure hunters, but with these digs, if it wasn't beautiful or valuable, it was discarded; even the most thoughtful of Victorian antiquarians was attracted to the out of the ordinary, something that might occupy the place of honour in a curio cabinet. There really wasn't that much to distinguish these investigations from the attentions of grave robbers. But for Pitt-Rivers, everything was interesting and it was this emphasis on the everyday items of the past and the careful, precise recording of exactly where everything was found, that laid many of the foundations for modern archaeology.

Augustus Pitt-Rivers, the faithful servant of the British Empire, was typical of another facet of the slowly coalescing new discipline: many of its techniques and technologies derived from the same techniques and technologies that had made the British Empire successful: surveying, cartography and the necessary logistical expertise to mount and maintain a military or an archaeological expedition. Meanwhile, the encounter with other cultures at markedly different levels of development provided an ethnographic avenue into exploring the past.

Ethnographers studying tribes who made their living through stone-age technologies could credibly argue that these primitive lifestyles (being confident Victorians, they saw no need to put scare quotes around 'primitive') could be read into the past. Taken together, these strands were starting to lay the foundations for productive archaeological theory. This was the era of the gentleman adventurer, of men like Richard Burton, Flinders Petrie and T. E. Lawrence, men who could, through mastery of language and mores, enter into an extraordinary variety of different cultures. For instance, Lawrence went to the Middle East ostensibly as an archaeologist, but while there he also gathered information on the Turks in preparation for the coming conflict. This was the apotheosis of the English public-school tradition and its production of men who, while born wealthy, could happily live in a cave for three years while excavating ancient ruins. The stoicism and tolerance of pain and discomfort inculcated by that style of public-school education no doubt had many drawbacks, but it did produce some extraordinary individuals.

The period after the First World War saw huge advances in archaeology as a result of the technologies developed during the war years. Aerial photography, for instance, made it possible to see patterns in the landscape that were invisible from ground level but it remained a science that was the playground of the rich amateur. The Second World War created a seven-year hiatus in the field, but when the war was over the Ministry of Works, which was created to remake the country after the ravages of wartime, tied archaeology into its programme of rebuilding. The war had also provided a huge collection of aerial photographs waiting to be deciphered. Meanwhile geophysical techniques developed in the exploration for oil and other resources began to be applied to archaeology.

Through its history, archaeology has been a magpie discipline, plucking its techniques and theories from all and sundry, first pursued by upper-class men with considerable personal resources and a general ability to withstand discomfort, before modulating into a pursuit for a wider variety of eccentrics with less money but access to a broader suite of techniques and technologies: the 'men-in-sheds' mentality of the Second World War translated into field studies.

As the effectiveness of archaeological techniques improved,

the confidence of archaeologists expanded too. With the discipline still in its infancy in the first half of the twentieth century, archaeologists were content to be the handmaids to historians, sifting through the earth with their trowels for physical examples of historical accounts. But in the decades after the Second World War the new discipline pulled itself out from under the skirts of the historians and started to assert itself: archaeologists were going to start doing it for themselves.

In Britain, what they found suggested much more cultural interaction and co-existence between the Angles, the Saxons and the native Britons than the historical sources and the old historical narrative suggested. For instance, the discovery of large amounts of Roman-style pottery and coins at the excavation of the West Stow site in Suffolk suggested to the excavators that, in this case at least, the inhabitants of what was indubitably an Anglo-Saxon village had settled alongside the previous inhabitants. The archaeologists were discovering a patchwork country of small settlements, widely separate from each other and not as yet united into kingdoms. The implication was that Anglo-Saxon villages were interspersed with the settlements of the native Britons, suggesting a history of gradual migration rather than the apocalyptic tides of conquest we read of in Gildas.

Perhaps the most cogent argument was presented by palaeobotanists. By looking at the pollen from deep core samples, they could work out the density of tree and arable coverage over the time of changes. According to this, there was very little difference in the proportions of forest, pasture and arable land throughout the period. This suggested that there was very little change in the area of land being farmed from the end of the western Roman Empire until the consolidation of England, Wales and Scotland into states. But if the period had been characterised by great displacements of people, then some land would have fallen out of cultivation, to turn back to shrubland and then forest. However, there was no sign of this in the pollen record so the same amount of land must have remained in cultivation throughout. In order to explain this, archaeologists argued that the agricultural communities remained in place: only the upper layers of society changed.

In the new interpretation of the evidence, the Angles and Saxons, rather than being an incoming horde driving all before them, were elite bands of warriors who arrived and fought the warrior elites of the native Britons, slowly cutting the tops off various local pyramids of power and placing themselves at the apex. In this view, with Angles and Saxons in place at the top of the social hierarchy their language and culture was gradually imposed upon the peasantry, whose day-to-day life was little changed by the alteration in power arrangements, but who had to adapt to the different language and culture of their new lords.

In the scholarly skirmishes that ensued, archaeologists tended to favour the new interpretation while historians, and in particular the specialists in the history of place names, remained convinced that the native British population had been largely displaced, at least in the eastern and central regions of the country. Both sides could marshal bodies of evidence in their favour. For the archaeologists, the patterns of settlement and, in particular, the palaeobotanical record told a tale of continuity, suggesting the continued settlement of the land by static farming communities.

The place name specialists disagree. Looking to the earliest names of places in England, they find few names that can be derived from Brythonic, the ancestor language to Welsh, Breton, Cornish and Cumbric. So how, ask the place name historians, could these names be English if they weren't bestowed by the English? Therefore, the English, or rather the Angles, Saxons and other tribes, must have been in possession of the land with either no or very few of the native Britons around to answer the question, 'Hey, what is the name of that hill over there?'

To settle this argument, new evidence was needed. It has come, curled up in the double helix of DNA. There have been many studies trying to answer the question of the origins of the peoples of the British Isles, looking at varying samples of the population from different parts of the country, and they have come up with wildly varying answers. But as the numbers of studies have increased, and the samples and areas they have examined have widened, an overall consensus on what these DNA studies are telling us has gradually emerged.

In this view, the onset of the Anglo-Saxons lies somewhere between the two opposing views described above. Yes, there was a meaningful movement of people coming to Britain, but it was a movement spread over centuries rather than being an invasion completed in one or two generations. But there was also significant emigration from Britain, with native Britons moving to the continent. At the top level of society there was what might be called genetic churn through the giving of princesses and other high-status women as brides to cement alliances. The young Norwegian woman found in the Bowl Hole cemetery might well be an example of this sort of exchange. There was also significant mixing at the bottom level of society through slave-taking and -trading.

Recent research using DNA studies on Anglo-Saxon settlement suggests that the earliest Anglo-Saxon cemeteries contain only Anglo-Saxon remains, which indicates an almost apartheid-like separation between Anglo-Saxon and Brythonic populations. But then, over time, the cemeteries start to include Brythonic bodies as well as Anglo-Saxon remains, before finally interring people of mixed heritage. However, there were areas of Britain that were never settled by the Anglo-Saxons. Think of a topological map of Britain, and then think of a tide coming in, washing through the lowlands but not reaching the high-lands. There seem to be islands of population whose genetic signatures have barely changed since the first humans arrived here after the retreat of the glaciers at the end of the last Ice Age. These populations have remained, static and relatively unmixed, as successive waves of incomers have washed through the 'lower' levels. So there are some corners of Britain that have been backwoods for ten thousand years while other regions have seen their populations change many times through the later centuries. This is undoubtedly a feature of natural geog-raphy: those areas isolated by mountains, moorland and remoteness have simply remained more or less untouched by later arrivals.

6

New Gods

On 14 June 1939, just as the lights were beginning to go off in Europe, the first real illumination of the Dark Ages in Britain shone into a buried chamber in Suffolk. Basil Brown, a farmer's son who had left school at twelve and taught himself archaeology (as well as Latin, Greek, French, German, Spanish, astronomy, geology and geography), had just stuck his finger into the chamber that months of patient excavation had gradually uncovered. But the sun was setting, and Brown had to cover over the dig for the night and return the next day to see what he had found.

The subsequent weeks of excavation revealed that Brown had made the most important archaeological discovery in English history. He had found an untouched ship burial of unmatched magnificence and significance.

The Anglo-Saxons who came to Britain in the fifth and sixth centuries were supposed to be barbarians – illiterate, pagan, destructive. In Britain they had supplanted the civilisation bequeathed by Rome and inaugurated a new age, a Dark Age.

But what teams of restorers gradually revealed was a culture that was, in some areas at least, of astonishing sophistication. Visiting the Sutton Hoo display in the British Museum, the most obvious aspect of this refinement is the metalwork. Extraordinarily intricate gold buckles and mounts, with cloisonnéd garnets, gleam and glister behind the glass. The materials used give evidence for trading networks far greater than had been suspected previously – the garnets came from India and Sri Lanka. Other objects in the burial chamber had also come from distant shores. The metal worker who created the buckles and brooches buried at Sutton Hoo was not content to rely solely upon the natural reflection of light to make the red of the garnets glitter. Instead, he helped them glow. On their mounting, he hammered little pyramidal indentations to which he fitted each garnet, a pyramid for each jewel. Sitting on a reflective golden pyramid, every garnet glows with a secret fire lit by the exquisite skill of the craftsman who put them there.

The magnificence of the finds suggested a royal burial. Dating had narrowed the possibilities to the first half of the seventh century, but that could indicate several candidates among the kings of the East Angles. The village of Rendlesham, which was one of the centres used by the Wuffingas, the kings of the East Angles, lay only three and a half miles northeast of Sutton Hoo, lending further credence to the belief that this was a royal burial. Sutton Hoo lies by the River Deben and, when the mound was built, it would have commanded the view of anyone sailing up the river.

The ruling dynasty of the East Angles traced their lineage back to a founding figure, Wuffa, hence Wuffingas, and according to their king lists Wuffa was followed by Tytila, Rædwald and Eorpwald. Of these, Wuffa probably would have been too early – if he existed at all, some historians consider him a quasi-mythical foundation figure – while Eorpwald converted enthusiastically to Christianity so seems an unlikely candidate for such a predominantly pagan burial. That leaves either Tytila or Rædwald. Tytila was a thoroughgoing pagan but Rædwald, according to Bede, was a man to bet each way with the gods: although he accepted Christian baptism from his ally and over-lord, Æthelberht of Kent, when he returned to his home he maintained a mixed Christian/pagan shrine, jumbling up religious objects and devotions. As such, Rædwald seems the best candidate for the man buried at Sutton Hoo. Buried with him were two silver christening spoons, marked 'Paul' and 'Saul' in Greek, while the ship burial, and the rich grave goods, is the epitome of a pagan burial. So while there is no way to definitively state who was buried in a ship in seventh-century East Anglia, Rædwald remains the most likely candidate.

Rædwald's death would have brought about a profound change in the fortunes of Edwin, the man he had installed upon the throne of Northumbria. Bede, monkishly appalled by Rædwald's shake and bake attitude to religion, does not mention him after his role in defeating King Æthelfrith, so we do not know exactly when he died, or how. But sometime around 627 seems likely for when, and some variation on natural causes, rather than death in battle, seems probable as to how. As the pre-eminent power in Britain, and with death not having involved the sort of catastrophic defeat that ended Æthelfrith's imperium, it might have been expected that Rædwald's surviving son, Eorpwald, would also assume his status as *Bretwalda*, high king over the realms of the Anglo-Saxons, but this was not what happened. Much scholarly ink has been shed over the exact meaning of *Bretwalda* and the power and status it conveyed, with so far little agreement, but it is clear that, along with kingship in general, it was a reflection of power rather than a title of power. The *Bretwalda* was the king with the most clout; it could not be claimed by birth, but only earned through strength and cunning.

As such, by the time Rædwald died, there was another power in the land: King Edwin of Northumbria. He had waited a long time for this. When, in 616, Rædwald had installed him on the throne of Northumbria, he had been the junior partner in the alliance. But in the following decade Edwin had steadily extended his power. He brought the Brythonic kingdom of Elmet, which today roughly maps onto the West Riding of Yorkshire, under his control early in his reign, and added the Anglo-Saxon kingdom of Lindsey, which approximates to modern-day Lincolnshire, sometime around Rædwald's death. Bede notes that Edwin also conquered the isles of Man and Anglesey during his reign, although the exact dates for these conquests are uncertain. However, the fact that such seaborne invasions were both recorded and credible tells us something about the resources an Anglo-Saxon king could command. While it's possible that the ships required for such an invasion could have sailed from anchorages on Northumbria's coast, up and around Scotland and down into the Irish Sea – there being records of other such ventures – it seems more likely that Edwin commandeered vessels on the west coast. But the sheer fact that his power extended to the west coast, despite Northumbria's east coast position, indicated his reach. The likely embarkation points for an assault on the Isle of Man were all in the Kingdom of Rheged, the Brythonic kingdom that had most vigorously contested Northumbrian power. So for Edwin to have assailed the Isle of Man from a port in Rheged suggests that he had brought it under his control. The petty kingdoms and statelets that had existed in the two centuries after the withdrawal of the

Roman legions were gradually being swallowed up by the most powerful.

If Bede's account of the night-time meeting with a mysterious stranger who persuaded Edwin to stay with Rædwald is true, then by the 620s Edwin must also have realised that the first two prophecies the stranger had made to him had come true: he had defeated his enemy, Æthelfrith, and he had ascended to greater power than any of his forebears. Now there was only the third to come true: 'If the man who can truthfully foretell such good fortune can also give you wiser and better guidance for your life and salvation than anything known to your parents and kinsfolk, will you promise to obey him and follow his salutary advice?'[1]

Many historians contend that Bede knew perfectly well who approached Edwin on that night of despair but chose not to mention the fact as it did not fit with his narrative. The man's name was Paulinus, and he was Italian. Paulinus had arrived in Britain in 601, part of the second group of missionaries Pope Gregory sent to reinforce Augustine's pioneering group of Italians in Kent. Given that Rædwald had been baptised, probably in Kent, with Æthelberht acting as his godfather and sponsor, there would have been good reason for a member of the Augustinian mission to have been either visiting or resident with Rædwald's court when Edwin was exiled there. Even if it was not Paulinus, whichever member of the mission had made those predictions would have been sure to have told Paulinus of them before he set off. For in 625, Paulinus was headed north, as part of the escort for Edwin's new wife, Æthelburh of Kent.

Edwin was nearing the height of his powers. By this time his supremacy was unchallenged in the north of Britain, at least as far as the Firth of Forth. But in the south there were two rising powers: the kingdom of Mercia, in the Midlands, and the West Saxons, in the kingdom of Wessex. As a young man Edwin had found exile with the Mercians, and sufficient favour from their king, Cearl, to marry his daughter, Coenburh, and father two sons, Osfrith and Eadfrith. But by the mid 620s, Coenburh had either died or Edwin had decided to repudiate her for a more favourable match with Æthelburh – we don't really know which, although the silence about Coenburh's fate might suggest death by one of the many hazards that attended life in the seventh century.

As for Edwin's intended, there are indications that Princess Æthelburh, although young, had already proved that she would play the full part in royal politics that Anglo-Saxon queens were expected to play. Royal women were 'peace weavers', the key dynastic pieces in the complex links of marriage and influence that were the other strand, alongside the military, that decided the hierarchy among the kingdoms of Britain. Her brother, Eadbald, had inherited the kingdom of Kent from his father, Æthelberht. Eadbald had struggled to match his father's authority and, seeking to shore up his own status, he had married his father's queen. While on the face of it this suggests something far too Oedipal for comfort, Æthelberht's queen wasn't Eadbald's mother. Queen Bertha, the Frankish princess who had given birth to Eadbald and Æthelburh as well as facilitating the acceptance of Augustine's mission, had died and King Æthelberht had taken a new wife, most probably from the local nobility. Unfortunately we don't know the name of this Kentish queen because our source, Bede, was appalled by the implied incest of a son marrying his father's wife, as were the contemporary Kentish clergymen. Deciding that the political benefits of the match outweighed the religious disadvantages, Eadbald went ahead with the marriage while going back on his religion: he abjured his faith.

This is where Æthelburh comes in. Eadbald's sister was the scion on her mother's side of the Frankish royal family. The Merovingians were the most prestigious royal line in northern Europe and they were deeply Christian. If Eadbald wanted his sister to play her part in the family's fortunes, she would do so as a Christian princess and she expected her brother to do the same as a Christian king.

The high status of the king of Kent among the kingdoms of Britain depended upon the king's links with the Franks and the prestige and sheer bling those links brought with them. When faced with a choice between the political advantages of strengthening ties with a local clan, through his marriage, or ensuring continuing good relations with the king of the Franks, there was really no contest as far as Eadbald was concerned. To his sister's great satisfaction, Eadbald put aside his queen and resumed his faith.

With her brother a Christian king again, Æthelburh was willing to play her part in Anglo-Saxon politics. Edwin was thirty-nine by this time, while she was still in her teens or early twenties, but this was not unusual for Anglo-Saxon kings. The negotiations between the two kings would have been intense and complex. By marrying Æthelburh, Edwin was entering into alliance with the most prestigious of the Anglo-Saxon kingdoms. According to their own tales, it was in Kent that the twin brothers, Hengist and Horsa, had landed with their warbands as mercenaries for the kings of Britain. Kent also had the longest pedigree of Romanisation and the strongest links back to Rome of anywhere in the country. There had been Roman villas in Kent from the first century. Anglo-Saxon kings, in common with other barbarian kings in Europe, loved to

show their quality by demonstrating their Romanitas, generally by the display of imported finery, which wasn't necessarily
Roman but which suggested Rome through its magnificence.

Edwin would also be bringing the whole east coast of Britain, from the Firth of Forth to the Isle of Thanet, under his
control. As the daughter of a Frankish princess and sister of
the king of Kent, Æthelburh would also be bringing the kind
of wealth that seventh-century kings coveted and required. A
king needed to be seen as magnificent, in his bearing and his
display. The great helmet uncovered in Mound 1 at Sutton
Hoo gives some indication of the magnificence to which these
kings aspired.

For his part, marrying Æthelburh to Edwin would give King
Eadbald of Kent the support of the most powerful warlord in
Britain. Together, they could face down the rising challenge of
Wessex and Mercia. But there was the question of his sister's
faith. Æthelburh had been instrumental in his own reversion
to Christianity: the young woman would have let her brother
know that she would not renounce it herself in order to gain
a husband. But Eadbald had every reason to emphasise his
sister's faith and to commend it to her prospective husband.
As negotiations progressed, Eadbald no doubt advanced the
proposal that Edwin convert to Christianity as part of the marriage settlement, thus winning both a bride and entry into the
larger family of European Christian nobility. Bede records a
telling detail of what Edwin's thinking on the nature of his
kingship was:

> . . . whether in battle or on a peaceful progress on horse-
> back through city, town, and countryside in the compa-
> ny of his thegns, the royal standard was always borne
> before him. Even when he passed through the streets

on foot, the standard known to the Romans as a *Tufa*, and to the English as a *Tuf*, was carried in front of him.[2]

Edwin was already consciously linking his kingship with the memory of Empire. While we think of the Roman Empire as pagan, for the Anglo-Saxons it had been a Christian empire. It was into the service of Christian emperors that they had first committed themselves as mercenaries, and it was from the Christian Britons, who most definitely still saw themselves as Roman, that they had wrested their own kingdoms. Thus by accepting conversion to Christianity, Edwin would be following the logic of his own reign.

However, there were serious ramifications to Eadbald's offer of conversion. Should Edwin convert to Christianity, then he would require a godfather as part of the baptismal ritual. The obvious candidate would be Eadbald, the sponsor of his conversion and the husband of the bride who would be the fruit of the conversion. However, within the context of seventh-century Britain, the taking of a king as godfather carried with it the implication of accepting him as overlord. While Edwin wanted an 'in' to the continental networks of patronage and power that the Christian Franks had access to, he was certainly not going to do so by publicly proclaiming himself the vassal of a young and relatively untested king such as Eadbald.

So the negotiations continued, most probably via trusted messengers sailing up and down the east coast of England, although fast horsemen may have made use of the Roman road system, which remained mostly intact and usable for communications between the old Roman entry ports in Kent and legionary capital of York.

In the end, the two kings settled on an arrangement where

Æthelburh would marry Edwin while she remained Christian
and he remained pagan. She, however, would bring her own
household to Northumbria with her, and included among them
would be sufficient clergymen to enable her to continue practising her religion. Eadbald managed to extract from Edwin
the promise that he would think about converting to Christianity: such a promise had been sufficient for his own mother's
marriage to Æthelberht. It was an arrangement that suited
both sides for it could be spun as a win for both parties. In the
summer of 625, Æthelburh arrived in York with her household.
They must have made a magnificent sight: the future queen,
with her brother, King Eadbald, and the soon-to-be Bishop
Paulinus, being met by King Edwin and his retainers, all
dressed up in the matchless finery of barbarian kings.

There were few other cities in Britain that recalled the
splendour of its Roman past better than York. With its city
walls and gatehouses still largely intact, it would have taken
little thought to imagine a legion marching from its gate. It was
an appropriate venue to celebrate the marriage of a king with
imperial pretensions to the daughter of the most prestigious
ruling family in Britain.

The marriage made, Queen Æthelburh soon fell pregnant.
While she and her household had leave to follow their religion
without constraint, the question of the religious status of their
children seems to have been left unanswered by the marriage
agreement. Æthelburh would have wanted her first child to be
Christian, but as a potential heir to Edwin – although he had
two grown sons from his first marriage, a son with Æthelburh
would have greater claims to the kingship, due to his mother's
prestige – the religious status for the baby was not hers alone
to decide.

Bede records two letters from Pope Boniface V (619–625) to

Edwin and Æthelburh respectively. In his letter to Edwin the pope emphasises, to a king who clearly thought about kingship long and hard, that kingship is conferred by God while pointing out that accepting the Christian God would bring Edwin into communion with the other kings of Europe. Boniface goes on to denounce idols as purely the products of men, with no more power to influence events than the wood and stone from which they were made, and finishes with an exhortation to Edwin to accept the new religion and thereby win eternal life. The pope sent Edwin gifts with the letter: a gold tunic and a cloak all the way from Ancyra (Ankara) in Turkey. Although there's no mention in the text, we can't help surmising that the cloak may have been dyed imperial purple. Edwin would have got the message.

In Æthelburh's letter from the pope she was urged to work on her husband, through prayer, explanation, by all means necessary, that he might accept the new religion, and he included gifts of a silver mirror and a comb made from gold and ivory.

For a man with Edwin's imperial pretensions, to hear a letter read out to him that had come from Rome must have made it seem as if the eyes of the world were on him. The story of Edwin's conversion is, justly, the most famous part of Bede's *Ecclesiastical History* but at least part of its fame rests upon its suspense: will he, won't he? Edwin hovers on the edge of decision for page after page, after sign and portent and prophecy, seemingly riven with indecision. But of course Edwin was not just deciding for himself: he was deciding for his kingdom. And while the ordinary run of people could go on in their own way largely undisturbed, Edwin's decision would affect the class of people who supported his rule. For him to convert to Christianity meant the conversion of his warriors and retainers too. The agonising would have been partly due to Edwin

weighing the odds of carrying these men with him. Failure to
do so would mean the weakening of his rule, possibly even his
overthrow, for Anglo-Saxon kings were most of all the judge-
ments of two harsh masters: battle and the estimation of the
warband as to whether the putative king looked like a winner.
Edwin had proven himself but would abandoning the gods
that had favoured him lead his men to fear the loss of the gods'
favour. Through history the foremost god followed by warriors,
though unspoken, has been Fortuna, in all her many guises:
amulets, charms, pendants, rabbits' feet, mascots. The great
question that hung over Edwin's deliberations was whether
abandoning the old gods would lose them Fortune's favour.

It was Easter 626. Queen Æthelburh was heavily pregnant.
The question of the religious status of the new child remained
unanswered. Then a messenger, from Cwichelm, king of the
West Saxons, arrived at Edwin's palace beside the River Derwent. The messenger's name was Eumer. He entered Edwin's
hall, gave his sword and weapons into the door warden's
keeping, and stood before the king as he sat at table with his
companions. The hall was high, and long, hung with tapestries and banners, and the trophies of conquered enemies. By
Edwin's side stood the *Tufa*, the symbol of his hopes and plans.
Eumer approached the king, his cloak still wrapped around his
shoulders from the long journey through the changing weather
of spring. Then he reached under his cloak, drew a knife and
leaped at the king.

Eumer must have known it was a suicide mission. Even if
he had succeeded in killing Edwin, he would die. We do not
know why he did it. It seems unlikely that Cwichelm simply
ordered him to carry out the assassination attempt. Such an
attack suggests a personal history, a man seeking revenge for
some loss or outrage unknown to us. Edwin was a very success-

ful warlord. Although there is no record of him campaigning against the West Saxons, it is possible that Eumer might have suffered some loss in a theatre of war, which made him offer his services to Cwichelm. Standing in front of Edwin, Eumer had the object of his revenge within range. All he had to do was strike. It did not even have to be a killing blow, for he had coated both edges of his knife with poison, so that even a wound would prove lethal.

Sitting near Edwin were his companions. They had probably accompanied him into his exile, moving from court to court, ever wary of assassins. Now, one of them, seeing Eumer move upon the king, jumped from his seat and flung himself forward. His name was Lilla. Bede calls him the king's 'best friend' which suggests that Lilla had been with Edwin through all the vicissitudes of his life. Although Bede does not name the 'loyal friend' who had discovered that Rædwald planned to hand Edwin over to Æthelfrith while he was in East Anglia, it is tempting to think it was Lilla.

In Anglo-Saxon thought, the bond between a king and his warband was stronger than any other human loyalty: it outweighed fidelity to wife, children, gods or life. But ideals endure as aspirations, being held up precisely because they are rarely achieved, and there is ample evidence of Anglo-Saxon warriors choosing to interpret their oaths of loyalty with flexibility. It was not unknown for men, seeing their lord dead, to decide, not unreasonably, that their oaths of loyalty to him had ended and, on being offered fresh terms by the victorious battle lord, switch sides.

Lilla, however, did not hesitate. According to Bede, having no weapon to hand, he made his own body into Edwin's shield, taking the knife thrust intended for the king. Such was the violence of Eumer's thrust that the knife went right through

Lilla's body, as he lay above the king, and pierced Edwin too.

Chaos erupted in the hall. Those nearest the king, having been temporarily paralysed with surprise, threw themselves at the would-be assassin. Eumer, struggling to finish the job he had come to do, fought off the men attacking him, killing another, named Fordhere, in the process. But with surprise lost, the weight of men told, and Eumer was dragged down while Edwin was pulled away, injured but alive.

On Fylingdales Moor in Yorkshire, about a mile to the northeast of the Ballistic Missile Early Warning station, is a barrow, raised in the Bronze Age, commanding expansive views of the moors around. On top of the mound stands a stone cross. It's weathered now: a broad upright that narrows at the neck, before sprouting two vestigial crosspieces, all capped with a little crown. There's a clear, deep 'C' carved into the centre of the crosspiece, and a cross, looking like a '+' sign, below it. There were words carved in it once, but they have weathered away over the years. It's called Lilla Cross, and it has stood there since at least the tenth century. Archaeological investigations into the barrow it sits on have revealed Anglo-Saxon and Viking remains. The name, and the reputation, say that this was where Edwin brought the body of Lilla, burying him high in the moors, in a place of honour. Whether that's actually the case, we don't know: the cross itself is generally dated to a time a couple of centuries after Edwin and Lilla lived, although it could feasibly have replaced an earlier cross. There is also the question of how Lilla's remains could have been preserved for burial, as Edwin was probably not in a fit state to travel far after Eumer's assassination attempt: not only was he wounded, but he had to recover from poisoning too, although Lilla's body would have received most of the poison from the blade, as it received most of the force of the blow.

That night, the queen, Æthelburh, gave birth. Perhaps the violence erupting in her home, and the injury done to her husband as well as the death of two of his closest companions, brought on premature labour. Amid all the confusion, the question as to how the new baby – it was a girl – should be raised remained open. When Paulinus brought Edwin news of the birth of a daughter, Eanflæd, the king offered thanks to his gods, the old pagan gods of the Anglo-Saxons. But, according to Bede, Paulinus told him that it was Æthelburh's own God, Christ, that had safely delivered her of her daughter after the traumas of the day.

We have little knowledge of the religion of the Anglo-Saxons before they adopted Christianity. What we do know – or rather suspect – is mostly based upon extrapolating forwards the accounts of Tacitus and other Roman writers, in the first and second centuries, of Germanic tribes, living in Germania, where the Anglo-Saxons came from, or reading backwards from Norse legends and sagas that were mainly written down from the twelfth century onwards. So we are trying to reconstruct the paganism of the Anglo-Saxons from accounts of German and Scandinavian religions written five hundred years before and six hundred years after the encounter between Christianity and Anglo-Saxon paganism. But one thing we do know about the pagan Anglo-Saxons was the high honour Woden held in their genealogies. Almost all the ruling dynasties of the Anglo-Saxon kingdoms had family trees that were rooted in Woden: Woden was king father. He was king father because he was the Lord of Battles, the god, or ancestor – there need not have been much to distinguish between the two ideas – who granted victory in war.

Before Edwin could countenance conversion to the new religion he had to know if Christ could conquer too. He told

Paulinus he would accept the new religion if it would bring
him victory in the battle he knew he must now fight: the West
Saxons had tried to kill him in his own home. He had no choice
but to return open vengeance upon them. For an Anglo-Saxon
king who became known as weak would attract scavengers and
raiders faster than a dead horse attracted blowflies. As surety of his word, Edwin offered his new daughter agreeing that
Eanflæd would be baptised into the new faith. The guarantee
was made easier for him by the baby being a girl: if it had been
a boy he probably would have wanted baptism delayed until
after victory had been won.

However, even when victory against the West Saxons had
been achieved – Bede records that Edwin killed five of their
'kings' although these kings were presumably tribal chiefs
or leaders of small sub-areas of Wessex – Edwin held back
from making the final public conversion. Before that could
be countenanced, he called together all the leading men of
his kingdom, so that they might discuss this matter of great
moment.

Since the eighteenth century, we have internalised the idea
that it is normal, even desirable, for kingdoms and states to
be divided into contending factions, into 'parties' represent-
ing sections of interest, with the proviso that, to put it simply,
the 'parties' will take it in turns to govern according to the
interests of those they represent. But this idea would have
amazed people of earlier centuries. Taking the family as model for the kingdom, the ideal was unity in diversity, all acting
together for the same ends and the common good. While on
first glance this is hard to discern among the warring statelets
of seventh-century Britain, it becomes much clearer when
we think how the king was selected by the assembly of the
leading men. It was no private matter for Edwin to put aside

the gods of their fathers, gods who had served them well and defeated the god Edwin was now asking them to accept. However, here Edwin had an advantage: Christianity was coming to Northumbria in a glamorous foreign package, rather than being proselytised by the priests of the Britons, many of whom still lived in Northumbria. Bede is emphatic that the Britons made no attempt to proselytise the Anglo-Saxons, but historians today believe that the story was far more complex than he portrays, with continuing Christian activity by Brythonic congregations in pagan-ruled Northumbria. However, there was no denying that that form of Christianity had failed to win in battles against Edwin and his forebears. But the form of Christianity that now stood, in the tall, saturnine form of Paulinus, before the assemblage of the most powerful men in Northumbria, looked very different from the Christianity that they had witnessed before. To begin with, the hair was different. Paulinus, and the clergy accompanying him, wore the Roman tonsure, which looked like a shaggy torus placed upon a shaved scalp. The Brythonic monks that they would have seen before wore the Irish tonsure, where the front of the head was shaved to the crown, but the hair was allowed to grow long down the back of the head.

Paulinus also carried the glamour of distant Rome: they lived among the relics of its works and used the roads that the legions had laid down across the landscape. So the Christianity that Paulinus proposed to the assembled men of Northumbria carried a different meaning from the kind they had seen before: it was the religion of Rome, it was the religion of exotic places far away and it was, Edwin could now assert, the religion of winners. And that was precisely how it was perceived, according to Bede's magnificent treatment of the debate, by Edwin's pagan priest, Coifi, who apparently announced to the council that his religion was worthless as it had brought him no advantage. But the most significant passage is also the most quoted, and it's worth doing so again, and to remember that while modern historians tend to view everything through the politically obsessed lenses of our time, for other ages different considerations held greater sway:

> Your Majesty, when we compare the present life of man on earth with that time of which we have no knowledge, it seems to me like the swift flight of a single sparrow through the banqueting-hall where you are sitting at dinner on a winter's day with your thegns and counsellors. In the midst there is a comforting fire to warm the hall; outside, the storms of winter rain or snow are raging. This sparrow flies swiftly in through one door of the hall, and out through another. While he is inside, he is safe from the winter storms; but after a few moments of comfort, he vanishes from sight into the wintry world from which he came. Even so, man appears on earth for a little while; but of what went before this life or what follows, we know nothing. Therefore, if this new teaching has brought any more certain knowledge, it seems only right that we should follow it.[3]

That a thegn, that is one of the ranks of nobles, made exactly this speech seems unlikely, particularly as Bede does not name him. But that such thoughts formed a core part of the decision is very likely: these men were all too familiar with sudden, usually violent, death. What we infer about Anglo-Saxon paganism's attitude to death, which is largely derived from later Norse myths, is that there was an eschatological imperative for a warrior to follow his lord to the death, for death in battle brought translation to Woden's mead hall and an endless round of feasting and battle until all battles ended with the death of the gods. But there was little comfort for ordinary people nor those who failed to achieve transcendence by glorious death. The eschatology of these northern myths is essentially an eschatology of the *skalds* (the Norse word for a court poet) and *scops* (the Anglo-Saxon equivalent) who venerated the deeds of the dead in astonishingly complex and intricate poetic metres. This was an afterlife predicated upon poetic strip mining: give the skald or the scop enough material to make a song of your death and then you would be assured a life both in this world and the next. If priests were the arbiters of the afterlife in Christianity (although at this time they weren't: they only assumed that position with the later elaboration of the whole complex of doctrines that encompassed purgatory, indulgences and atonement), the scops and skalds held that position in the paganism of the Anglo-Saxons and the Norse.

However, the adoption of this new religion also brought with it new paths to renown. As well as providing a different career path for young men and women of the higher social classes, the entry into the wider Christian world offered a chance of a new and different fame: a fame that might be immortalised in words on a page that were read as far away as Rome itself.

Thus Christianity offered a hope the old pagan religion did not. Coupled with a now recognised ability to provide victory, plus the prestige of its associations with Rome, with the Frankish power across the Channel, and the arcane but clearly transformatory technology of writing that the Christian clergy brought, Edwin and Paulinus had a winning proposal to put before the assembled thegns of Northumbria. According to Bede, such was the enthusiasm with which the new religion was adopted that Coifi, erstwhile chief pagan priest, promptly rode off on the king's stallion – as a pagan priest, custom only allowed him to ride a mare – to the nearest sanctuary at Goodmanham, where he proceeded to demonstrate the powerlessness of the idol there by sticking a spear into it before ordering the sanctuary burned. As such, Coifi demonstrated considerably less tolerance than Pope Gregory who had instructed Augustine and his missionaries that 'the temples of the idols among that people should on no account be destroyed'.[4]

Having received the consent of his people – or at least, those among his people who mattered enough to be consulted – for his conversion, Edwin (and Paulinus) moved fast. A year after Eumer's failed assassination attempt, on Easter Sunday 627, which that year fell on 12 April, Edwin, king of Deira and Bernicia, king of Northumbria, high king of Britain, was baptised into the new life of the Catholic Church in the hastily built church of St Peter the Apostle in York. Pope Gregory's original plan, when he had dispatched Augustine to Britain more than a quarter of a century earlier, was for the church in Britain to have two archbishops, one in London and one in York, reflecting the old Roman division of the country into Britannia Inferior, governed from Eboracum (York), and Britannia Superior, ruled from Londinium (rather than casting aspersions on northerners, 'Britannia Inferior' means 'Lower Britain' and 'Britannia Superior' means 'Upper Britain'). The political realities of seventh-century Britain had necessitated Augustine and his successor archbishops making Canterbury their episcopal see, but now that Paulinus was in the north, and a bishop, he wanted to stake his claim upon York.

For his part, Edwin's choice of York as the place of his baptism showed the depth of his thought about what he was doing.

Even if he had not known it before, Paulinus would have been able to tell him that no less an emperor than Constantine the Great, the first Christian Roman emperor, had first been acclaimed as emperor by his legions in York. By being baptised there, Edwin was stating his claim to imperium, and wrapping himself in the glory of the Roman past and the expansiveness of the Christian present in Europe.

It was an astonishingly daring move on Edwin's part, but one of a part with his appropriation of imperial regalia and the dignity of Roman office. Such was the peace engendered by Edwin's political and military dominance that, it was said, 'a woman could carry her new-born babe across the island from sea to sea without fear of harm'.[5] While there is always a tendency, particularly in medieval literature, to look back at earlier periods as golden ages, it's very likely that Edwin's dominance brought an end to the single greatest threat to peace at this time: roving parties of warriors, led by petty kings, ravaging each other's kingdoms. Nothing is more calculated to disturb the peace than groups of young men with weapons and no constraints. After all, much of the history of humanity can be read as the story of the various attempts to rein in and control roving groups of violent young men. But with Edwin so firmly in charge, these petty wars largely stopped.

With his change of religion made public and accepted by his power base, Edwin moved quickly to Bernicia, where nostalgia for his old rivals, the Idings, would have been strongest. There, at the royal palace of Ad Gefrin, in the shadow of Yeavering Bell, the hill of goats, Paulinus preached for thirty-six days, baptising those he received in the cold, clear waters of the River Glen, which runs a little to the north of the palace. Ad Gefrin was where the tribute of the hill peoples was brought to the kings: cattle and goats and sheep, herded into a huge stockade. It would have been customary for people to gather at Ad Gefrin when the king and his entourage came round, on their annual peripatism, to present their offerings to him and to seek justice and royal adjudication in law, so it would have been straightforward for Edwin to have put out a further call for all the people of the neighbourhood to come to hear the new proclamation.

And this is where, according to Brian Hope-Taylor, we find one of the few occasions where archaeology meets history. For in his excavations at Ad Gefrin, Hope-Taylor found the remains of a unique wooden structure. Think of a section of an amphitheatre, with a podium at its focus. Rows and rows of benches in stepped tiers, with the podium backed by a wooden screen to reflect sound towards the listeners. And standing at that podium was the tall, aristocratic, saturnine Paulinus expounding the new faith to the people who had come in from the countryside at their king's call. The majority of these people would have been Britons and many of them might well have been Christian already, so it was no great step for them to receive baptism from a Roman prelate.

The scope of Edwin's ambitions was astonishing. In conjunction with Paulinus, he was planning to reconstitute an imperium, to make something that would encompass much of Britain if not the entire island, and to create a state that could endure after the death of its founder. For Edwin had seen one thing clearly: none of the petty kingdoms that rose and just as quickly fell in Britain at this time could survive the death of their king. Indeed, the more successful, the more fortune-favoured a king was, such as Æthelfrith, then the more rapid and complete the dismantling of whatever he had achieved in life upon his death. The early medieval kingdoms of Britain were short-lived things, dependent on success in war and the men that that success could attract. There was no shortage of young men with weapons and the desire to make names for themselves: any king gaining a reputation as fortune's favoured would quickly find himself welcoming a steady stream of these landless men to his retinue, particularly if he was generous: gifts were the exchange items of the oath-giving economy, and a good gold arm ring would secure the oath of most young warriors. It was, however, a system that demanded feeding: glory and gold were the attractors that pulled young men to a king's court, so he had to fight regularly, pillage continually, and give generously. It was an economic system that ensured a constant flow of exchange – gold was not left to moulder in treasure hoards but was given out almost as soon as it came in – but there was nothing to hold it together when the centre – the king – died.

So Edwin set about creating something that would endure. Paulinus began building a stone church on the foundations of the wooden church of St Peter in York, which had been hastily thrown up for the king's baptism. There could be no more tangible token of their desire to make something permanent than the decision to build in stone. They were surrounded by the stone-built remains of the Romans, two centuries after the legions had left. While the wooden halls of the Anglo-Saxons displayed great skills in carpentry, wood did not endure. Also, the church they were building in York, and the churches they were building elsewhere in Northumbria, were filled with the sound of chant after the manner of the church in Rome, for Paulinus had with him a companion, James the Deacon, who knew the chant of Rome and set about teaching it to the Northumbrians.

But the building of something permanent requires one thing more than anything else: time. And time was not something that Edwin and Paulinus were granted. Early in October 633, right at the end of the campaigning season, Edwin received word that enemies were marching against him.

Cadwallon ap Cadfan was king of the Brythonic kingdom of Gwynedd. Edwin had conquered Anglesey, the breadbasket for the kingdom of Gwynedd. In response, Cadwallon entered into alliance with another kingdom that had grown fearful at the rising power in the north: Mercia. Its leader was Penda – it's not entirely clear if Penda was king of Mercia at this time but he had command of the Mercian warband. So in order to defeat Edwin, a Christian Brythonic kingdom joined with a pagan Anglo-Saxon one, illustrating again the maxim that the enemy of my enemy is my friend.

Edwin was the most experienced war leader in Britain. He had defeated Æthelfrith. He knew the perils of being caught unprepared. So when the news reached him, most probably in York, that enemies were advancing on his kingdom, he could have taken time to plan. York's walls were still largely intact. Besides, few warbands of the time had any experience, and even less skill, in siegecraft. He could have waited but instead he rode out to meet them. We don't know if he received faulty intelligence, suggesting that he faced a small force of raiders. Bede, who disliked Cadwallon more than anybody else mentioned in his history, was not going to credit the king of Gwynedd any more than he had to, but possibly Cadwallon managed to mislead Edwin as to the number of men he was bringing to battle. But for whatever reason, on 12 October 633, most probably somewhere in the barren marshlands of Hatfield Chase, in south Yorkshire/north Lincolnshire, the warbands met. Much of the area was drained in the seventeenth and eighteenth centuries, and those areas that weren't drained were, until very recently, strip-mined for peat, leaving a bleak, lonely landscape.

We have no details of the battle. All we know is that it was as catastrophic a defeat for Edwin as the defeat he inflicted on Æthelfrith seventeen years before. Edwin was killed. Pretty well all his warband died alongside him, or in the chaotic aftermath of the battle. His eldest son, Osfrith, was killed too. Eadfrith, his younger son from his first, ironically Mercian, wife, was captured or surrendered to Penda, the Mercian leader. If he was hoping for mercy, or some sort of alliance with Penda, that hope was spilled with his blood. As soon as Eadfrith's usefulness to Penda came to an end, Penda put him to death.

As to what happened, and how such an experienced war leader could lose so badly, we simply do not know. But the history of this period is replete with accounts of battles such as this, where dominant war leaders suffer catastrophic, and usually terminal, defeats. Unlike later wars, these were battles fought on a small scale, with the number of combatants in the very low hundreds. The king was both the focus and the target: the rallying point and the dissolving point. He could not leave the battlefield without his battle line dissolving, thus making it very difficult for a king to retreat.

But sometimes, when forced into a corner, as Edwin and Rædwald had been by Æthelfrith, a king would decide to risk all on a throw of the battle dice. We do not know why Cadwallon and Penda had come to the conclusion that it was worth risking everything on the throw of their defeating Edwin in battle, but they rolled the dice and they won. In the aftermath, at least one or two of Edwin's men must have escaped, and ridden back to York, where the queen and Paulinus waited, with the surviving young children she had had with Edwin: Eanflæd, the daughter born on that extraordinary Easter Sunday of 626, and a little boy, Wuscfrea. Hearing of the death of her husband, along with most of his warband, and knowing that the warbands of Cadwallon and Penda were only twenty-five miles away, Æthelburh had little choice. For the safety of her children, she had to leave, and quickly. Paulinus went with her, taking the rich gold cross and chalice and much of the rest of the royal treasure so that it would not fall into the hands of Cadwallon and Penda. York is a riverine city; the refugee party must surely have taken a ship, sailing down the River Ouse to the Humber Estuary, and then down the east coast to Kent. Along with her own children, Æthelburh took Yffi the young son of Osfrith, Edwin's grandson, into exile too.

But there would be no glorious return for these boys. Wuscfrea and Yffi died in childhood, in the kingdom of the Franks, where Æthelburh sent them for greater protection. Only through Eanflæd did Edwin's line endure. As for Æthelburh, she founded a double monastery, that is one for both men and women over which an abbess – Æthelburh was the first – presided at Lyminge in Kent, which is currently being excavated.

Paulinus was reassigned to the bishopric of Rochester in Kent. As far as we know, he never went north again. His old companion, James the Deacon, remained behind however, ministering quietly to the people around Catterick and living to such an age that Bede records him alive in his own time.

King Edwin had dreamed of creating something that outlived him, and had begun putting into place the elements required to achieve that. But the time was not long enough, and the foundations were too shallow. When he died, everything that he had hoped for died with him. An Anglo-Saxon kingdom, it seemed, could not endure without its king.

7

Does it All Mean Anything?

So much of archaeology is down to chance, and Paul Gething became an archaeologist by chance. He'd had a succession of jobs after leaving university: tomato picker, furniture removal man, DJ and nightclub doorman among them. On his way to a meeting he walked past an open gateway and happened to glance in. There was a deep excavation going on and he was drawn to it, as so many people are, by the sight of a group of people standing around a big hole in the ground. He caught the tail end of a site tour, but rather than leaving when it ended Paul hung around and asked questions. He never made his meeting. Instead, the archaeologist took Paul on a tour of the site, answering every question through a life-changing couple of hours. Within a week Paul had a job on an archaeological excavation, funded by the long defunct Manpower Services Commission scheme that so many archaeologists started on in the 1980s. Within three months he was a trusted member of staff.

All this was fuelled by the visceral thrill he felt when he

uncovered his first piece of pottery and held in his hand
something that had lain hidden for centuries. Fourteenth-
century green glaze, a rim sherd. The image of it is still vivid
in his memory, waiting only for him to close his eyes and reach
back to that thrill of knowing that he was the first person to
touch that piece of pottery since it was lost to the soil seven
hundred years ago. This connection to people who had long
since become dust completely changed his life. It lies at the
heart of why archaeologists spend hours on their knees in
pits in the ground and it was why Paul and Rosie Whitbread,
Graeme Young and Phil Wood set up the Bamburgh Research
Project. In the years since the project started, over two thousand people have worked on the digs there, from teenagers
trying out an interest to see if it will become a passion, through
many archaeology undergraduates receiving practical, hands-
on training, to laymen and women, inspired by reading and
programmes such as *Time Team* and *Meet the Ancestors*. Some
found that a day's digging was enough, some have returned
many times, others have gone on to careers in archaeology;
there have been marriages, friendships, feuds, and reunions.
But it's been a memorable experience for everyone who has
got involved, and almost all of them have felt that same visceral thrill that first transfixed Paul: the electric charge of holding
some object from the deep past. And for field archaeologists
at least, pottery will track them through their careers, the
broken plates, jugs and dishes of past times and civilisations
mapping out their professional lives more accurately than any
other measure, whether they be papers published, academic
citations or professional reputation. It also poses the silent
question: does it all actually mean anything?

Theoretical archaeology is a discipline in itself. Put ten
archaeologists in a room and you'll get two hundred and fifty

opinions, two fights, a marriage and a lot of empty bottles. All of human life is there, tied up with the most modern techniques and the most ancient disputes. Like the story of humanity, it is complicated. Its complexity is best illustrated by the story of one of the most important archaeologists of the twentieth century. Lewis Binford (21 November 1931–11 April 2011) never made any important archaeological discoveries, nor is his name attached to a famous excavation and he was, by many accounts, an appalling human being, but he transformed archaeology.

By the middle of the twentieth century archaeologists began to realise that their methods created huge sampling biases. There you are, an archaeologist, with trowel in hand and funding in place, but where do you dig? The obvious answer is somewhere old, monumental and mysterious: Stonehenge and its environs has been more extensively excavated than anywhere else in the country. It's easy to see why. And archaeology has largely followed this pattern of digging among the ruins. But it slowly dawned that this tendency to dig in the shadow of the acknowledged past was creating a huge recording bias in the data they were collecting.

Around the same time some archaeologists were also becoming dissatisfied with archaeology's traditional role as handmaiden to history and were pushing for it to be recognised as a science rather than a branch of the humanities. It is this group, and Lewis Binford in particular, that today's archaeology undergraduates can thank for the lectures on multivariate analysis and the other tools of statistical modelling that they have to take as part of their degree. Although Binford's ideas are now seen as having been anticipated by Walter Taylor in 1948 in *A Study of Archaeology*, at the time they were seen as revolutionary.

Binford championed the idea that archaeology, despite the

fragmentary nature of its data, could interrogate every aspect
of the past. It need not follow along in the footsteps of the
historical record but could strike out on its own, seeking fresh
insights into the past. He urged a change in the focus: from the
excavated artefacts to the societies that produced those artefacts. Archaeologists needed to develop specific hypotheses,
test them against the evidence, and analyse the body of data
through statistical sampling. In the 1960s there was a sense
that the old fuddy-duddies in charge of archaeology were too
hidebound to understand this 'new archaeology'. According to
Sally Binford, one of his ex-wives (he had six) and an important early collaborator, he was 'extremely smart, but extremely
crazy and aggressive'. Although the couple allegedly had a vol-
atile relationship, it's still worth quoting what she said about
Binford's intellectual capacities:

> He was an extremely brilliant guy, but couldn't write
> a sentence that made sense – that had a subject and
> a predicate. His writing was unspeakable. My job in
> the marriage became to translate what Lew wrote into
> English and to get him his Ph.D. . . . I served another
> trickier function: one of Lew's fatal flaws is that he's a
> pathological liar – and most of the time he didn't know
> he was doing it. He is truly incapable of distinguishing
> what he wants to believe from what is real. He had a
> distressing tendency to 'improve' data. He would gener-
> ate a large number of original and intriguing ideas – 90%
> of which bore little or no relationship to reality, but the
> 10% that were valid were great. I would attempt to steer
> him away from his more imaginative notions and help
> him in finding data to support the sounder ones, then
> help him write them up in comprehensible English.[1]

Whatever Binford's alleged shortcomings, his great service to archaeology was to first put it on firmer scientific foundations and then to demonstrate the limits of certainty within this new paradigm.

Binford's great research interest was the hunter-gatherer societies of prehistory – the most notorious of his many academic feuds was his battle with the eminent French archaeologist François Bordes over the interpretation of Mousterian flint remains. The great problem of archaeology is that the people being studied are dead; they can't be asked if this shaped flint was used for skinning animals. But Binford reasoned that there are societies that still live in ways comparable to the hunter-gatherers of prehistory. So he went and studied them. These were the Nunamiut of the Arctic north. The hunter-gatherers of Europe during the Ice Age would, Binford reasoned, have faced similar difficulties and would probably have found similar solutions. He asked a group of Nunamiut hunters who were using a cave during the hunting season to record what they did there. The record of what they'd done in the cave was given to the team of archaeologists but, crucially, the archaeologists did not look at it. Instead, with the cave now empty, they went there and excavated it, treating it as an archaeological site. They then wrote the site report, blind, and compared the site report to the Nunamiuts' own account of what they had done in the cave. This was the great test of the truth of archaeology and the interpretations it makes of the past.

When they compared the site report to the diary that the Nunamiut had kept of their activities, to their horror the archaeologists found that their accuracy was ludicrously low – less than 5 per cent accuracy. Middle-range theory was developed by Binford as a response to his frustration with the limitations of traditional archaeology. He believed that by excavation, combined with observation of current indigenous peoples practising ancient technologies, we could arrive at a better understanding of how ancient people acted and lived.

This was a wake-up call for archaeology but one that has been largely ignored because no one really wants to know that they're wrong most of the time and that there's very little chance of improving on that because anyone who could tell them what actually happened is dead. There were also reports that Binford had skewed the data and that he tried to hide it. This led to feuds with other people and ended with his findings being somewhat discredited.

However, this work did set off a major reappraisal of how archaeology was done making archaeologists take a more functional approach, looking at typologies and the way things were used, and a more cognitive approach, looking at the thought processes and the way archaeological data is analysed. It also set off the second wave of archaeological theory, producing a variety of modelling strategies. Archaeologists began to realise that going to a castle and digging was self-fulfilling: obviously, there's a monument there, it's sitting in as dominating a position as its builders chose, so there's going to be history attached to the castle and an accompanying archaeological record. The question was how to correct this bias towards the obviously historical.

The first answers were things like blind sampling, test-pitting and surveys of aerial photographs. While people had been looking at aerial photographs for years, this was now done on a larger scale and in a more systematic way. All of the techniques, theories and modelling strategies coalesced to form modern archaeological practice: the expansion of a theoretical framework, an increase in the range of techniques, and the recognition that there is an inherent bias in the modelling strategies used by archaeologists. As such, please remember, when reading this book, that it's probably wrong. The past is a different country, and we try to reach it, but the fact remains that when Binford put archaeology to the test it was found wanting. The chains of deduction and inference that allow conclusions to be made are only as strong as the weakest conclusion, which makes them fragile – and thus all the more fiercely guarded by many archaeologists. The apparent hole into which Brian Hope-Taylor seems to have dug himself in order to safeguard his work is evidence of how easily even the best archaeologists can fall into this trap.

Paul and the team at the Bamburgh Research Project try to remind themselves that being wrong is not wrong: it's right. It's the removal of one error from the vast barrier of errors that seal us off from the proper appreciation of our past. Removing a bad interpretation of the past is one of the most valuable things an archaeologist can do, although it attracts considerably less acclaim than finding the skeleton of Richard III in a car park (and demonstrating that he really was Richard 'Crookback', despite the confident averrals of a generation of historians that his twisted back was solely the product of Tudor propaganda. It's not just archaeologists who should cultivate a decent measure of humility with respect to their discipline.).

8

The Sea Kingdom

Standing on the Antrim Hills, you can see Kintyre, Islay and Galloway. The passage across the Straits of Moyle is only thirteen miles. So it's no surprise that the Irish, a seafaring and adventurous people, began venturing across the straits in the fifth and sixth centuries. Known as Gaels, they were viewed in a less flattering light by the people they encountered, who called them *Scoti*, meaning, according to one derivation, pirates. And the name would stick, and spread, so that the country they migrated to came to be called after its immigrants.

Having sailed east, the new residents called their new land Ear-Gaidheal after themselves, that is the Eastern Gaels, which became Argyll in time, and named their kingdom Dál Riata after its progenitor in County Antrim. But soon it became a kingdom in its own right with King Fergus Mor Mac Erc, regarded as the traditional founder of Dál Riata, ruling around about AD 500.

A land of peninsulas, islands and channels, Dál Riata was a quintessential sea kingdom. Its most famous and most enduring resident, Colm Cille, St Columba, thought it beautiful beyond compare. He called Iona '*I mo Chridhe, I mo Ghraidh*'; that is 'Iona of my heart, my darling.' Iona, the place where he walked through most of his earthly life, became sanctified in the imagination of the people of northern Britain: the most powerful among them sought burial there in the belief that being interred on Iona would rub away the stains of their earthly sins and gain them heaven. It is said that forty-eight Scottish, eight Norwegian, four Irish and four kings of the Isle of Man lie there. John Smith, leader of the Labour Party and the man who would have been prime minister instead of Tony Blair if he had not died of a heart attack at the age of fifty-five is buried there too, indicating that the sense of sanctity has not left Iona even now.

While Iona was the spiritual centre of Dál Riata, its political heart beat upon the rock of Dunadd. Today that rock lies a couple of miles from the sea, but fifteen hundred years ago it's probable that the flat, marshy land that separates rock from sea was much narrower, with an easy channel to the stronghold. The original Pictish inhabitants of the area probably made some sort of fortification on Dunadd, and for seaborn newcomers, the rock made an irresistible base: it guarded the land entrance to the long, pointing finger of the Kintyre peninsula, pointing to the old homeland, while also guarding the sea lanes to the west coast islands. The geology of the site, a rough jumble of rocks rising to a twin-humped summit, provided a series of natural defences, pushing anyone attempting to climb the rock into natural defiles that were then further defended when the Dál Riatans built walls, snaking over the rocks to create defences, and then, higher up, an inner wall guarding the upper fortress. Little remains of the defensive walls now, but the defiles that made the path up to the summit are still clear.

At the top, carved into the bare rock of the summit, are a circular bowl and a foot-shaped impression. The purpose of the bowl is not known, although the way it collects water suggests that it may have been used for collecting a liquid; the footprint historians believe was used in the anointing of the kings of Dál Riata. The new king, silhouetted against the sky, standing at the top of the stronghold of his people in sight of them all lined up below, would place his foot into the rock in a symbolic union with the land he was about to rule.

Dál Riata was close to the height of its power in the early years of the seventh century. King Áedán mac Gabráin had suffered a serious defeat against Æthelfrith at the Battle of Degsastan around AD 603, but his successor, King Eochaid Buide, who reigned from 608 to 629, avoided further conflict with Æthelfrith or his successor, Edwin, and consolidated his rule. Eochaid was an unlikely king. His father, Áedán, had three older, grown-up sons, any of whom would have expected to ascend to the throne – or, in the case of Dál Riata, put their foot in it – but they each died, as apparently foretold by Colm Cille:

> . . . the saint questioned King Áedán about a successor
> to the kingdom. The king answered that he did not
> know which of his three sons would be king, Artuir,
> Eochaid Find or Domangart. The saint then spoke to
> him thus:
>   'None of these three will be king. They will all be
> slaughtered by enemies and fall in battle. But if you
> have other, younger sons, let them come to me. The
> one whom the Lord has chosen will run directly to my
> arms.'
>   They were called, as the saint instructed, and

Eochaid Buide went as soon as he entered and leant
on the saint's bosom. The saint kissed and blessed
him, and said to the father: 'This one will survive
to be king after you, and his sons will be kings after
him.'

Afterwards, all these things were wholly fulfilled.
Artuir and Eochaid Find were killed soon afterwards
in battle . . . Domangart fell slaughtered in battle in
England. But Eochaid Buide succeeded his father
as king.[1]

Apart from indicating that the laws of kingly succession in
Dál Riata were far from settled at this time, the passage also
indicates the enormous influence Colm Cille and, by extension, his successors on Iona, wielded upon the kings of Dál
Riata. To be anointed by the saint was to ensure the blessing
of heaven and success in battle.

Although Áedán died around 608, the memories of the disastrous defeat at Degsastan would still have been vivid in 616.
So it was probably something of a surprise for Eochaid Buide
when the wife and children of King Æthelfrith, the man who
had defeated his father, fetched up at Dunadd, bedraggled,
tired and desperate. Why did Acha believe that she and her
children might find refuge with her husband's enemies?

A clue to answering that question lies among the dead of
the Battle of Degsastan. Among the piles of Irish dead, which
probably included Áedán's son Domangart, was a Northumbrian. His name was Hering and he was the son of the man
who had been king of Bernicia before Æthelfrith. The Battle of Degsastan sounds, therefore, very much like an attempt
by Áedán to remove Æthelfrith and install a king beholden
to him upon the throne. The attempt failed. But when King

Eochaid Buide received the party of Northumbrian refugees he must have thought long and hard about the advantages and disadvantages of giving shelter to an ætheling of Northumbria. There was a new king in Northumbria, Edwin of Deira (who was also Acha's brother of course). The two boys standing before the king of Dál Riata with their mother were sons of the man who had defeated his father and killed his brother. Vengeance was there for the taking: Eochaid Buide could all but expunge the seed of Æthelfrith from the earth (there was one other older son, Eanfrith, apparently the son of a previous marriage by Æthelfrith, who took refuge in Pictland, presumably because his mother was Pictish).

As Eochaid Buide heard Acha make her plea for refuge, he looked on the boys standing bravely beside their mother, then counted the men standing behind them. The Northumbrian thegns had given their weapons to the doorwarden of Dunadd before being allowed into the king's presence, but even so, his own household warriors stood ready. Eochaid Buide assessed the men with the practised eye of a warrior king, checking for armour, age, bearing, ornament, all the markings of experienced warriors. They were men who knew how to wield sword and spear, but they were few; certainly too few to make any attempt to wrest the throne of Northumbria back from Edwin.

Edwin had killed Æthelfrith the Twister. Tales had reached even Dál Riata of Æthelfrith's long pursuit of Edwin. Now, Eochaid Buide learned, the hunted had turned on the hunter, like a boar at bay, and gored his pursuer to death. This was news indeed. In deciding what to do with the Northumbrian refugees, Eochaid Buide would have turned to his counsellors. Clothed with the mantle of Colm Cille – and the saint's prophecy that had foretold Eochaid Buide's unlikely ascent to the throne – the words of the representative from Iona carried great weight.

A later abbot of Iona, the Adomnán who wrote the life of Colm Cille, was also responsible for promulgating the *Lex Innocentium*, the Law of the Innocents, and persuading a convocation of Irish, Dál Riatan and Pictish kings and monks to accept it at the Synod of Birr in 697. The Law of the Innocents protected women, children and non-combatants from the depredations of warfare, with harsh punishments on anyone who broke the law. In particular, a man who killed a woman was to have his right hand and left foot cut off, and then be put to death. However, the law accepted its own logic with respect to women, so that even should a woman be convicted of murder, she should not be executed but rather cast adrift in a boat with a single paddle and minimal supplies. Thus, while death was the likely result, the final judgement as to her fate would rest with God. Long before Adomnán's law, Patrick himself had managed to enjoin protection for monks and religious people from the warring Irish tribes, although it was an injunction often overlooked. However, this indicates the long history of attempts by the Church in Ireland to ameliorate the endemic warfare that characterised early medieval society.

When considering the fate of Acha and her children, Eochaid Buide could also see the possible long-term advantage in raising æthelings to the Northumbrian throne. Kingship was precarious in the early medieval period and there was no telling when a vacancy might occur in Northumbria. There was no doubt that Oswald, when he grew to manhood, would have a strong claim to the throne. After all, not only was his father the king of Bernicia, but his mother was the daughter of the previous king of Deira, and came from the Deiran royal line. But Eochaid Buide was still looking at the wife and children of the man who had killed his brother. Were these considerations enough to outweigh the obligations to vengeance, to bloodfeud?

As further encouragement to mercy, Acha may have returned some Dál Riatan hostages to Eochaid Buide. A usual consequence of a military defeat was the giving of hostages. If Æthelfrith had demanded them after his victory at Degsastan, Áedán would have been hard put to refuse. Although thirteen years would have been a long time to be held hostage, it was possible that Acha came to Eochaid Buide with some relatives he had not seen for a long time.

There is another possibility too. Around 629, the Annals of Ulster include a report of a battle between King Conadd Cerr of Dál Riata (who appears to have ruled alongside Eochaid Buide for the final few years of his reign) and the Dál nAraid, a northern Irish kindred. The Battle of Fid Eoin was a disastrous defeat for Dál Riata in which Conadd Cerr lost his life. But alongside him among the dead was listed a 'Saxon', that is an English man named Osric whose full name suggests he was the grandson of King Áedán mac Gabráin. If King Áedán, King Eochaid Buide's father, could have an English grandson, then it appears likely one of his daughters married into the Northumbrian royal line.

Look at the names of these boys. Osric, Oswald, Oswiu. It was normal practice for Anglo-Saxon royal clans to indicate their lineage by making use of a common prefix. Without surnames, it was one of the easiest ways of indicating a relationship between different people. Anglo-Saxon names were formed by joining a stock prefix to a suffix. Each had a meaning, so the full name was a combination of both. For example, Edwin combines the prefix 'Ed' (which could be written in many different forms including 'Ead', 'Aud' and 'Od'), meaning 'wealth' or 'prosperity', with the suffix 'win' (also written as 'wine' or 'wyn'), which means 'joy' or 'friend'. Thus Edwin could be read as 'friend to riches' or 'joyful prosperity'. Reading through Anglo-Saxon king lists and genealogies, it is clear that, unlike the Normans and later rulers of England, they did not repeat names. Even in the oldest families, it's rare to find names repeated. What's even more remarkable is that the names of the founders of the ruling houses were not given to later children. Thus Ida founded the ruling house of Bernicia, making his descendants the Idings, but none of the later kings are called after him. The same is true of the founders of other Anglo-Saxon royal houses. The East Angles, the Wuffingas, traced themselves back to Wuf-fa, but there were no other kings by that name. This was true even for the House of Wessex, the most long-lasting of all the Anglo-Saxon royal families: claiming descent from Cerdic, no later king shares the name of their founder. The Anglo-Saxons tried as much as possible to create a unique name for each child. This practice appears to have had its origin in a pre-Christian belief that the name and the person were, in some senses, one, combined. Thus for a person to share the name of somebody else was to dilute them both, and make them liable to magic directed against the other person of the same name. While names became slowly more conventional over the centuries, there remained a strong tendency to find unique names. However, to indicate relationship in a time before surnames, parents would often use the same prefix for their children. Two and a half centuries later, this was still the case, as seen with the elder siblings of King Alfred the Great: Æthelstan, Æthelswith, Æthelbald, Æthelberht and Æthelred.

Therefore we have some indication that Osric was related to Oswald and Oswiu. So if Osric was a grandson of King Áedán, and thus possibly nephew to King Eochaid Buide, then Oswald and Oswiu and their sister Æbbe must have been related to

Eochaid Buide too, most likely as cousins. In a world where kin relationships mattered deeply, there was little distinction between different degrees of relationship: they were all blood. Indeed, some languages conflate kin relationships, so that the same word will cover 'brother' and 'cousin'.

So when Acha lined her children up in front of King Eochaid Buide, she was hoping that he would see not the sons of the man who had killed his brother, but his own blood, his cousins, and help them accordingly.

He did.

Eochaid Buide, king of Dál Riata, accepted the tired and bedraggled party of refugees into his household. Safe for the moment, Acha and her young family slip from the pages of history into obscurity. There is no record of Edwin pursuing them in the way that Æthelfrith pursued him. The boys would grow to manhood among the sea raiders and cattle rustlers of Dál Riata, learning the language of the Gaels as fluently as their native Anglo-Saxon. So many were the languages of early Medieval Britain that a facility with languages must have been one of the great unsung abilities for anyone seeking to travel more than a day's journey from his hearth. Just on the mainland of Britain, there was Old English, with pronounced regional variations, Pictish, Welsh, Cornish, Cumbric (closely related to Welsh and spoken in the Brythonic kingdoms of the Old North), Old Irish and Latin.

While Edwin expanded his imperium over the other kingdoms of Britain, Acha's boys grew up. It was common practice among the ruling families of the time to send boys, from about the age of seven, to be fostered and raised by another allied, or sometimes even opposing, family. Without any strict rules of succession, the struggle to succeed a dead king to the throne was Darwinian. Only the strongest survived. To have sup-

port from another ruling clan in this struggle could be vital
– it would prove to be for Oswald – and the family that had
raised the new king could, once the king was installed, call
in the debt he owed them. So having accepted Acha and her
family into his kingdom, Eochaid Buide would have taken the
boys on as his foster sons, raising them alongside his own sons,
fostering friendships, facilitating rivalries, doing all in his
power to turn boys into the sort of men who could be kings.

9

The Making of
Warriors

In previous times, it was not unusual for people living by the
sea to be unable to swim. Those who lived on the sea feared
and respected it so much that there seemed little point in
learning to swim. Should the sea decide it wanted you enough
to sink your boat, then being able to swim was not going to
save you: only the sea god, an unpredictable and capricious
divinity at the best of times, could decide that. Learning to
swim was to tempt the sea to do its worst, and its worst was
more than any mariner could endure. Better to respect it, pro-
pitiate it, retreat and wait for another day when its mood had
turned than try your luck when the sea was against you.

Oswald, growing up, was often by the sea. Bamburgh sat
upon a rock that was washed by the waters of the North Sea
at high tide. Northumbria was a kingdom with a long coast
but also an expansive hinterland. In the peripatetic round of
kingship, royal villas and palaces were generally close enough
to each other that the wagons containing the paraphernalia
of the royal household – ox-drawn and slow-moving – could

go from one to the next in a day or two. While Oswald, and his younger brother, Oswiu, travelled by boat, they would not have needed to learn too much of the skill of seafaring, for any sea voyages they took would have been limited to short coastal hops, near enough to shore to seek immediate shelter should a squall blow up. For these sorts of journeys, there were always mariners among their retainers, or men could be hired. River journeys were more common, but they required little more skill than the ability to row. Oswald was still a boy, while Oswiu was barely more than a toddler, so they wouldn't have been tasked with rowing. This was left to the slaves. Any of the king's thegns looking to build up strength and endurance would have joined in too.

However, if Oswald and Oswiu were boys who lived by the sea, the son of Thunder, the warrior from the Bowl Hole, lived *on* the sea. The kingdom of Dál Riata was a maritime kingdom, spanning the Straits of Moyle, the sea lochs of Argyll and some of the Western Isles. The three kindreds who made up the Dál Riatans were assessed not in terms of mounted warriors or troops of soldiers, but by how many shiploads of men they could contribute to marine assaults. According to his skeleton the son of Thunder had had a privileged upbringing for his time. There were no stress markers in his skeletal remains. Growing children are a bit like growing trees: they lay down layers of growth in their bones. Feed them well, ensure they get plenty of exercise and sunlight, and they will grow steadily, their growth marked in their bones. But if the family suffers privation this will be reflected in the child's bones and their later life. This does not just apply to the early medieval period. When the British were recruiting soldiers to fight the Second Boer War (1899–1902), the recruiting officers were appalled to discover that half the working-class volunteers were medically unfit to serve as a result of their health and growth being stunted by childhood diseases and malnutrition. In the First and Second World Wars, British Tommies were, on average, shorter and lighter than their Australian comrades.

None of the human remains excavated at the Bowl Hole show the stress markers for childhood deprivation and malnutrition. Given that the Bowl Hole was in use as a cemetery for over two hundred years it's inconceivable that there would not, in that time, have been periods when the harvest failed and there was famine. The fact that none of the skeletons excavated from the Bowl Hole show signs of malnourishment is evidence that the families of the people buried there were rich enough to acquire sufficient food for their children even during times of general scarcity.

The son of Thunder was one such child. He grew up in a family that ensured he always had enough to eat, allowing him to grow at an optimal rate. As such, and given that he was buried so far from where he grew up, we can confidently say that he belonged to the upper echelons of Dál Riatan society. His father, likewise a member of the warrior caste, went raiding, coming back with tales to tell his wide-eyed son, but the son of Thunder grew up near to one of the Dál Riatan fortifications, so that whenever raiders came to threaten his family's land and cattle he was bundled into the stronghold and kept there safe. We can imagine the lad throwing insults and stones at the men below before being dragged back into cover by his exasperated mother. His father, though, told her to let be and, taking the boy's hand, led him back to where they could peer over the walls and see the men below.

His father pointed them out, the men below, telling the boy their kindreds from the weave of their clothes, the designs of their brooches and buckles, and the symbols on their shields.

Some of the men below announced themselves, shouting their lineage up to the watching men, reciting the tale of their forebears. A thousand years later, in the final great confrontation between the Gaelic and Anglo-Saxon worlds, the assembled clansmen, arrayed in family groups before the redcoated squares of the Duke of Cumberland's infantry, chanted their lineage too. The year was 1746 and they were standing on the boggy ground of Culloden Moor. Drawn up in family groups, brother standing next to father standing next to uncle, they stood with the most experienced and bravest men at the front. The Highlanders that made up the majority of Charles Edward Stuart's army relied upon breaking the enemy with a headlong charge. As they waited for the battle to begin, the Highlanders recited their long family histories, their names and the names of their forebears tied to the land that had bred them. But they waited a long time, while Cumberland's artillery, having got the range, wrought death and destruction on the Jacobite forces. For some reason, the prince did not issue the order to charge. He may have hoped that Cumberland would advance first, allowing his men the chance to counter-attack. But Cumberland had no need to order a general advance: he could simply allow his cannons to pound the static Highlanders.

Culloden is flat and pretty well featureless. There's not much in the way of cover. For an hour, Cumberland's artillery pounded the Highlanders and the order to charge, 'Claidheamh Mòr!', did not come. In the end, Clan Chattan charged without order. The other clans, seeing them advance, unable to bear the dying without doing anything, charged as well. The attack, funnelled into a much smaller front by the boggy ground, was insanely brave and, in the face of disciplined volleys of musket fire, doomed. A handful of men broke the British lines, they even managed to claim one of the colours of the 4th Foot, but the few who broke through were cut down by British reinforcements. The Highland rising was broken, and with it the culture that supported it. Within a few years, the Highlands were being cleared and the great emigration of Scots to America had begun.

But when the son of Thunder was a child, growing up in Dál Riata, the culture that ended on Culloden Moor was still all-encompassing. The wild bravery that saw men armed with swords charge lines of musket-shooting infantrymen was born in the battles and raids of the Gaels, and celebrated in song and poem by the *Táin Bó* ('cattle raid') genre of Irish literature, which includes *The Cattle Raid of Cooley*. Bravery was the cardinal virtue of all the warrior societies of early Medieval Britain, but there was a certain reckless, devil-may-care quality to its Gaelic strain, which prized individual over collective bravery, that endured through to the field of Culloden. That was the spirit that the son of Thunder's relatives instilled in him as he grew up. Weapon-training started as play, waving a wooden sword around, shooting arrows at targets and then at birds, learning to ride and, for the child growing up on one of the islands of Dál Riata, learning to sail and handle the many different types of boat available, from the coracle, that floated light as a feather upon the water, to the ocean-going currach. But the great training ground for the warrior classes was the hunt. The pursuit of game, preferably large and potentially dangerous animals, on horseback or on foot, bred strength, the ability to coordinate groups of men, courage and tactical awareness – as well as providing a welcome extra supply of food. The most prized export from Britain to Europe at this time was hunting dogs (the second most valuable was slaves). With their packs of dogs the inhabitants of early Medieval Britain cleared the island of the dangerous animals that inhabited it:

the last bear was killed around AD 1000, the last wild boar four hundred years later, the last wolf in 1680. The son of Thunder's early years may also have included going after aquatic mammals, such as seals, porpoises and dolphins, and even the smaller whales. While he and his family were probably not members of the ruling families of Dál Riata, as retainers to the king they were given a share of the dues paid to the king by his people. It also meant that, growing up, the son of Thunder saw and interacted with kings and queens, abbots and warriors: the highest echelons of early medieval society. He was at home among them.

Training as a warrior was not solely physical. An ancient Irish board game, called *fidchell*, was another method of teaching tactics and strategy. Although we are not sure, now, of the rules of *fidchell*, Irish epics tie the game to the outcomes of battles, with the tide of fortune on the battlefield matching the changing fortunes of the *fidchell* players. There are many variants on these ancient board games. The Vikings introduced their own variants called *tafl* games, where the attacker had a 2 to 1 advantage over the defender, accurately depicting the advantage usually accruing to a surprise Viking attack.

Winter evenings in the north are long. The Isle of Iona lies at 56°N. The longest night of the year at this latitude lasts for nearly eighteen hours. That's a lot of time to spend inside. While moonlit nights would have allowed for time outside, and the eyes can adjust to the most minimal of light conditions, winter inevitably meant long evenings sitting inside near the fire. Weaving, particularly tablet weaving, was a useful winter pastime. A practised weaver could do the weaving by feel, passing the thread through the tablets, which was a polygon, usually a square or hexagon made from bone or wood with holes in the corners and one in the centre through which the thread was passed. Bone tablets survive quite well in the ground, and many have been found during excavations, including those at Bamburgh. More complex patterns could have a score or more tablets through which the threads passed, but once the thread was inserted through the holes in the tablets, it was a straightforward matter for the practised weaver to turn the tablets, making the patterned edging. Although weaving was mainly women's work during the months of sunlight, in the winter any pastimes were helpful, and particularly useful as a way of curbing the energy of young boys. It was also a useful skill in that it enhanced manual dexterity. For the warrior, the ability to 'feel' his weapons, to know where the tip of his sword was without looking at it, was crucial. All the skills that used the fingers were helpful in developing the necessary manual dexterity, although there would have been specific exercises taught to the young boys as they practised with, first, wooden swords, and then blades with dulled edges before moving on to battle weapons.

Another way of passing the time would have been conversation and reminiscence. Tale-telling. Although Christianity had brought with it the world-transforming technology of writing, early Medieval Britain was still an oral society. People defined themselves by the tales they told of their origins and their heroes. It is no accident that among the most common surviving documents from this era are king lists. Genealogies were the mark of the past upon the present: they spelled ownership and legitimacy in the only way possible before the invention of written deeds of ownership. Written deeds were to come soon, however, as the Church realised that it needed proof that the lands gifted to it by kings and the nobility really did belong to it. But this was not just a list of names. There were stories associated with the list of forebears, tales that told of

courage and endurance and cunning: all the qualities necessary to make a warrior.

Winter nights were story nights. They were when the son
of Thunder learned, in the flickering firelight, who his family
was, where they came from and what they expected of him.
Some of the stories were told in prose, others in poetry, many a
combination of both, since the Gaelic languages have a musi-
cality that makes it almost impossible to reduce them to blank
prose, devoid of rhythm and melody. The oldest extant written
vernacular poetry in Europe is in Old Irish, taking the form of
marginalia scribbled in Christian manuscripts by the scribing
monk. Not having much space – most of the page being devoted to the book the scribe was copying – the marginal jottings
had to be concise. In these jottings, the stanza is most usually
a quatrain of seven-syllable lines with the couplets rhyming.
Longer Irish vernacular works such as the 'cattle raid' genre
were mixed prose and poetry, with the language switching to
poetry to emphasise moments of particular importance in the
story. The marginalia of these long-dead Irish monks provide
some of the purest, most intimate glimpses into the lives of
people who lived centuries ago. They are whimsical, playful,
complaining and lyrical.

The stories the Gaels, the Angles, the Britons and the Picts
told themselves had, with respect to their martial cultures,
many similarities. The early medieval cultures of Britain naturally all extolled bravery and loyalty but there was another
strand: cunning. Tricks, stratagems, riddles and ruses were all
ways to make a warrior look at a situation from a different angle
and, looking where no one else has, seeing a way of getting
the drop on an enemy. This was not the tactic of epic poetry,
celebrated in *Beowulf*, but the legacy of Woden, the one-eyed
god of deception and trickery. The Greeks celebrated Odys-

seus's trickery, the Anglo-Saxons appear to have been slightly embarrassed about it, while still seeing its necessity. The Britons and Gaels were less ambivalent about cunning as a proper attribute of the warrior, celebrating it in poem and song; the amphibious warfare that the men of Dál Riata specialised in depended on misdirection and surprise.

Growing up on the other side of Britain, the young Oswald heard the tales of his people, but those were told in Old English, with its very different sounds and rhythms. The basic metre of Anglo-Saxon verse was the four-stress line, with three of the stressed words alliterating, and a pronounced caesura midway through the line. Lines did not generally rhyme: the beat and music was provided by alliteration, assonance and the naturally strong four-beat measure of Old English and, indeed, Middle English and modern English.

Among the finds at Sutton Hoo was a lyre. Another was found in the tomb excavated at Prittlewell in Essex in 2003, which proved to be the richest Anglo-Saxon tomb excavated since Sutton Hoo. Although the men buried with the lyres were not scops, the presence of the lyres indicates that the songs and tales told as the main form of entertainment by the Anglo-Saxons, in this world and the next, were accompanied by music. The Anglo-Saxon lyre normally had six strings, although there are examples with five and seven strings, and looked like a long washboard with rounded ends and a similarly shaped sounding hole in the top half of the instrument. The strings were gathered together at the base of the instrument and then splayed out over the sounding hole before being pegged at the top of the lyre.

Both Anglo-Saxon scops and Gaelic bards seem to have played the lyre by strumming rather than plucking individual strings like a harp, although it's likely that both techniques were employed depending on the occasion and the accompaniment. Kings had their own resident poets, whose job was to magnify the exploits of the king, praise his accomplishments, record his deeds and generally ensure that his name and fame spread throughout the kingdoms of Britain, thus ensuring a constant supply of young men wanting to make their names going to his court.

The young Oswald and our young warrior, the son of Thunder, grew up in societies that were related by their martial orientations, their oral cultures and common technological levels, which produced extraordinarily high-quality arms and metalwork but had very limited civil engineering capabilities, and were divided by religion, language and history. So when they met, brought together by the vicissitudes of fortune that had driven Oswald and his family into exile among people who were ancestral enemies, there was much that would foster mutual understanding between them.

Oswald remained in exile for seventeen years, from the age of twelve to about twenty-nine. He grew to manhood as a refugee among people who spoke a different language and followed a different religion. It was sometime during these years that he first met the son of Thunder. As to where and how they met, there are two main possibilities as there were two main foci of the kingdom of Dál Riata: Iona and the king's court, which was itinerant but had its main stronghold at Dunadd. At Iona, they would have met as pilgrims. At Dunadd, they would have met as warriors.

For Oswald growing up in Dál Riata the natural quid pro quo for the refuge given to him and his family would have been to lend his sword, and the swords of the men who had accompanied the Idings into exile, to King Eochaid Buide. It was what was expected and the natural way for an exiled ætheling to start making a reputation for himself. As such, Oswald came to learn and understand a very different martial tradition from that of the Anglo-Saxons.

The defining formation of the Anglo-Saxons in battle was the shieldwall. It was not an Anglo-Saxon invention, having been perfected by the Greeks and then the Romans centuries before. A shieldwall consisted of warriors, with their shields held in the left hand and spear or sword in the right hand, forming a line of interlinked shields and advancing, standing firm or retreating together. This remained the bedrock of Anglo-Saxon military formation from the fifth century to the eleventh, ending finally on Senlac Hill. Anglo-Saxon warriors did use horses, but they were the transport arm of the warband, ferrying men to battle but not actually used for fighting. For battle, the key weapons were the shield, the spear and, for the highest class of warriors, the sword.

The Northumbrian shield was generally made from lime wood, which is light but strong enough to absorb or deflect most blows. If lime wood wasn't available, then rowan and alder could have been used as they have similar properties. The shield was usually round, with an iron boss at its centre that served to protect the hand holding the shield. Its size varied, anywhere from eighteen inches to four feet in diameter, but the norm was for a shield to be three feet wide. This was big enough to protect the torso and to allow the warrior to duck his head behind it for further protection. Shields were usually made of planks of wood, reinforced with metal bands, and covered with cowhide. The Laws of Ine, a law code promulgated by the king of Wessex at the end of the seventh century, specifically requires shield-makers to use cowhide when covering shields, which suggests that some shield-makers used inferior but cheaper sheep hide. A leather or cowhide edging was often applied to the circumference of the shield, the hide being put on wet since on drying it shrinks, thus holding the planked construction together more tightly. Excavated shields show traces of paint confirming what one would expect: they were painted in vivid colours and designs, telling the tale of the warrior who bore them, or his clan or warband.

Although a shield's obvious function is defensive, Anglo-Saxon shields were also important as offensive weapons. The central boss was extremely hard and could be used to ram into any part of the enemy left exposed. In the clash against an enemy, the power and momentum of a well-drilled shieldwall would be enough to overwhelm, by sheer weight, all but the strongest and most determined opposition. But it wasn't just the central boss that could be used as a weapon. The edge rim was used too. It could be rammed into an unprotected face or throat with devastating effect. Excavations have uncovered very few helmets from this time, suggesting that only the richest and most renowned warriors wore them. A man without a helmet was vulnerable to having the shield edge uppercut into his throat or jaw. A blow like that could crush the windpipe or break teeth and jaw, leaving him incapacitated and easy to finish off. In the final stages of a battle, the shieldwall would generally dissolve into a melée. In the chaos, a shield could be employed very effectively horizontally.

While the big round lime shield was almost as characteristic of the Anglo-Saxon as the ubiquitous long knife, the *seax*, the Gaels and the Picts used smaller shields. It was in the use of this sort of shield, called a targe, that the son of Thunder was trained in Dál Riata. Targes were about eighteen inches wide and round. They could be made of wickerwork or wood, often yew, and occasionally bronze, painted in the swirling Irish fashion, and usually covered in concentric circles of studs.

Shields that were covered in hide were then whitewashed with chalk or lime, white being a popular colour for Irish shields. In battle, the chalk or lime flew off in clouds when the shields were struck, making for a popular poetic trope in Old Irish battle tales. Some targes had a detachable iron spike set in the centre to use as an additional weapon (it was detachable so the shield could be carried around without the spike sticking out). Targes remained the northern shield of choice right into the dawn of the modern era: many of the Highlanders on Culloden Moor carried targes. The fighting style with a targe was different from that employed with the Anglo-Saxon shield. Dál Riatan warriors, and the Gaels in general, were skilled at skirmish encounters, and valued acts of individual bravery highly. The targe is light and when combined with a short sword or long knife makes for an efficient fighting style. The aim would have been similar to that of a boxer dealing with a taller opponent with a longer reach: to get inside his opponent's guard where his speed and short-range weapon can finish off a slower-moving enemy. Gaelic literature has many examples of champions meeting in battle and the typical war gear of warriors facilitated such encounters. The sword and targe combination resembled the Thracian weapon set used in gladiatorial contests during the Roman Empire, which typically pitted a fast-moving, lightly armed Thracian gladiator against the slower-moving murmillo, whose sword and shield resembled the typical weapons of Roman legionaries.

Dál Riata was a sea kingdom, its borders were its beaches, and warriors learned the skills of amphibious warfare. From the Vikings right through to the Marines, the principles remain the same. Stealth in approach, local surprise, dawn attacks, prepared fall-back positions for evacuation. Without the bludgeon of the shieldwall, the warriors of Dál Riata had to rely on different tactics for battlefield success. When facing Anglo-Saxon enemies, the key tactical objective was to achieve surprise, thus denying the enemy the chance to form the shieldwall properly and dissolving the battle into a general melée where the mobility and practised one-to-one combat skills of the Dál Riatan warriors had a greater chance of success. If it proved impossible to stop the enemy forming a shieldwall, the Dál Riatan war master's objective was to turn the flank of the enemy, to try to attack his side or rear so that the shieldwall could be disrupted and broken up. To prevent that, the Anglo-Saxon war master sought to anchor the wings of the shieldwall in impassable terrain: a river, a marsh, thick woodland. Failing that, a reserve would be kept behind the main shieldwall detailed with the task of meeting and repelling any attacks to the flank or rear, while the shieldwall itself advanced upon the enemy.

But while the tactics of the Dál Riatans and the Northumbrians were as different as their shields, there was one weapon that was common to both. The spear. Although we tend to think of swords as the typical medieval weapon, in the early medieval period the spear was far more common. In fact, it was so ubiquitous that there is good reason to think that it was viewed as an everyday tool rather than a weapon. Where a weapon was buried with a body, in most cases it was a spear. For the Anglo-Saxons, the spear was the mark of the freeborn man; slaves were not allowed to carry spears. Spears were as common then as hats were for the Victorians and mobile phones are today. A spear served as a walking stick, general poking device (particularly valuable for checking to see how deep that water is) and weapon against thieves and animals. Spears lay stacked in the corner of rooms, ready to be picked up before going out. While a sword marked out a warrior as high born and wealthy, a spear was the go-to weapon of everybody at this time. They had iron heads, but few spear shafts have survived to be excavated. The few samples that survive, when coupled with information from experimental archaeology and ethnographic parallels, indicate that ash and hazel were the woods most commonly used, with apple, oak and maple used less frequently. To make an effective spear shaft, the wood had to be dense, strong and with a slight but not pronounced flex.

In battle, the spear allowed men with less combat training to engage enemies at arm's length. A disciplined line of men, holding spears, was very hard to break apart, although a heavily armoured and experienced warrior with a shield would be able to break past the line of spear points and get in close. At close range, a trained warrior, a man whose life was dedicated to war, would wreak havoc on a spear line: it paid to keep such men at bay.

We have unique pictorial evidence that the Picts also used the spear as a main weapon. In the churchyard and the nearby road at Aberlemno in Angus, Scotland are five standing carved stones, one of which shows scenes from a battle, often identified with the Battle of Nechtansmere on 20 May 685, when a major Northumbrian army, which had gone north into Pictland under the command of King Ecgfrith (the son of Oswald's brother Oswiu and, until his ill-fated expedition north, the most powerful king in Britain), suffered a catastrophic defeat at the hands of the Picts. The Battle Stone, as it is called, has a beautifully embossed Celtic cross on one face, its circle centre inscribed with six spirals arranged in a hexagon around a central spiral. But it is the other side of the stone that gives it its name. Yes, it shows a battle. There are three lines of figures set one on top of the other. On each line, the figures depicted on the left have long, flowing hair, while those on the right are wearing helmets. Given that it's the men on the left who are shown as the winners, scholars have identified these figures as Pictish warriors defeating the helmet-wearing Northumbrian army of King Ecgfrith.

The top line shows a mounted Pictish warrior, supremely confident on horseback, chasing after a fleeing Northumbrian who, in his panic, has dropped his sword and shield but is still clutching his spear. The centre line shows three Pictish warriors on foot, armed with spear, swords and shields. It's possible that this carving might actually show the typical battle formation of Pictish warriors. If so, they were arranged in three lines. The foremost man is armed with a sword and shield, the man standing behind him has a spear and appears to be guarding the front man, using his long spear to keep back the mounted Anglian warrior who is trying to attack them. The third and rearmost man would therefore be the reserve, ready to be called up into the battle line to replace fallen warriors, or used to attack targets of opportunity.

The bottom line shows two mounted men, a Pict and a Northumbrian, confronting each other, while on the far right a Northumbrian warrior is apparently being pecked by a raven. He is presumably dead. If the interpretation of the scene as the Battle of Nechtansmere is correct – the idea looks less secure now than it did twenty years ago but is still possible – then the bottom line might show the one-on-one battle between Bridei, king of the Picts, and Ecgfrith of Northumbria, while the dead man on the right would be the corpse of Ecgfrith being eaten by ravens. If the stone is an accurate depiction, then it shows both sides used horses and horse-riding warriors, as well as infantry – although another interpretation might be that the raiding party of Northumbrians, riding deep into Pictland, were ambushed and tried to fight their way out on horseback, knowing that if they abandoned their horses they would never make it back to their homes. This would seem more likely, as there are no other suggestions that the Anglo-Saxons fought on horseback, while there are indications that the warriors of the Brythonic kingdoms sometimes did so.

Given the later mastery of the medieval battlefield by men on horseback, the question arises why the armed warriors of the Picts and the Britons were not more effective against the Anglo-Saxons. The first part of the answer is that it's difficult for a mounted warrior to break a line of disciplined and determined warriors on foot. Even William's knights at Hastings, who had trained their entire lives as mounted warriors, failed to break Harold's line on Senlac Hill. It was only the attrition of the long day's battle and the fortuitous, from the Norman point of view, death of Harold that broke the Anglo-Saxon shieldwall.

However, the mounted warriors of the Picts and Britons were not as formidable an opponent for warriors on foot as Norman knights. They rode bareback or with light saddles, without stirrups, making it far harder for the horseman to sustain heavy contact with a warrior on foot. Attacks, using spears, would have had to be fast and light, with spears jabbed rather than thrust with the full force of the medieval knight. Also, the horses ridden by the Picts and Britons were much smaller than the war horses of the later period. Such large animals have to be bred carefully, with mares and stallions carefully selected and the breeding stock continually monitored. Horses, left to their own desires, breed downwards in size, making for animals not much bigger than modern ponies.

Twelve at the time of going into exile, Oswald received a solid grounding in the tactics and weapons of his foster people: the amphibious assault, the facility with horse and spear.

But serving alongside him in the Dál Riatan warband were men who had accompanied him and his family into exile and these men would have taught the young ætheling the ways of his people. So Oswald would have grown to manhood accomplished in two schools of war.

Iona was becoming the school of kings. Colm Cille had anointed Áedán king of Dál Riata and prophesied Eochaid Buide's unexpected rule. His successors as abbots of Iona continued the close relationship with Dál Riata. The monks taught the princes of Dál Riata the new religion, with its concomitant civilisation and learning, and protected them through prayer and fasting. Oswald's conversion was deep and wholehearted. He learned the language of the Ionan monks fluently; he learned their characteristic methods of prayer, which became so habitual that he always sat with his palms upward on his knees, in a position of praise and thanksgiving. Although the deep workings of a man's soul are inaccessible to history, there is no reason to doubt that Oswald was what his later hagiographers made of him: a genuinely devout man. This was a time when Christianity exploded like a hope bomb among the Anglo-Saxons; there is a grim courage to the eschatology of the old gods, but there is no hope. Our perception of Christ and Christianity is filtered through the prism of two thousand years of history, a history that veers from the sacred to the profane, from saints to sexual abusers. It's a history encompassing the best and worst of humanity. But in seventh-century Northumbria, all of that is yet to come. How did Oswald view Christ? A Norse legend of Odin has him hanging on the world tree for nine days as he seeks knowledge. Assuming that the Anglo-Saxons had a comparable story about Woden, then Oswald was already familiar with the figure of a god sacrificing himself. But Christ, according to the testimony of the monks whom he had come to revere, had done more than that: he had defeated death itself.

In a world where death was apparent and real in a way that is almost impossible for us to imagine today, this triumph over death called to a man whose job was dealing out death in battle. Christ was the warrior who had turned the tables on the great devourer and overcome the most impossible of odds. To Oswald, Christ was a man of destiny, isolated at times, abandoned at the end, but who came through his abandonment to a triumph beyond hope. For Oswald, there were significant parallels. What's more, the church that proclaimed the truth of Christ had its seat in Rome, which itself still held a mythic power. It was the city of the legions, of ancient emperors who had raised works beyond the comprehension of men of his day. The power of Christ and the myth of Rome were intertwined.

That power was felt widely among the first generations of Christian kings for whom Oswald's piety was not hugely exceptional: other kings renounced their thrones for lives of prayer, or put aside rule to make a final, life-defining pilgrimage to Rome, the seat of the Apostles Peter and Paul and the site of the tomb of Pope Gregory. Indeed, King Sigeberht of East Anglia was so devoted to his new monastic life that he had to be dragged from his monastery to face an army of Mercian invaders by the king who had succeeded him. But Sigeberht, having achieved that reputation by killing many men, wanted no more on his conscience. On giving up the crown and becoming a monk, he had vowed to put aside the sword. When thrust, unwilling, onto a battlefield, he still refused to take up the sword again. Sigeberht died a martyr in the true sense of the word: a witness to a belief that enjoined its followers to love their enemies. Such a love was unknown in a warrior society. Respect for a worthy foe was one thing, but love? Even Oswald, eulogised by Bede as the perfect warrior saint, could not summon it at

the end; on the battlefield where he fell Oswald prayed for his
men but there was no mention of prayers for his enemies. But
nonetheless, there was something about this new religion that
presented something different, something new to the warrior
societies of early Medieval Britain.

After two millennia of Christianity, and the sins and crimes
committed in its name, it's difficult for us to see the religion
fresh, unexpected: as full of promise as a new-born baby. But
that is how Oswald saw it. He also seems to have embraced
some of its asceticism, unlike his younger brother. The two
brothers were a long time in exile. They grew to manhood in
Dál Riata, living a life where death was a constant prospect.
Young men living with the risk of death often seek release
from the constant tension with young women, and Oswiu certainly did: at some point during the brothers' exile he fathered
a child by an Irish princess. Her name was Fina, and her father
was the high king of the Northern Uí Neíll. There is no record
that Oswiu and Fina were formally married, but they called
the boy Aldfrith and, many years later and in rather unusual
circumstances, he would become king of Northumbria. But as
far as Oswald is concerned, there is no record of any dalliances
before the necessary marriage he undertook when he returned
to Northumbria. Given the glamour that attached to the exiled
young prince, he must have decided to avoid such entanglements and the most likely reason was the ascetic example of
the monks of Iona.

As for the warrior, he married. He married in Dál Riata, a few
years before the end of the princes' long exile. When did he
first meet the Northumbrian exiles? As a member of the Dál
Riatan nobility, it's likely he knew the two young aethelings
during his youth. King Eochaid Buide, as did every king of the
time, required his nobility to attend him regularly. Loyalty was

personal. It needed to be refreshed and reinforced by regular meetings. So the warrior would have met the party of Northumbrian exiles when his own father went to see the king. The king's retinue was the central clearing house for news and gossip: the death of Æthelfrith and the flight of his family would have been the talk of the north for many a long winter night.

But the kingdom's other focus was Iona and it's just as likely that Oswald met the son of Thunder there. Oswald became close friends with the fifth abbot, Ségéne, who succeeded to the abbacy in 623, although Oswald had known Ségéne when he was a simple monk. The young Northumbrian was a frequent visitor to Iona, so any contacts with the warrior would have been reinforced on the holy island when the two men met there for the major Christian festivals.

Loyalty was personal and patriotism local. But a new loyalty to a prince fortune seemed to smile on and who had the favour of the saint could outweigh the ties of place, particularly if the adventure might bring glory and great gains. During his exile, Oswald had gained sufficient reputation to be given a nickname by the annalists: *Lamnguin*. This is a Gaelic word, which can be translated as 'Whiteblade', or 'Blessed hand'. Anyone growing up in the 1970s will, though, favour another translation: 'Flashing Blade', for Oswald did 'fight for what you want, for all that you believe'. The name indicates that Oswald had garnered a considerable reputation as a warrior and fortune's favoured son. Such a man would attract young warriors to his cause. However, a member of the Dál Riatan nobility could not simply go off in service to another lord without his king's permission. But so long as Oswald served Eochaid Buide, then it would be acceptable for a young warrior to join his retinue. In the same way that Oswald had learned the ways of war of Dál Riata, so a warrior joining Oswald's ranks would learn the war ways of the Northumbrians. No bad thing, for the power of Northumbria was waxing and an ambitious young warrior would want to know their secrets. Even so, as long as Edwin reigned supreme among the kings of Britain, there was no possibility of Oswald returning to Northumbria to stake his claim to the throne. Nor does he seem to have had any desire to do so. What is notable is that there is no evidence that Edwin pursued his young nephews in the way that Æthelfrith, Oswald's father, had pursued him. While it is true that Edwin might have seemed beyond reach, and it was clearly sensible to avoid confrontation with him, yet young princes denied the thrones they think are rightfully theirs have often acted with no thought to what was most sensible. That there is no evidence that either party made any effort to overthrow the other suggests that some measure of sibling regard remained between Edwin and Acha: he left her and her children alone on the implicit understanding that they would not attempt to win back the kingdom. Whether that tacit agreement was meant to extend beyond Edwin's lifetime to include his heirs we do not know: perhaps if Edwin had passed on his kingdom to his grown-up sons from his first marriage to Coenburh the Mercian princess, or had lived long enough for his young son, Wuscfrea, by Queen Æthelburh of Kent, to inherit, then there would have been conflict between the cousins as to who should rule Northumbria.

But Edwin did not live long enough to secure the succession for his sons. As we have seen, he fell in battle on 12 October 633. His eldest son, Osfrith, died with him that day. A later chronicler tells of the surrounded king, at bay, standing over the body of his dead son, until he too fell.

10

To Take Back What is Ours

'The king is dead . . .' The news of the high king's overthrow went whispering through the land and over the islands. Edwin, who had reclaimed the throne of Northumbria in 616, had reigned with increasing dominance for seventeen years, his mastery only growing in the years following King Rædwald's death. That he should be brought down in such catastrophic fashion was a disaster for his house and for the religion he had espoused in his last years. Bishop Paulinus fled south with Queen Æthelburh and Edwin's surviving family. Northumbria was left to the wolves.

The wolves in question did not see themselves that way. They were Cadwallon, king of Gwynedd, and Penda of Mercia. Of the two, Cadwallon was the senior partner, but it was an unlikely alliance. Cadwallon was a Briton, a Christian and, in the self-description of his own house, a Roman. Penda was a pagan, an Anglo-Saxon and, possibly, not even king of Mercia. Given the long history of conflict between the Britons and the Anglo-Saxons, it was not the most likely of partnerships. But amid the small kingdoms of the isles of Britain in the seventh century there was one truism that held sway over all others: the enemy of my enemy is my friend. Edwin had ravaged Anglesey, possibly in the year 629. The *Annales Cambriae* (Annals of Wales) suggests that Edwin might have besieged Cadwallon during his attack, stating in its laconic way, 'The besieging of King Cadwallon in the island of *Glannauc*' (Puffin Island, a 69-acre island off the east arm of Anglesey. The puffin population that had given the island its name is now slowly recovering following the extermination of the brown rats that all but wiped them out, after a ship was wrecked on the island in 1816: yes, the rats abandoned the sinking ship).

There is some late evidence that the conflict between Edwin and Cadwallon was more than the ordinary competition between rival kings. The twelfth-century monk Reginald of Durham wrote that 'Cadwan, who reigned on this side of the Humber, brought up Edwin with his own son Cadwallon.'[1] 'This side of the Humber' suggests that Reginald may have had access to material from south of the Humber estuary. The *Red Book of Hergest*, a late fourteenth-century manuscript kept now at Jesus College, Oxford, contains Welsh prose and poetry, including the *Mabinogion* and Triads. The Triads were a way of grouping material together to make it more memorable, each triad giving a subject and three examples. For instance:

> Three Fortunate Princes of the Island of Britain:
> Owain son of Urien,
> Rhun son of Maelgwn,
> Rhufawn the Radiant son of Dewrarth Wledig.[2]

The longest and most detailed of the Triads, number 26, 'Three Powerful Swineherds of the Island of Britain', concludes:

And at Llanfair in Arfon under the Black Rock she brought forth a kitten, and the Powerful Swineherd threw it from the Rock into the sea. And the sons of Palug fostered it in Môn, to their own harm: and that was Palug's Cat, and it was one of the Three Great Oppressions of Môn, nurtured therein. The second was Daronwy, and the third was Edwin, king of Lloegr.[3]

Môn is the Welsh word for Anglesey and *Lloegr* is the Welsh word for the lands of Britain outside the regions where the Cymry live, apart from the people of Devon and Cornwall, who were closely related to the Welsh and whose land was called Dumnonia. Lloegr was expanding. At the end of the sixth century its western edge stretched roughly from the Severn to the Humber estuaries, and included all land to the south except for modern-day Devon and Cornwall. But as the power of the Anglo-Saxon kingdoms grew, Lloegr expanded, until it became roughly coterminous with England. Triad 26 supports the idea that Edwin, 'king of Lloegr', was raised in the Brythonic kingdom of Gwynedd, then invaded and ravaged Môn. However, the question remains as to how much credence can be placed upon sources that derive from hundreds of years after Edwin's lifetime.

Nonetheless, reading through and between the sources, there does seem to have been a greater degree of enmity between Edwin and Cadwallon than normal between rival kings. Cwichelm, king of the West Saxons, attempted to assassinate Edwin and, while Edwin naturally then mounted a punitive expedition against Wessex, he seems to have allowed Cwichelm to live, although the living was presumably predicated upon Cwichelm's public submission to him. And there the matter rested for both kings. But our fragmentary sources say that

Edwin invaded and ravaged Cadwallon's possession of Anglesey, forcing Cadwallon into exile. Triad 29 commemorates:

> Three Faithful War-Bands of the Island of Britain:
> The War-Band of Cadwallawn son of Cadfan, who were
> with him seven years in Ireland; and in all that time
> they did not ask him for anything, lest they should be
> compelled to leave him.[4]

But when Cadwallon returned, he wreaked his revenge upon
Edwin and his people. According to Bede, following the Battle of Hatfield Chase, Cadwallon 'was set upon exterminating
the entire English race in Britain, and spared neither women
nor innocent children, putting them all to horrible deaths with
ruthless savagery, and continuously ravaging their whole country'.[5] Bede visits more vituperation upon Cadwallon than any
other person mentioned in his work: if the *Ecclesiastical History*
has a villain, Bede casts him as Cadwallon, King of Gwynedd.
Bede was born in 672, four decades after these events, and finished his history around 731, a century later. Yet the memory
of what, for the Northumbrians, had been a most evil time was
still vivid.

Taken all together, the evidence does suggest a level of
hatred between Edwin and Cadwallon that might originate in
the betrayal of a youthful friendship. However, medieval writers
could see a good story just as well as modern ones: if Lew Wal-
lace could see the narrative punch of making Judah Ben-Hur
and Messala childhood friends, the anonymous writers of the
Welsh Triads could also see the story value of such a link. History has to be suspicious of the natural human tendency to turn
fragmentary, disjointed events into a story, particularly when
one of the major players is turned into an out and out villain.

There was more to Cadwallon than the ravaging murderer portrayed by Bede. To see this, travel to Wales and pass through the valleys and passes of Snowdonia. Here the kings of Gwynedd had their castles and strongholds; here the Welsh people held out longest against the domination of the English crown until Edward I crushed Welsh independence under the stone weight of his castles at Harlech, Conwy, Caernarfon and Beaumaris. Beyond the slopes of Snowdon, across the turbulent waters of the Menai Strait, is Anglesey, Ynys Môn. Where the scree and granite of the mainland support little but sheep, the fields and pastures of Anglesey are rich and fertile. Cross Thomas Telford's elegant suspension bridge, completed in 1826, that afforded the first permanent link to the mainland. Before it was built, the cattle, made fat by the island's green pastures, had to be swum across the Menai Strait, with many being lost to the currents. Across the bridge, take the A4080 that winds round the south-west corner of the island until it passes the flat expanse of Malltraeth Sands. Just a mile further along the road is the quiet hamlet of Llangadwaladr. About a hundred yards before the junction with the road to Bethel is a tarmac track on the right. Down the track, hidden behind a screen of trees, is the church of St Cadwaladr. It's a quiet country church, mostly dating from the twelfth century although the chancel was built in the fourteenth and the two chapels in the seventeenth. The church breathes silence.

Almost opposite the door, set into the middle of the bare, whitewashed wall, is a rough rectangular slab of stone. It's above head height but, reaching up, it is possible to touch it.

There. That is the rough grain of raw history under your fingertips. The slab is covered with incised markings carved into the surface. On first sight, the markings appear almost random, a collection of curves and diagonals and crosses arranged in columns. But it's those crosses that first resolve. And with a sudden twist of perspective, the stone becomes clearer. For it was not originally built into the wall of a church but stood, upright, in the ground. Now, as part of a wall, it is on its side. At the far left, which would have been the top of the stone, is a cross. Arranged below the cross, in four vertical columns, are letters, but these are turned at ninety degrees to the cross, with the largest letters making up the top two columns. So when the stone was first set into the ground, anyone reading it would have had to tilt their heads to the right to see the letters the right way up.

CATAMANUS REX SAPIENTISIMUS OPINATISIMUS OMNIUM REGUM

It's Latin. Carved into a stone first erected sometime around 626 on an island off the coast of Wales. The legions had left more than two hundred years earlier. Yet the knowledge of the language of Rome had been kept alive through the centuries and inscribed in memoriam.

The inscription says: 'King Catamanus, wisest, most renowned of all kings'.

Catamanus is the Latin form of Cadfan. Cadfan ap Iago was king of Gwynedd from about 616 to roughly 625. His son was Cadwallon, the scourge of the Northumbrians, the man portrayed by Bede as the most savage and cruel of kings. But it was Cadwallon who had this memorial to his father erected. While the words may not have been his, the sentiments were, for gravestones tell of the living not the dead. That Cadwallon called his father 'wisest' showed that he wanted to link him to the biblical ideal of the ideal king: *magnificatus est ergo rex Salomon super omnes reges terrae divitiis et sapientia* (King Solomon exceeded all the kings of the earth in riches and wisdom,

1 Kings 10:23). But 'sapientisimus' also had a more direct meaning for Cadwallon and the people reading the stone. 'Most wise' was the epithet used by Irish annalists for the most learned of scholars. Gildas castigated an earlier king of Gwynedd, Maelgwn, for his vices but admitted his learning. The court of the kings of Gwynedd retained into the seventh century an ideal of learning and wisdom in the exercise of kingship; their aspirations were equal to the barbarian kings who had supplanted the emperors in continental Europe yet who still used superlative Latin forms to memorialise themselves and their works: Theoderic, king of the Ostrogoths, was memorialised as the 'most famous and glorious' on the aqueduct he repaired outside Rome.

The stone itself, carboniferous quartz arenite, was quarried nearby. The monk who composed the epitaph in Latin first wrote out the words on a wax-covered wooden tablet, inscribing them with a sharp metal stylus. This was how scribes learned to write, as vellum was far too expensive for writing exercises. Some examples of these wax-covered boards were found in a bog in Ireland; the Psalms that had been written on them were still legible. The inscription written out, it was then painted onto the stone as it lay on the ground, and the mason carved the outlines of the letters before chiselling out the rest. The letters were probably then painted to make them stand out more clearly before the stone was set into the ground to mark the grave of Cadwallon's father.

The church of St Cadwaladr is named after Cadwallon's son who acquired a reputation for holiness very different from his warlike father. The church was probably dedicated to a different saint when first built, but was renamed in honour of the saintly and peace-loving Cadwaladr. Llangadwaladr lies a mile east of Aberffraw, the site of the primary royal residence of the kings of Gwynedd. It seems strange that they didn't have a church closer – except that there was one there, probably before the church of St Cadwaladr was built. Half a mile west of Aberffraw is the tidal island of Cribinau. On it is a small twelfth-century church dedicated to St Cwyfan – Kevin. St Cwyfan was Gaelic and while the current church is twelfth century, the original was probably founded in the seventh century. Its exposed position, which makes the site horribly open to westerly gales blowing in over the Irish Sea, was just the sort of penitential site that appealed to Gaelic monks. But while it would have appealed to Gaelic monks, tramping into the face of a force 8 probably did not hold as much appeal for the kings of Gwynedd and their court. A church inland, and easterly, was a more appropriate location for the burial and remembrance of kings.

But if the king commemorated at the church was 'wisest' and the king after whom the church was named was a saint, the king who came between them was the 'furious stag' who burst from the mountain strongholds of the Britons. Cadwallon was the last great Brythonic king, successor to Arthur – if he existed anywhere outside the tales the Britons told themselves of their lost lands – and, for a year, it seemed that the king of Gwynedd would indeed restore the fortunes of the Britons.

It is clear that Cadwallon did not fight by the normal rules. After their victory at Hatfield Chase on 12 October 632, Penda returned to Mercia with his spoils and Eadfrith, the younger of Edwin's two sons by his first, Mercian, wife. Eadfrith had survived the battle that killed his father and elder brother, apparently by surrendering to Penda. He would have been a useful hostage, particularly as there is some doubt as to whether Penda was actually yet king of Mercia at the time. But being able to tout Eadfrith, the son of a Mercian princess, as his hostage would cement Penda's growing reputation as a winner. But the point is that Penda did return to Mercia but Cadwallon did not go back to Gwynedd.

Communications, particularly by land, were slow, and Gwynedd was a long way even from Deira, the southern half of Northumbria. Normally, the aftermath of battle was for the victorious king to impose terms and tribute upon the people whose king he had defeated. If the defeat had been fatal, and a new king was required, then that new king would have to be acceptable to the victor, and swear submission to him. But once that was settled, the victor would return to his own land and his people. While his immediate warband were tied to him, the greater part of his warriors had land of their own to manage, families to maintain and the harvest to bring in. The battle of Hatfield Chase had taken place in the first half of October. Winter was the time to return to one's own hearth, spin tales of battle, and wait for spring. But Cadwallon stayed.

His victory would have meant little to most of the peasant farmers who cultivated the land. And since the Northumbrian expansion was relatively recent, it's likely that many if not most of these peasant farmers were Britons. Cadwallon and his men spoke their language. So while Cadwallon razed the halls of the Anglian elite and expropriated their land, the native Britons probably helped him by paying their renders with more than customary willingness and providing him with intelligence. Cadwallon and his men overwintered in Deira, making their quarters in what Bede called an *oppido municipio*, a municipal town. This was probably not York, which was a Roman *colonia*, making it one of only four towns in Britain to be accorded this highest legal status. Looking at Cadwallon's strategic situation, he would have wanted quarters with the best communications that were possible, which meant a town lying on the old Roman road network, and with clear lines of advance and retreat. The Roman settlement of Calcaria (Tadcaster) lay on Icknield Street, which provided a clear line of retreat to the south-west, and commanded the River Wharfe, while also covering one of the main approach roads to York. Doncaster, which guarded the Ermine Street route between London and York while avoiding a boat passage over the Humber, was another possibility, as it lay reasonably close to the site of the Battle of Hatfield Chase and would have allowed wounded men to recover there without them having to travel much. Another possibility, north-west of York, is Isurium, modern-day Aldborough, which guarded both Dere Street, the main Roman road up to the Antonine Wall, and a secondary road connecting the northern extension of Watling Street to Luguvalium (Carlisle).

During the winter of 632, what was left of the Deiran nobility gathered together, probably in York, the capital of the Yffings, to find a new king, and one capable of leading them to victory against Cadwallon. By this time, it must have been clear to them that Cadwallon had embarked on a war of conquest rather than plunder. Over the previous fifty years there had been a slow expansion of kingdoms, with the stronger polities swallowing up the weaker ones. But while kings might attack distant kings – as Edwin attacked the West Saxons – they went home afterwards. They only conquered neighbouring kingdoms. So during his reign Edwin conquered the Brythonic kingdom of Elmet, which occupied what is now the West Riding of Yorkshire, but ravaged the more distant islands of Man and Anglesey. The Deiran nobility who had survived the disaster at Hatfield Chase would have expected Cadwallon to follow the same pattern, particularly as Gwynedd was a long way away and winter was approaching. When he did not leave, they had little choice but to find a new king.

The man they chose was Osric. He was the son of Edwin's uncle, Ælfric, making Osric first cousin to the dead king. Although not mentioned by name, he must have taken part in the great debate Edwin had held with his nobles about the adoption of Christianity. As with the other nobles he had accepted the decision of the king's council and Paulinus had baptised him into the new religion. But now Paulinus was gone, fled into the south, and the new God had failed his new adherents in the most visible way possible: he had left their bodies dead on the battlefield.

Religion, for ancient and indeed most modern people, is a practical matter: the obtaining of favours and blessings from gods or a God who might, according to his advertising, be loving but is usually inscrutable. For Edwin and his council, one of the key considerations in the debate had been the this-world benefits of following the new god. While Bede's dramatic reconstruction of the debate is just that, too dramatic to be true, the study of the psychology of conversion suggests that the words he puts into the mouth of Edwin's pagan priest Coifi would have played their part in the debate.

> Your Majesty, let us give careful consideration to this new teaching; for I frankly admit that, in my experience, the religion that we have hitherto professed seems valueless and powerless. None of your subjects has been more devoted to the service of our gods than myself; yet there are many to whom you show greater favour, who receive greater honours, and who are more successful in all their undertakings. Now, if the gods had any power, they would surely have favoured

myself, who have been more zealous in their service.
Therefore, if on examination you perceive that these
new teachings are better and more effectual let us not
hesitate to accept them.[6]

But if 'this new teaching' had been 'more effectual' for a
while, leading Edwin to the zenith of his power, it had now
failed utterly and apparently conclusively. During the council where Osric made his claim for the fealty of the surviving
Deiran nobility, he also abjured the new God who had let
Edwin down: if they would accept him as king, he would lead
them back onto the road of their fathers. Amid the shock of
the defeat there must have been few voices raised in favour
of keeping the new God. Taking Osric as their king, the
witan (the king's advisers) chanted the list of his ancestors,
the fathers and forefathers of the Yffings, through to the All-
Father, Woden.

And secure in the conviction that the old gods would accept
their repentance and lead them to victory, Osric led the gathered remnants of the Deiran nobility to where Cadwallon had
his quarters and laid siege to it. It's close to impossible that
Osric could have commanded enough men to lay siege to York
and its extensive Roman walls, providing further evidence
that Cadwallon had made his headquarters in another town
rather than the capital of the Yffings. According to Bede, Cadwallon's forces launched a surprise attack from their place of
besiegement, taking the Deirans by complete surprise. Osric,
king for a few months, joined his cousin Edwin in death. The
Deiran warrior elite was further reduced. In less than a year
Cadwallon had killed, taken hostage or driven the Yffings into
exile. Deira was now well and truly his.

And in the surprise of his attack, we can dimly discern the

help given to him by the Britons. York and its surroundings, as capital of the Yffings, would have been one of the areas most densely settled by Anglians. But in the other, smaller, Roman towns and villages the old Brythonic language was still spoken. The inhabitants stood silently aside as Cadwallon and his battle-confident men crept past their houses, swords muffled by strips of cloth, footfalls deadened with wrappings, to catch Osric and his warriors off guard. The slaughter was swift and complete.

If the new God had failed the Deirans, so had the old ones. It must have seemed that heaven's face was turned from them. But for Cadwallon, the wrath of God was finally being visited upon the Yffings. If there was a deeply personal element to the conflict between the kings of Northumbria and Gwynedd, then Cadwallon could see that God's favour rested with him – Roman, Christian, Briton – rather than with the Yffings – barbarians, pagan/Christian/pagan again. It was the implicit, if not explicit, belief of these kings that heaven showed its favour in the most direct way: by who left the battlefield alive and who lay on it as food for the crows.

Cadwallon had killed the high king. He had destroyed the remaining warrior strength of Deira. The Yffings were dead, broken or fleeing. The kingdom was his. Now he turned his attention towards the northern half of Northumbria, to Bernicia, the kingdom of the Idings, with their stronghold at Bamburgh and their royal palaces at Yeavering, Maelmin and elsewhere. With no one left to oppose them in Deira, they raided the royal villages scattered through the kingdom, looting the tapestries and fittings, the gold and silver. Associated with each royal village were warehouses and stockades, the places where the local farmers came to leave their render to the king. The king was dead but for many of the peasant farmers it made little difference who came to consume the food they put aside for the men with swords. With Osric dead and the Deiran warrior nobility broken, Cadwallon's passage north was easy. As a conqueror, he may have installed his own men in halls along the way, displacing the Anglian families. With their menfolk either dead or gone into exile, there would have been little that the women, children and servants could have done to stop the expropriation of their homes.

The most likely route north for Cadwallon was Dere Street. This was the old Roman road that ran from York north to Hadrian's Wall and then on to the Antonine Wall. 'Dere' is not a Latin word. The Roman name for the road was lost. 'Dere' derives from the kingdom that Cadwallon had conquered, Deira. Dere Street crossed Stanegate, the east–west Roman military road that preceded Hadrian's Wall, at Corbridge. Excavations of the two roads, Dere Street and Stanegate, have shown that they were the same width, 25 feet (7.5 metres), but that Stanegate is much deeper than Dere Street (28 inches compared with 12 inches), which suggests that Stanegate was much more heavily trafficked and required more frequent resurfacing, which pushed its foundations further into the ground.

Going north on Dere Street, the road passed through the wall at Portgate. Nothing remains to be seen of Portgate today, but when Cadwallon's men went through it the gate was still a substantial Roman fort. As excavations at Vindolanda and elsewhere have shown, some of the Roman sites along the wall remained occupied after the legions left. It's quite likely that a small community used Portgate as their home. Most probably, the inhabitants of the semi-ruined gate hailed Cadwallon as he and his men arrived. With the Anglian kingdom of Bernicia only having been established for at most eighty years, most of the inhabitants would have been Britons, speaking the old language.

North of the wall, Dere Street continued into Redesdale, but it's likely that Cadwallon branched off east of Dere Street at Portgate, taking what is now known as the Devil's Causeway. The modern A697 follows part of its route. As with the majority of Roman roads, the original name has been forgotten but it runs for 55 miles from Portgate to Berwick-upon-Tweed, where there was a Roman fort. A dedication slab at the Roman fort of Hunnum (Halton Chesters) near the start of the road says that Legio VI Victrix built the road. The garrison in the third century was a cavalry troop raised in Pannonia (Hungary), the *Ala I Pannoniorum Sabiniana*. Then there is silence until the seventh century, when the hooves of the horses of Cadwallon and his warband thudded upon the worn stone. They were, we think, heading to Ad Gefrin.

In his excavations at Ad Gefrin, Brian Hope-Taylor teased meaning out of marks in the soil. He 'elucidated a sequence from an awesomely complex stratification of inter-cuttings and from this he developed a model of phasing and chronology'.[7] Without carbon-14 dating Hope-Taylor relied on a small number of datable objects – pottery, loomweights and a buckle – and two key features in the stratigraphy of his excavations. These were catastrophic fires that would have left only charred stumps of wood above ground – and Hope-Taylor used these two fires to fix the chronology of the palace. For Bede of course states that Cadwallon ravaged Northumbria following his defeat of Edwin on 12 October 632. What more likely place for Cadwallon to burn than the great hall of the kings of Northumbria in the north of their kingdom? But . . . we don't know that Cadwallon burned down Ad Gefrin. Neither Bede nor any other source states that he did. The second burning Hope-Taylor assigned to a later incursion north by Penda, the man who would become the great foe and nemesis of the two Northumbrian kings after Edwin, the brothers Oswald and Oswiu. But again, there is no definite evidence that Penda's depredations included burning down the rebuilt hall at Ad Gefrin. Both burnings could have been accidental, or related to other attacks or raids that were simply not recorded.

This illustrates the problem of tying archaeology to history. While there's a good chance that the hall was burned by Cadwallon and Penda, the identification is based upon inference: we can't state it as a certainty. A great deal of archaeology is like this.

But let us assume that the identification is true. During the year 633, Cadwallon and his men turned west from the Devil's Causeway, and came riding along the valley of the River Glen. To their left rose the twin-humped peak of Yeavering Bell, with the salmon-pink stone of the ramparts of the hill fort on its summit. The great hall of the Idings stood in the middle of the field at the bottom of Yeavering Bell, its painted timbers glowing in the slanting northern light. There were servants and slaves there, but there was no obligation upon them to lay down their lives for their lord: they stood aside as the warband rode up. Cadwallon dismounted and looked up at the hall. It was magnificent. Beautiful. A building upon which all the talent for decoration revealed in the armour at Sutton Hoo was displayed in wood and carving and paint.

'Burn it.'

And in the burning of the hall, Cadwallon was demonstrating to all the remaining nobility in Bernicia that there was no one to come to their aid, no one to protect them from him and his warband. He had killed Edwin. He had killed Osric. They could place their trust in the sons of Æthelfrith, but as the smoke rose into the sky Cadwallon was showing all who saw it that the sons of Æthelfrith could not stand against him. By now news had reached Cadwallon that one of those sons had returned to the ancestral stronghold of the Idings at Bamburgh and raised his banner, calling the warrior nobility of Bernicia to him, to stand with him against Cadwallon. His name was Eanfrith.

Æthelfrith, the Twister, had twisted his marriages too. Before he married Acha of Deira, mother to Oswald, Oswiu and Æbbe, he had been married to a woman named Bebba. Æthelfrith and Bebba had one recorded son, and his name was Eanfrith. After Æthelfrith's death at the Battle of the River Idle, Eanfrith fled the kingdom but, unlike Acha and her children, he took refuge among the Picts. Given that Acha sought refuge among relatives, then the assumption is that Eanfrith likewise looked for sanctuary among the kin of his mother, Bebba. Eanfrith was clearly accepted by the Picts: he fathered a son with a Pictish princess who became their king in 656.

It is possible that Eanfrith may have had some sort of informal contact with Cadwallon before the king of Gwynedd launched his assault on Northumbria. Unlike Oswald, who was Edwin's nephew, Eanfrith had no family connection to Edwin and being able to call on the ancestral loyalty to the Idings would have made him a useful ally, particularly if he could draw some men away from Edwin's army. Subsequent events suggest that Cadwallon may have played it this way, for after Edwin's death Eanfrith did come south and claim the throne of Bernicia. It's notable that he made no claim upon Deira.

But for Bede, it was Eanfrith's apostasy that was significant and, ultimately, fatal. As with the sons of Acha, Eanfrith had also become a Christian during his exile. While Oswald and his family clearly became attached to the monastery at Iona, it is far less clear how Eanfrith became a Christian. Much of the history of Pictland is obscure. However, Martin Carver's excavations at Portmahomack on the Tarbat Peninsula in the Moray Firth have uncovered a Pictish monastery, the first to be found by archaeologists. The monastery was established as early as AD 550 and flourished for two hundred and fifty years before its destruction by fire around 800, probably because of an attack by Vikings. Carver and his team found evidence of a veritable monastic factory: vellum production for the making of books, sculpted stone, and glass-making. Portmahomack was a monastic powerhouse like the monastery on Iona.

Eanfrith went into exile in 616. The monastery at Portmahomack was already well established. Eanfrith probably chose to become a Christian during his exile, but when he returned to Bernicia to claim the throne he forswore his new religion, returning to the ways of his father, Æthelfrith. The Bernician nobility had adopted the new religion of Edwin, their imposed Deiran king, but reluctantly. So long as the new religion brought military success they accepted it, but following Edwin's death its hold was loosened. The most likely scenario is that the Bernician nobility agreed to accept Eanfrith as their king so long as he returned to the ways of their fathers.

Eanfrith's conversion to Christianity may have been political in the first place: a conversion consequent to his engagement to a Christian Pictish princess. His apostasy was similarly political: Bamburgh was worth abandoning the Mass for. Besides, it seems that he had made some sort of arrangement with Cadwallon. For when Cadwallon came north into Bernicia, Eanfrith went to meet him with only twelve men as companions. That he should have thought it safe to meet Cadwallon with such a small retinue suggests that there had been an accommodation between them beforehand. Cadwallon was now the dominant force in Britain, so Eanfrith came to him as a supplicant. Together with his oath to support Cadwallon, he probably brought gifts of gold and silver.

But it wasn't enough.

Cadwallon was fighting a different sort of war. He did not want a client king. He had broken Deira and its Anglian nobility. Now he was going to do the same to Bernicia. Although Eanfrith had come to him under the generally agreed conditions for safe passage, Cadwallon ordered his men to seize the king and his companions. As his chief quarrel was with Edwin and the Yffings, there is reason to hope that Eanfrith's end was swift. But it's unlikely that his body was allowed to rest in peace. Cadwallon was intent on sending a message to the Bernician nobility, the men who had accepted Eanfrith as king but had not accompanied him when he went to meet Cadwallon.

The only man who remained with any claim to the throne of Northumbria was Oswald, son of Æthelfrith, nephew of Edwin. By his links to both Bernicia and Deira, Oswald's claim was possibly stronger than anyone else's. But he had gone into exile as a child. He had had no chance to forge the relationships and loyalties that tied the local nobility to him. Besides, during his exile Oswald had evinced no interest in reclaiming the throne.

For Cadwallon and his warband, a long way from their homes, it must have seemed that the war was done. If Cadwallon was set upon conquering Northumbria and remaking it, then he had all but completed the job.

II

The White Blade

Oswald was twelve years old when his father was killed and his world was turned sideways. People remember their flight into exile: the panic and the fear but most of all the uncertainty. The seventh century was a much more uncertain world than our own: death was a present companion. But the son of a king, particularly a king as powerful as Æthelfrith, always had food and drink, shelter and companionship, until he had to flee. Oswald's brother, Oswiu, was only four at the time and his family's flight would have been only slightly more memorable than the normal everyday wonders that fill the life of a four-year-old. Oswald, at twelve, was laying down the memories that would provide the foundation for his adult life: flight, and loss, fear of pursuers and the crumbling of everything that had seemed strong and secure.

In exile, in Dál Riata, Oswald found what he had lost. He found a home, a faith, a name. The *Lamnguin*, the White Blade. He had fought with the warband of Eochaid Buide. He had splashed ashore on the white sand beaches of the Western

Isles, sword in hand. He had sat, hands upturned on his knees, in silent prayer as the monks on Iona chanted the Divine Office. He had a life and it is clear that he was content with that life. During the long reign of Uncle Edwin, Oswald made no effort to reclaim the crown of Bernicia, even though there were many men who had been loyal followers of his father, Æthelfrith, and who would still remember Æthelfrith's son. Even after Edwin's death, in the long chaos of Cadwallon's depredations, Oswald did not act. He left the field to his elder half-brother, Eanfrith. Perhaps he was making preparations, gathering a warband together. Or perhaps he was waiting for his birthday. Sometime in 634, Oswald turned thirty. It was an age that had a resonance for him. Jesus was thirty when he went to the River Jordan, was baptised by John and seized by the Holy Spirit, beginning his public ministry after fasting for forty days in the desert.

By the latter part of 634 Eanfrith was dead. If Oswald's elder half-brother had hoped for men and arms from Pictland to come to his aid against Cadwallon, they had not arrived, and he had been forced to try to parlay with Cadwallon. Now his head was on a pole and Ad Gefrin burned.

While there were common laws, and the legal code first prom-ulgated in writing by King Ine of Wessex was based on the legal customs adopted through the years by the Anglo-Saxons, there was little in the way of restitution against the powerful: for injury by such a man, the only recourse was the feud, the vendetta of one family against another, the shedding of blood for blood. Thus there was considerable cultural pressure on Oswald to avenge his half-brother's death, and even the death of his uncle, although that uncle had doubled as his father's killer.

But against this was, to put it simply, fear. Fear of death and fear of failure. Oswald, a warrior, knew the levels of violence employed in the sort of face-to-face, life-or-death battle he would be joining should he decide to return to Northumbria and lay his claim to the throne, but it is difficult for us, today, to get any sort of visceral understanding of the nature of this sort of warfare. However, one of the men buried in the Bowl Hole told, in horrifying detail, the story of early medieval warfare.

It was right at the end of the first season. On the last day of the dig, Paul uncovered two graves. As they were overlapping, he had to excavate them both at the same time, to establish which grave came first while not disturbing the other. But they had to leave the site the next day so that meant excavating two skeletons in eight hours.

Any archaeologist will tell you that simply can't be done. Working with Rosie and a team of students removing and sieving the spoil as they went deeper, Paul soon uncovered the two skeletons. The good thing was that the graves only overlapped in one corner and the skeletons were separate. The normal practice would be to work out which grave was dug first, excavate the other one, and then excavate the original grave, but there simply wasn't time to do this. So he excavated both graves simultaneously, working out the order in which they were dug in the post-excavation examination of the evidence.

One of the skeletons was buried face down and the other was on its back. This presented particular difficulties as a body buried face down is excavated the wrong way round, with the bones appearing in what seems the wrong order: it's one of the mind-melts peculiar to archaeology. Why he was buried in this position remains open. The usual reason given for prone burials is that it's a final insult: a post-mortem punishment for some pre-death disgrace or crime and it is true that some of the excavated prone burials appear to be of individuals who were executed. Another interpretation is that prone burial signifies a sinner who died before completion of penance. But it does seem to be a laborious way of disrespecting the dead. If the object is simply to heap a last humiliation upon the deceased – as was done in later centuries when people executed for treason were quartered and their remains either displayed on spikes or disposed of – then throwing a body to the dogs and pigs, or heaving it into the sea would seem simpler options. Furthermore, the archaeologists already suspected, and would later confirm, this was a high-status burial ground; it was the seventh- and eighth-century equivalent of being buried in Westminster Abbey. Why would a traitor or a murderer or a thief be buried in such exalted company, even face down?

One possible answer came in a conversation with Dominic Powlesland, director of the West Heslerton Project. He suggested the main reason for prone burials is a simple mistake. In the days before a corpse could be kept in a cold drawer and preserved, the body was generally wrapped in a winding sheet. But even wrapped in a burial shroud, many bodies would start to bloat as decomposition gases inflated internal cavities. In these cases, and with the attendant smell, there would have been little to indicate to the men interring the body which way was up, while there would have been every incentive to get the body into the ground as quickly as possible. Under such circumstances, it would be easy to put the body into the ground the wrong way up. So, in common with Dominic, Paul thinks the reason this body was buried face down was simple human error. However, this is still contentious and archaeologists continue to argue about it. For instance, Andrew Reynolds, professor of medieval archaeology at University College London, asserts that it is impossible to mistake the front and back of a shrouded corpse, however bloated.

Whatever the reason for the prone burial, the individual buried next to the man laid to rest on his front was buried on his back. But, as Paul excavated this more conventionally buried skeleton, he realised that layers of past and present were meeting all around. For as he brushed away the sand and soil, he saw that where the skull should have been, there was only a stone. The words of the old lady came back to him: 'Only the strange thing was, it had no head. Where the skull should have been there was a stone, a big stone.'

Apart from the missing skull, for an early Christian burial it appeared normal: there were no grave goods although they found the remains of a belt buckle and a seax knife, and the grave was aligned roughly but not exactly east–west. Archaeologists suspect that the reason the alignment for these early Christian graves is often haphazard is that this was at a time when bodies needed to be buried quickly; it would have been easy, when hastily digging a new grave, to get the alignment slightly wrong.

Paul and Rosie were digging almost as quickly as the grave-diggers all those centuries ago. They mapped, photographed and did the context sheets before lifting the skeletons. The process was so quick that they did not have time to look at the skeletons in any detail. Once lifted, the remains were taken to Bamburgh Castle to be stored over winter until they could be properly analysed.

This was the task of the project's bone specialist, Sarah Groves. When she laid out the skeleton of the headless man, she discovered something extraordinary about him. There was

a cleft running through the bones from his – she had quickly established the remains belonged to a man – from his left
shoulder diagonally downwards to his waist. The man had
been cut almost in two, the cut breaking collarbone and ribs
and spine.

The news was transfixing, and perplexing. The likelihood
was that the man had been a warrior, although they would
need further analysis to confirm this. But while Sarah had discovered what had caused his death, the archaeologists found it
difficult to understand how he died. For it is no easy matter to
cut a man in two like that, severing bone after bone after bone.
The first thought was that he might have been struck with a
Dane axe, one of the two-handed battleaxes that tenth- and
eleventh-century Vikings were famous for wielding, and which
became the weapon of choice for the house carls who stood
beside Harold in his battle line on the top of Senlac Ridge. But
the archaeologists already suspected that these graves predated the Viking age (generally dated from 793 to 1066), making it
unlikely that it was a Dane axe that had inflicted such wounds.
But if it was a sword, how could it have dealt such a devastating injury? Even assuming that the warrior had been unlucky
enough to face an enemy with a sword sharp enough to do so
much damage, the simple physics made it all but impossible
that one man standing in front of another could deal such a
blow. Even raising the sword above the head and bringing it
down upon the shoulder does not give enough leverage, and
the cutting angles were all wrong.

Could he have been cut down by a man on horseback?
That would have allowed greater weight to the blow, as a man
standing up in stirrups could perhaps have brought a sword
down onto the shoulder of a man standing below him with
the necessary force to cut his enemy in half? But, while the

evidence is partial, it seems reasonably certain that the stirrup was not employed by mounted troops in Britain until much later. However, the angles worked much better if the warrior had been killed by a man standing over him.

Standing over him. That was the clue. The man dealing the killing blow had been standing over him, which meant that the warrior had been brought down upon his knees. Perhaps in the mêlée after the shieldwall had broken down, the warrior had received a blow that had stunned him and dropped him to his knees. Before he could rise again, an enemy warrior, seeing him incapacitated and temporarily helpless, had closed on him and, standing over the warrior, had brought his sword down in a massive arc from over his right shoulder and down upon the warrior's left shoulder, cutting down through collarbone and ribs, and ending his life in a single, devastating cut.

Such was the way of death for many in the early medieval period – particularly those who belonged to the warrior elite. This was a time of endemic raiding and frequent warfare. The archaeologists of the BRP would have loved to find out this man's background, to see whether he was local to the area through isotopic analysis. Unfortunately, isotopic analysis works by tracing the strontium and oxygen signatures in tooth enamel and, without a head, let alone teeth, this was impossible in this case. This bifurcated warrior was buried just a few feet away from where Paul found the Ionan warrior, the son of Thunder. If only his head had remained intact, it would have been possible to find out where he was born, to see if he was another warrior who had come with Oswald to reclaim the kingdom. But that is something we cannot know.

The question remains, however, as to why Oswald finally decided to make his play for the throne. One possibility is that the two half-brothers, Eanfrith and Oswald, were in contact and had agreed that the elder should try first. But such cordial contact makes it likely that, with Eanfrith in place in Bernicia, Oswald would have returned with his own warband to support his half brother against Cadwallon. But instead, he left Eanfrith to drift in the shallows of half-hearted support.

Bede portrays Oswald as the saintliest of individuals, but an alternative reading of the evidence would see him as a skilled and dangerous politician: perhaps he encouraged Eanfrith to make his play for the crown with the promise of support, only to leave Eanfrith on his own. Any battle between Eanfrith and Cadwallon would erode the strength of the victor, as well as removing the loser from the equation, leaving an easier foe for Oswald to face. That Eanfrith should choose not to fight, but be killed during a parlay, would not have figured in the calculations.

However, there is more direct evidence for the view of Oswald as a reluctant king and devout Christian. Since March 623, the abbot of Iona had been Ségéne mac Fiachnaí. Oswald and Ségéne were close friends, and Ségéne was also the man Oswald turned to for spiritual advice and counsel. The monks of Iona had received a party of refugee pagan Anglians from Northumbria and transformed them into Christians. Mission was fused into the very heart of Irish Christianity: Patrick had gone, as a missionary, beyond the edge of the world to preach to the Irish. In Iona, they had raised and nurtured two Anglo-Saxon æthelings and seen them grow into fine young men (given Oswiu's relations with Irish princesses, one of them had perhaps a little too much vim for the austere monks). While the successors of Colm Cille were ascetic monks, with their geographical position at the crossroads of the waterways that crossed the Irish Sea and their social position as spiritual guardians to the kingdom of Dál Riata, they were also ideally placed to affect the shifting currents of fortune in the kingdoms of Britain. For two generations, the kingdom of the Northumbrians had been ascendant, its power waxing under kings Æthelfrith and Edwin. For most of that time, it had been a pagan kingdom, and while that did not forbid marriage links between its daughters and the sons of Dál Riata, it made it difficult to support. However, Ségéne now had at his monastery a Christian ætheling, a man who had received his faith from Iona, a man who was a devoted son of Colm Cille.

In his *Ecclesiastical History*, Bede seeks to demonstrate that the Britons were deprived of their country because they had become unworthy of it as a result of their reluctance to preach to the pagan Anglo-Saxons. There are two chief elements in his case against the Britons. The first of these is that, by their moral failings and degeneracy, they had lost God's favour. In establishing this, Bede makes fairly shameless use of Gildas's polemic against the rulers of his day, turning a theological jeremiad into an historical account, and making the urging for the moral regeneration of the Britons into a case for their prosecution. But the second and, in Bede's mind, stronger reason for condemning the Britons is their steadfast refusal, again according to Bede, to preach the new religion.

Today, scholars are inclined to believe that there was far more proselytisation by Brythonic Christians of the pagan Anglo-Saxons than Bede was willing to admit. However, given the long history of conflict between the two peoples, and the relatively small inroads of Christianity among the Anglo-Saxons by the seventh century despite their having had two centuries of contact with Christian Britons, then we can accept Bede's overall point. There should be little surprise at that. If we look at situations in the world where two peoples live in proximity and conflict, then the markers of identity become more prominent, and the changing of these markers all the rarer. In Northern Ireland, during the Troubles, how many Protestants became Catholics, or vice versa? Similarly, in Israel, few Palestinians have converted to Judaism, nor have many Jews embraced Islam. For there to be an avenue to conversion for the Anglo-Saxons required a different pathway to conversion. Paulinus had provided one for Edwin. Now Ségéne saw that Oswald, a convert to a Christianity that had as its languages Gaelic and Latin rather than the proto-Welsh of the Britons, and had as its culture a Gaelic/Irish Sea perspective that was largely free of the history of conflict with the Anglo-Saxons, could offer a new pathway to Christianity for his people too.

But the king who now had the kingdom in his fist was also a Christian. Cadwallon's Christianity was very similar to that of Iona. There was a long history of contact between the Christians of Britain and the Christians of Ireland, going right back to Patrick himself, a Briton taken as a boy as a slave to Ireland who had returned there after gaining his freedom to preach the new religion to the Irish. So the question remained for Ségéne: should Iona support the king of Gwynedd, a man allied to the island by religion and long resistance against the pagan invaders, or should the monks give the blessing of the saint to one of their own, a man raised on their island, who they knew intimately and believed in. Iona chose Oswald.

For King Domnall Brecc it was an easier call. The links between Dál Riata and Gwynedd were no stronger than those with the other Brythonic kingdoms. Oswald, on the other hand, was a kinsman, a sword hand and a bondsman. By supporting Oswald's bid for the crown, Domnall Brecc would, at worst, lose a man who had been a trusted part of his warband (and the other warriors who chose to accompany Oswald). But if he won . . . Ah, if Oswald won, then Domnall Brecc would have installed upon the throne of the most powerful kingdom in Britain a man who owed him. Looking out from the stronghold at Dunadd, there really wouldn't have been much doubt. Indeed, the only doubts seem to have been Oswald's. Perhaps he had to be persuaded to make this play. Dunadd and Iona, and desperate emissaries from his exiled home coming all together to Oswald and his family, asking him, in the name of his forsaken kin, for the honour of his adopted home, and for the glory of the saint, to accept the task appointed to him: raise a warband and fight to claim the throne.

But first Oswald had to raise a warband. He had with him, of course, those retainers who had hustled the young family into exile, protecting them in their hurried flight west. But that had been eighteen years ago. Many of those old retainers had died in the intervening decades, or were too old – maybe not for the fighting, that was something where an experienced warrior's guile could overcome the strength of a young man – but for the travelling. Because Oswald, raised to military manhood among the Dál Riatans, already had his strategy in mind: to strike fast and hard and in surprise. Though he could not launch the sort of dawn amphibious assault on Bernicia that he had taken part in so often in Dál Riata, he could adopt the elements of the surprise dawn assault that formed such a large part of the Dál Riatan strategy. But for that to work he needed young men, men who could ride hard and fight at the end of such a ride.

One of the men in Oswald's warband was the warrior, the son of Thunder. But if Oswald was initially reluctant to take on the fight, so too was the warrior. For while tied by bonds of friendship and loyalty to Oswald, there were other ties holding him to Dál Riata: ties of family and love. For the warrior was married now. He had a son.

12

Father and Son

It was the colour that was the first clue. Rather than the bright yellow of the surrounding sand, the ground that Paul was look-ing at was darker, an ochre rather than the mustard yellow of the area around it. Touch was next. He bent down and touched it, scooping some up with his fingers. It had a different feel: less abrasive, finer grained. Then sound. Digging his trowel into the ground, the metal made a different, slightly softer sound as he pushed it in. He scooped up the material with the trowel, then tilted the trowel so the load fell off. On the tilting trowel, it held on for longer, then fell more suddenly than the sand. Yes, there was something different here.

The natural soil in the Bowl Hole is clay with sand over-laying it. But when, centuries ago, the gravediggers dug into the ground to make the grave, they dumped the spoil they excavated in a mound beside the newly dug hole. The body was then consigned to the ground and the necessary rites per-formed before the diggers shovelled the heap of clay and sand back into the grave, covering the body. But by this process of digging, piling up and then refilling, the gravediggers created a mixture of the clay and sand, leaving a subtle clue for the attentive archaeologist that here he might be on to something. The mixture of clay and sand holds water differently from the surrounding areas, where the sand and clay are layered, giving the ground a different colour, a different feel, a different sound even. The clue was in the sound of the backfill slipping off the side of the trowel. All the different mixtures of clay and sand and soil make characteristic sounds, both as the trowel digs into the ground and then again as the scoop is turned off the trowel's blade. So Paul already suspected that he was excavating something interesting when he saw the oblong of the lintel in the ground. A lintel grave is a burial where the sides of the grave are demarcated by slabs, usually of stone or wood, that act as battens but where the bottom of the grave is earth.

Not all the lintel grave had survived: some 80 per cent remained. Paul carefully removed the fill in the grave to get to the remains buried in the earth but, within that fill, there was an area of discrete fill, and in that area was a collection of bones. However, looking at the stratigraphy, it was impossible to tell what came first: this small area containing a discrete set of bones or the larger area containing the body of the warrior, the son of Thunder. One possibility, that archaeologists see often in their work in burial grounds, is that when the gravediggers were digging the grave for the warrior, they found in the ground human remains from a previous burial whose marker had been lost. Finding the bones, they then gathered them carefully together and reinterred them with the warrior when they laid him in the ground. However, Paul's profound feeling, both at the time and on reflection, was that what he found was not that. It was not the ad hoc actions of gravediggers dealing with disturbed bones, but something part and parcel of the burial of the warrior. When gravediggers find human remains, they immediately know they're cutting through a burial and try to avoid it. So normally, archaeologists find a few reinterred bones. But this was a virtually complete skeleton. Someone had gone out of their way to dig up this skeleton and move it here, to be by the warrior.

The warrior's grave was dug, the warrior was laid to rest in the ground and the other bones were placed in the grave either at the time of the warrior's burial or very shortly afterwards. But who did these bones belong to? They were disarticulated and there were no teeth. Without teeth, it was impossible to conduct the sort of tests that had allowed the BRP to establish that the warrior had been born on Iona and the islands of Dál Riata. But Sarah Groves, the BRP bone specialist, in her analysis of the warrior, also looked carefully at the assemblage of remains that were buried with him.

It was the body of a child. A boy. He had been between three and four years old when he had died. Then he was buried, laid to rest in the ground. But at some point after his death, his remains were exhumed and placed with that of the warrior, the son of Thunder. Why? Why dig up the body of a child and place them with the body of a grown man? The only answer that makes any sort of sense is that the boy was the warrior's son. He was placed with his father so that his father could protect and care for him in eternity as he had tried to do in this life.

Nowadays we expect to see our children grow up, to reach adolescence and then adulthood. It is a tragedy when a child dies young. This is new. We forget how astonishing this is, how unusual, how much grief we are spared. Most of human history is the silent tale of tears shed for lost children. Some historians and anthropologists, maybe seeking to spare history this unsupportable burden of sorrow, argue that children were regarded differently by their parents in previous times' cultures; knowing the possibility of loss, they were not accorded full acceptance into the community until they had reached the sort of age where it was reasonably likely that they would survive.

But this boy had a name. The warrior had known him, had dandled him on his knee and listened to him and heard him. He had buried him, in the cemetery at the Bowl Hole, in sight of the sea that washed the shore of his home. Then, when the warrior followed him into death, the ones who had loved them both exhumed the remains of the little boy and buried him with the warrior, so that father and son might voyage into eternity together.

The Bowl Hole is not an ordinary cemetery. Most of the burials are atypical in one way or another: of the remains that were most closely analysed, the great majority were not locals. At Bamburgh there is a church, St Aidan's, which is very old and its graveyard (which contains the grave of Victorian heroine Grace Darling, as well as a memorial to her) has been in use for centuries. The church was probably first founded by St Aidan in the mid-seventh century. The BRP archaeologists think this graveyard was used for the burial of local people, and the Bowl Hole cemetery was a graveyard for visitors, people who had come to Bamburgh to visit or serve the kings.

One area in the Bowl Hole cemetery was reserved for members of the Dál Riatan nobility who died while in the service of the kings of Bernicia. With a reasonable number of Dál Riatans living in Northumbria, and clergy having come from Iona, it was possible at Bamburgh to perform a burial rite like those carried out in Dál Riata.

Although near the sea, the church of St Aidan and its graveyard is not particularly well located to see the sea. The Bowl Hole cemetery, on the other hand, situated on the ridge running down from the castle, does have excellent sea views. The earliest burials predate the adoption of Christianity in Northumbria, but these too seem to have been burials of strangers and sojourners. There may have been an aspect of pagan belief that wanted to give these exiled dead a sight of the grey, shifting road that had brought them to Bamburgh. Christian belief states that, at the end of days, the dead will rise from their graves to meet the returning Christ. So the dead are buried in an east–west orientation, with their feet to the east, so that when they stand up from the grave they will be facing east, and looking into the face of Christ. But the Christian dead at the Bowl Hole would also see, on their rising, the sea by which they had come to the place and, seeing it, remember the path by which they came to be there, far from their original homes.

There is further evidence for a discrete Dál Riatan section of the Bowl Hole cemetery in the number of lintel graves that the BRP archaeologists found there, clustered together. Lintel graves are not common; the nearest ones to those in Bamburgh, geographically and typologically, are at Whithorn, near the western end of Dumfries and Galloway in Scotland. Whithorn is the oldest Christian site in what is now Scotland, dating to AD 397, when St Ninian founded a church and community there, the church being given the name *Candida Casa*, the 'Shining White House', presumably on account of it being built with white stone or being painted with whitewash. Whithorn was also where the oldest Christian memorial in Scotland was found, recycled into the wall of the medieval cathedral. The Latinus Stone dates from 450 and is inscribed:

(ET) DOMINU(M)/LAUSAMUS/LATINUS/ANNORU(M)/XXXV ET/
FILIA SUA/ANN(ORUM) IV/(H)IC SI(G)NUM/FECERUT/NEPUS/
BARROVA/DI. ('We praise you, Lord. Latinus, grandson

of Barravados, aged thirty-five, and his four-year old
daughter made this sign.')

Whithorn was only officially part of the Roman Empire for a
short time, during the period when its borders extended north
to the Antonine Wall, yet even in 450, a generation after the
last legions had left Britain, there was a Christian community
at Whithorn that could still write Latin and which, according
to the archaeological finds, maintained trading contacts with
the Mediterranean. During its long history, Whithorn came
successively under Dál Riatan, Northumbrian, Norse and
Scottish control. During the first half of the seventh century
it was under Dál Riatan control. The lintel graves found at
the Bowl Hole mirror the features of the lintel graves found
at Whithorn, strongly suggesting that a number of people of
Dál Riatan origin were buried at Bamburgh according to the
manners and customs of their people.

But why did people bury the dead in lintel graves? One possibility is that the lintel grave was conceived of as a physical
vessel made to carry the dead person to the land of the dead.
It is similar in a way to the urns used to collect the remains
of people who have been cremated. Urns containing physical
remains were often decorated, sometimes, in the Roman context, even painted with a portrait of the deceased. In effect, the
urn became a surrogate body. The lintel grave acts in the same
way. There are parallels also in the treatment of ossuaries, the
containers used to move the bones of revered saints. The monasteries of northern Britain quite often had buried, near the
altar, a box with the bony remains of a saint. Lintel graves are
like this, and also hark back to the rock-hewn tomb into which
Jesus's body was laid after his crucifixion. Indeed, the crypt
at the church in Hexham, built not long after the warrior was

buried, was constructed to mirror the physical dimensions of the tomb of Christ. Being shrouded in stone brought the dead of these newly Christian peoples closer to Christ at the point where he became most completely and helplessly human: lying cold and dead in the tomb. By uniting with him in death, how much greater the hope of being united with him in his defeat of death and joining him in his resurrection.

Cultures change, but there is enough commonality across times and cultures to make it possible to reach across the gulf of years and stand beside the mourners as they laid the warrior to rest in the Bowl Hole, within sight of the sea, and put his son with him. We can't know, but perhaps Oswald was standing among the mourners that day. For it was devotion to Oswald that had brought the warrior to Northumbria.

13

The Return of the King

In Dál Riata, the old king, Eochaid Buide, had died in 629. He had ruled as king of Dál Riata from *c.*606 to *c.*629. It was Eochaid Buide whom Colm Cille had prophesied would succeed his father, Áedán mac Gabráin, despite his many elder brothers. The records are sketchy but Eochaid Buide seems to have attempted to anoint his son Connad Cerr ('Left-handed Connad') as his successor, ruling jointly with him for the last two years of his life. But Connad Cerr was killed at the Battle of Fid Eoin, *c.*629, while Eochaid Buide was still alive. Having lost his heir, Eochaid Buide installed another son, Domnall Brecc ('Freckled Donald'), as king. Domnall Brecc would prove to be a less than successful king of Dál Riata, having an unfortunate tendency to lose battles. He survived three defeats before being killed in a battle against the Brythonic kingdom of Strathclyde. This final defeat was so well known that it was even added to the Welsh poem *Y Gododdin*, which commemorated the defeat of the three hundred riders of the Gododdin at the Battle of Catraeth in *c.*600.

I saw an array that came from Pentir,
And bore themselves splendidly around the
   conflagration.
I saw a second one, rapidly descending from their
   township,
Who had risen at the word of the grandson of Nwython.
I saw great sturdy men who came with the dawn,
And the head of Dyfnwal Frych, ravens gnawed it.[1]

'Dyfnwal Frych' is the Welsh for Domnall Brecc. But the meal for ravens lay in the future. In 634, Domnall Brecc had to decide what to do when his cousin – somewhat removed but a cousin nonetheless – and exiled ætheling, Oswald, came to him to request his support in a bid for the Northumbrian throne. Domnall Brecc knew of Eanfrith's death. He had heard how Osric had been surprised and killed. He could gauge the rising power of Cadwallon. There was no gainsaying Oswald's claim on the throne; but there was much doubt as to whether he could take it.

It is unlikely that Domnall Brecc would have risked many men on such a venture. The odds of success were low. But allowing some men to accompany Oswald would mean that he had a stake in Oswald's success if, against the odds, Oswald prevailed. Not too many men, mind. Maybe a dozen, two dozen at most. Of these, most were young men, raw, eager and relatively untried, but keen to make names for themselves. But one at least ranked among his more experienced retainers. The warrior was married and he had a son. As such, he had left the bachelor pack of warband retainers to become a man of means: he had land and status. Why should such a man risk so much to join Oswald in such a desperate venture?

The most likely reason is simple friendship. The bonds

forged between men in combat are deep and lasting and as strong today for men in the forces as they were then. As mentioned before, at the Battle of Fid Eoin ('Owen's Wood'), the Dál Riatans suffered a devastating defeat. As well as losing their king, Connad Cerr, two other grandsons of King Áedán, and one of the Bernician exiles, Prince Osric, were killed. Given the shared prefix with other members of the Northumbrian ruling families, it's reasonable to suppose that Osric was related to Oswald and Oswiu (although given that another Osric came from the Deiran ruling family, this Osric need not have been a brother). It's very hard to think that Oswald did not take part in that battle; that he survived is testament to his skill in rallying men who are routing. The men Oswald saved then would have been even more closely tied to him than before. So maybe that is why the warrior, the son of Thunder, agreed to accompany Oswald on his desperate venture: he owed him his life. As a member of the warrior elite of Dál Riata, he may even have been to Bamburgh before, since the place was a formidable stronghold and a magnet for trade, craft and diplomacy.

Once he had agreed to go with Oswald, the warrior had to get permission from his king, Domnall Brecc, as did all the other Dál Riatan warriors who wanted to go. So long as the numbers going did not compromise the kingdom, Domnall Brecc was happy to give them his blessing. It was an excellent way to keep young and restless men occupied, as well as providing them with invaluable experience. Oswald was probably a respected war leader by this stage. His forays into Ireland were so successful that he was one of only a handful of individuals to be named in the tales of these times. For many of the men he had fought with, Oswald would have seemed more Gael than Northumbrian. He spoke their language fluently and shared their religion.

However, Domnall Brecc was dancing a delicate diplomatic game. If Oswald's gambit failed, he did not want to have to deal with an incensed Cadwallon. So it is probable that the Dál Riatans accompanying Oswald went on the condition of deniability: if any of the Dál Riatans should be caught or killed, the king would disavow any knowledge of their actions. But if the king was trying to play for both possible outcomes, there is some evidence that Iona had placed its bet, and its blessing, upon Oswald. The *Red Book of Hergest*, the medieval sourcebook for old Welsh tales and poems, including the *Mabinogion*, includes an encomium to Cadwallon, 'the fierce affliction of his foes, a lion prosperous over the Saxons', but ends with three lines of lament:

> From the plotting of strangers and iniquitous
> Monks, as the water flows from the fountain,
> Sad and heavy will be the day for Cadwallawn.[2]

Although the *Red Book of Hergest* was written around 1382, it contains much ancient material. Its portrayal of Cadwallon as the lion of his people suggests that it preserves the view of Cadwallon taken by the Britons, of whom he was the last truly effective champion. The mention of 'iniquitous Monks' suggests a memory of monastic double-dealing in his downfall, for which the obvious candidates are the monks of Iona. When Adomnán came to write his *Life of St Columba* there was no doubt whose side the saint had been on:

> Some kings were conquered in the terrifying crush
> of battle and others emerged victorious according to
> what Columba asked of God by the power of prayer.
> God who honours all saints gave this special privilege

to him as to a mighty and triumphant champion, and it remained as true after he quit this flesh as it had been in this present life.

We shall provide one example of this special honour granted by the Almighty from heaven to the honourable man. This was revealed to the English King Oswald on the day before his battle against Cadwallon, the most powerful king of the Britons. While this King Oswald was camped ready for battle, he was asleep on a pillow in his tent one day when he had a vision of St Columba. His appearance shone with angelic beauty and, as he stood in the middle of the camp, he covered all of it except one far corner with his shining robe. The blessed man revealed his name to the king and gave him these words of encouragement, the same the Lord spoke to Joshua, saying, 'Be strong and act manfully. Behold, I will be with thee.' In the king's vision Columba said this, adding:

'This coming night go out from your camp into battle, for the Lord has granted me that at this time your foes shall be put to flight and Cadwallon your enemy shall be delivered into your hands and you shall return victorious after battle and reign happily.'[3]

The Welsh elegy for Cadwallon suggests that Iona supported Oswald against Cadwallon in the lead-up to the battle. But what could that support have consisted of? First and foremost, it was spiritual. The seal of Colm Cille's blessing and prophecy had seen King Eochaid Buide take the throne of Dál Riata: there could be no greater sanction that heaven was on Oswald's side. In the sort of battle where men fought face-to-face, the belief that God had granted victory even before battle began was of incalculable worth. But further, with Iona's approval, it would have been much easier for Oswald to receive Domnall Brecc's permission and then his backing. Domnall had seen first-hand what the saint could do: he would do well to go along with his wishes.

Some historians even suspect that Abbot Ségéne may have had at his disposal a squad of warrior monks. Many of Iona's monks came from the warrior class, either the younger sons of nobility or retired or converted warriors. They would have had considerable martial prowess and a wealth of knowledge about tactics. Most of the monks on Iona would have trained with weapons before entering the monastery. Some may have continued the practice even while on the island: the world was a dangerous place and all it took was one shipload of armed men willing to risk God's wrath to reap the richest of harvests. The British Isles were known throughout the rest of Europe as a rich source of slaves. The endemic raiding was directed as much at taking captives as amassing silver and gold. As Colm Cille's fame spread, fewer and fewer men within the ambit of the Irish Sea would have been willing to risk the saint's disfavour, but when the Vikings, men ready to risk Colm Cille's ire, came calling in 795, and again and again and again in the years afterwards, they found that his spiritual shield could be breached by sword and spear.

That lay in the future, though, as Abbot Ségéne prepared to bless Oswald and his companions before their leaving. Standing with Oswald, his brother Oswiu, the returning Northumbrians, and contingents of young Dál Riatan warriors and Ionan monks, was the son of Thunder. Along with the saint's blessing, the abbot may have given Oswald a relic of the saint, a tangible badge of his presence with them. Not the main relics of Colm Cille, for those were reserved to his monastery and it was only after a series of Viking raids, and nearly a century after the first, that Colm Cille's reliquary was finally removed from Iona and taken to Kells in Ireland. But with the saint's provisional backing, and the king's cautious support, Oswald was ready to go.

Speed and surprise were the tactical doctrines Oswald had learned fighting for Eochaid Buide and Domnall Brecc. North and east lay the country of the Picts, who seem to have given only minimal support to Eanfrith, despite his marrying into their royal line. It would have made no sense for Oswald to go that way: there would have been no support and probably little in the way of supplies, in particular the horses that he would need to make his warband into a fast-moving strike force.

For speed, the faster approach would have been to sail south from Iona, past the long finger of Kintyre, across the Firth of Clyde and around the hammerhead of the Rhins of Galloway before sailing up the Solway Firth. Landing somewhere near Carlisle, Oswald and his warband were in the ancient Brythonic kingdom of Rheged. Two generations earlier, the greatest of the kings of Rheged, Urien, had besieged his forefather, King Ida, on Lindisfarne, only for Urien to be assassinated by a jealous ally. But by this time Bernicia and Rheged had become cautious allies, with Bernicia the stronger power. Relations were good enough, and Rheged regarded highly enough, for Oswald's brother, Oswiu, to marry a princess of Rheged, named Rhieinmelth. We have no date for this wedding, but given that their son, Ahlfrith, was accepted as a sub-king of Deira in 655, they must have married around 635. Perhaps the king of Rheged made his help for Oswald and his warband conditional on Oswald laying down his brother for the cause. The match would have been conditional on victory, but what a match it would be, for a king and a kingdom down on their fortune, should Oswald and

Oswiu emerge victors and Rhieinmelth become a princess of
Northumbria.

But what Oswald would have wanted from Rheged far more
than princesses was horses. He needed to travel faster than the
news of his arrival, and for that he needed to ride. Given the
betrothal of Oswiu and Rhieinmelth, the horses were probably
forthcoming, and the warband set off.

From Carlisle, the easiest road is the old Roman Stanegate.
This was the military road the Romans constructed before
they built the wall that lies just to the north of it, and which it
supplies and reinforces. The Stanegate runs from Luguvalium,
Roman Carlisle, to the Roman fort at Coria (Corbridge), where
Stanegate meets Dere Street at its bridge over the River Tyne.
Unlike most Roman roads, the Stanegate avoids steep gradi-
ents, winding to find the easiest path, rather than taking the
straight way. As such, it must have been a relief for the legionaries manning the wall to use it when double-timing from one
fort to another. In the seventh century, the Stanegate offered
the swiftest road across the country to Cadwallon and his warband. The legions could march from Luguvalium to Coria in
three days, two if force-marched. On horseback and without a
baggage train, Oswald and his warband could have made it in
a day's long ride: it's around forty miles from Carlisle to Corbridge. Two days would have allowed them to keep horses and
riders fresh, and a more cautious approach allowed Oswald to
send scouts ahead to check for possible ambushes. There were
places along the Stanegate where Cadwallon could have set
watchpoints. As Oswald's entire strategy depended upon surprise, it was vital that any lookouts be located and dispatched
before they could get word back to Cadwallon. At the Roman
fort of Magnae Carvetiorum, near the modern-day village of
Greenhead, Stanegate and the wall run close together through

a narrow pass: it would have been the ideal spot for Cadwallon to leave sentries, or even a small force waiting in ambush.

But it seems that either Cadwallon was ignorant of Oswald's approach or that, having been victorious so often during the previous two years, he was supremely confident that he could deal with whatever force Oswald was bringing against him. But what Cadwallon did not realise is that God, or the gods, or Fortune, was turning against him.

We have heard Adomnán's account of what happened the night before the battle, a story that was passed down from one abbot to another. Bede, living in Monkwearmouth, the joint abbey that had churches near the mouths of the rivers Tyne and Wear, relates a different account of the events of that night:

> When King Oswald was about to give battle to the hea-
> then, he set up the sign of the holy cross and, kneeling
> down, asked God that He would grant His heavenly
> aid to those who trusted in Him in their dire need. The
> place is pointed out to this day and held in great vener-
> ation. It is told that, when the cross had been hurriedly
> made and a hole dug to receive it, the devout king with
> ardent faith took the cross and placed it in position,
> holding it upright with his own hands until the soldiers
> had thrown in the earth and it stood firm. This done
> he summoned his army with a loud shout, crying, 'Let
> us all kneel together, and ask the true and living God
> Almighty of His mercy to protect us from the arrogant
> savagery of our enemies, since He knows that we fight
> in a just cause to save our nation.'[4]

The two accounts are not necessarily mutually exclusive, but they do indicate a nervous, expectant night. They also indicate that Oswald knew where Cadwallon was. Actually finding the enemy is one of the most difficult military tasks, so the fact that Oswald knew this suggests that he had intelligence on their whereabouts. If Bede's account of the depredations of Cadwallon and his men is anywhere near the truth, then Oswald would have been welcomed back by the people of Bernicia as their deliverer, and they would have been keen to give him all the information they had. At the same time, Oswald was still trying to keep his approach as secret as possible. Bede tells us where Oswald and his men camped on the eve of the battle:

> This place is called in English Hefenfelth, meaning
> 'the heavenly field' . . . It lies on the northern side of
> the wall which the Romans built from sea to sea. . . .
> The brothers of the church of Hexham, which lies not
> far away . . . have recently built a church on the spot.[5]

There is a church there today, named for Oswald, naturally. Although the present church is largely a Victorian rebuilding of a Norman church, remains of an older, early medieval church were discovered in the 1950s. Pushing open the heavy red wooden door of the church today and stepping into the simple nave and looking up towards the unadorned chancel, it conveys a palpable sense of history. The silence is almost overpowering. A second look shows the candleholders in the walls and the big, glass, globed gas mantles dangling from the ceiling. The church remains resolutely grounded in the past, and is not connected to mains electricity, gas or water.

But why would Oswald want to camp in an exposed field, rendering himself easily visible? He didn't. In 1959, archaeologists found the underground remains of what is prosaically called Turret 25B, part of the defences along Hadrian's Wall.

Nothing remains above ground now, but it would have made a good place to pitch camp, providing both shelter and, as it lay on the declining slope of a ridge, cover from eyes to the south.

While Oswald probably had monks from Iona with him, among his assembled warband there were Christians and pagans. The raising of a tree before a battle would have answered to the religious sensibilities of those men who followed the old gods as well as those who followed the new one, for the World Tree, as represented by an upraised pole, appears to have been part of the belief system for the old religion. Even the words that Bede records Oswald as saying were carefully chosen: every man kneeling on Heavenfield could join with them.

What's more, if any of the warriors who had accompanied Oswald from Dál Riata had been wary of lifting their spears against Cadwallon on account of his kinship and the long friendship between Gwynedd and Dál Riata, those misgivings would have been assuaged by the dream vision of Colm Cille that had been given to Oswald. The saint had spoken: his favour lay upon them.

Could Oswald have made up the vision to encourage his wavering men? It is possible, but unnecessary. Oswald would have ridden towards this defining battle looking everywhere for a sign of the saint's favour; he would have expected it. This was not a time when signs were unforthcoming: they were everywhere – in the unexpected recovery from disease, in the finding of a milk-skin washed away by the tide, in the turn of the wind. With the saint's favour, the warrior monks of Iona and the retainers of the king of Dál Riata who had accompanied Oswald's small band of Northumbrian exiles had divine sanction to join battle.

They rode at dawn.

14

Battle

It was a battle that took place nearly fourteen hundred years ago. Outside the small field of historians specialising in early medieval history, historical re-enactors and readers interested in the early history of Britain, hardly anyone has heard of it. But the Battle of Heavenfield between the forces of Oswald Iding, ætheling of Bernicia, and Cadwallon ap Cadfan, King of Gwynedd, was among the most important battles in British history. In its ramifications, it's at least as crucial as Hastings: perhaps only the battles of Nechtansmere (20 May 685) and Edington (May 878) were as important in deciding what Britain would be. For the last thousand years Britain has contained three kingdoms, of varying degrees of independence: England, Scotland and Wales. Looking back from our vantage point it seems that it was always going to end up this way. But it really didn't have to be this way.

Under the Romans, Londinium in the second century had the largest forum north of the Alps; even so, the country always remained set apart from the rest of the empire. While the

Romanised Britons considered themselves Roman, the lack of almost any notable Roman Britons suggests that the rest of the empire wasn't so sure. Through the four centuries of Roman rule – a period that if moved forwards would run from the end of the Civil War to the present – there were no senators from Britain, or any notable Romano-Briton. The only Briton to achieve broader fame was the heresiarch, Pelagius, and he did so after leaving the country, never to return.

Within Britain, use of Latin and the native Brythonic languages continued in parallel even after the legions left: many Britons still thought of themselves as Roman, an identification that was heightened by the arrival of the Anglo-Saxons, who were resolutely neither Roman nor Christian. By the seventh century, Anglo-Saxon kingdoms were established in the south and east of the country, but the extent of Anglo-Saxon domination was far from settled. There were natural barriers in the Pennines, and long-standing Brythonic kingdoms that had weathered the first two centuries of Anglo-Saxon expansion. Kings Æthelfrith and Edwin had apparently tilted the balance in the north decisively towards the Anglo-Saxons, but the way their kingdoms disintegrated on their deaths showed that the boundary between the Brythonic and Anglo-Saxon kingdoms was still fluid.

Imagine Cadwallon victorious. The north would have belonged to the 'furious fiery stag' who had restored the dignity and the territory of the '*combrogi*' the 'men of the same country', the word that became *Cymry*. Yr Hen Ogledd, the Old North, had declined but there was still strength in it, in kingdoms such as Strathclyde. Bernicia's downfall would have allowed Rheged's rebirth. In the north, the Picts and the Dál Riatans would have continued their long struggle for northern Britain without having to constantly guard against the expansionist tendencies of the Northumbrians.

In the later centuries of the long Welsh struggle against the Normans and the Plantagenets, the fundamental strategic weakness of the Welsh kings was the custom of partible inheritance: on death, a lord's holdings were split between all his sons, with often his surviving brothers and nephews wanting a cut too. When due was not given, brother would fight brother in what proved ultimately to be a suicidal fratricidal conflict. The last prince of Wales, Llywelyn ap Gruffudd (*c.*1223–11 December 1282) lost his life and his kingdom to Edward I of England in part because of the betrayals of his brother, Dafydd ap Gruffydd, unhappy with his part of the inheritance. It's not clear if the custom of partible inheritance applied in the seventh century, but it's difficult to believe that a custom that proved so disastrous did not have deep cultural and historic roots. But Cadwallon, as king of Gwynedd and now king of Northumbria, had more than enough land for however many sons he might have. He could have placed his heirs in the key locations in an arc running from north Wales across the Pennines to the Firth of Forth. In the space of two years, a strategic situation that had seen the Brythonic peoples pushed back and starting to be hemmed into the more mountainous, less fertile regions of the country would have been reversed: the Anglo-Saxon kingdoms would have seen themselves surrounded, threatened and in retreat.

If Cadwallon had had another twenty years as king of Northumbria there would probably still have been a division of the country between Anglo-Saxons, Britons, Picts and Scots, but the proportions would have been different. One can imagine an 'England' confined to the south and east, bounded by the Pennines and the Humber marshes or even the Wash. While this area still contains much prime agricultural land, there would have been sufficient good farmland in the rest of the country for the Brythonic kingdoms to not suffer so markedly from the economic disadvantages of being confined to unproductive areas. As a result, fortune's dice would not have been loaded so heavily for the English. In the north of Britain, the complex and still little understood process by which the Dál Riatan *Scoti* merged with the Picts to the eventual elimination of the Pictish language might still have taken place, but there would have been much greater input from the Brythonic men of Yr Hen Ogledd: the kingdoms of Strathclyde, Rheged, maybe even the Gododdin.

How these kingdoms would have fared before the Viking assault of the ninth, tenth and eleventh centuries is anyone's guess. Maybe the 'great heathen army' would have completed its conquest and Britain would have become a country split between Norse- and Gaelic-speaking populations. Each successive move from history's timeline makes subsequent events harder to predict.

Neither Bede nor Adomnán tell us anything about the battle. For them, and for their narratives, it was a victory ordained by God, a sign of his divine favour and his will; the tactical details were of little interest. It's left to us to try to understand what happened from the few clues. Bede is quite specific about where the end came: 'the infamous British leader was killed at a place known by the English as Denisesburn, that is, the Brook of Denis'.[1] Bede is not usually so precise in his locations. Unfortunately, while the English of Bede's day might have known where the Brook of Denis was, the English of later days did not. It was not until the nineteenth century that a charter was discovered, dating from 1233, that mentioned the

Brook of Denis as land made over to Thomas of Whittington: 'Twenty acres of land from his waste in Ruleystal, between these boundaries, namely between Deniseburn and Divelis, beginning to the east upon Divelis and rising to the great road which leads up to the forest of Lillewude.'[2]

The Divelis is the Devil's Water, a tributary of the Tyne that rises on the moors south of Hexham. So Oswald camped before battle near the site of the present-day St Oswald's Church, just to the north of Hadrian's Wall. The Welsh annals name the battle Cantscaul, which comes from the Old English word for Hexham, *Hagustaldesham*, which lies due south of there, and Bede says the final end of the battle took place another five miles further south, on the Devil's Water. However, Hexham Abbey was founded in 674 after the battle took place by that most turbulent of Northumbrian saints, Wilfrid. Hexham lies on the south bank of the River Tyne. The river is broad. It is not an obvious place for a warband to cross, nor for an army to be able to retreat over: if Cadwallon's army had been caught on the north side of the Tyne, across from Hexham, they would have had to make a stand there.

This makes Hexham an unlikely candidate for the first clash between the two armies. A more likely possibility is Corbridge, three miles east. Corbridge is the site of an old Roman town, it lies at the junction of Dere Street and Stanegate, and the Romans had built a bridge over the River Tyne that was probably still standing. As such, Corbridge is a likely candidate for the place where Cadwallon had camped with his army.

With these places in mind, we can hazard an attempt at reconstructing what happened. It's probably wrong but then, as Lewis Binford showed, so is most archaeology. Here goes.

It was a dawn attack. Cadwallon's army outnumbered Oswald's warband. The retellings have Cadwallon's army in the thousands, but it's extremely unlikely to have been as large as that; at most a few hundred with Oswald's warband in the low hundreds. It may not even have made it into three figures.

Cadwallon's army had been campaigning for over a year, plundering and moving on. One thing we know about victorious armies like this is that they accumulate followers and hangers-on: women, pedlars, merchants, chancers, not to mention captives dragged along until the time arises to sell them as slaves. The army had even been in the field long enough for some of the accompanying women to have conceived and given birth. Even more importantly, the army would have acquired a huge baggage train to carry its accumulated plunder. They had ravaged two kingdoms, and while much Anglo-Saxon wealth was portable, pillaging soldiers are notoriously indiscriminate – they will take anything that isn't nailed down, and attempt to take out the nails from the stuff that is. So Cadwallon's army would have bloated – from an elite and mobile fighting force to a much slower moving and more static, although larger, army, with attendant hangers-on and a large baggage train.

Cadwallon was probably camped in or near Corbridge, where he could guard the bridge over the River Tyne, as well as Dere Street and Stanegate. The local people, tired of the depredations of Cadwallon's army, likely gave intelligence as to his whereabouts to Oswald and his men, and helped to ensure that no news of their approach got to Cadwallon. Oswald woke before dawn at their camp just north of the wall and, having bowed before the cross/tree, they set off, riding through the dark. To keep their movements secret, they would have muffled their horses' hooves, wrapping them with cloth and straw. The men's swords and spears, their belts and buckles and armour were tied down or dipped in wax to stop them chinking. With local guides, they made their way towards where Cadwallon was camped, moving into position before dawn, ready to attack as soon as there was light enough to see.

The success of the attack depended on surprise causing confusion and panic. One possible scenario is that Oswald sent a team of men to attack, and fire, the baggage train. Much of the personal loot of Cadwallon's soldiers was stored in those wagons. Carried out correctly, it would initially have seemed like a raid by bold thieves. As such, and waking to hear cries, and fires breaking out, many men would have rushed to secure their own riches without arming themselves properly. That was the time to launch the second wave of the attack: an all-out charge. Depending on the ground where Cadwallon was camped, this could have been on horseback or on foot, but the aim was to cause maximum impact, throwing the enemy into panic, and dividing Cadwallon's forces.

It must have succeeded beyond Oswald's fondest hopes, for Cadwallon began to retreat, falling back over the bridge. Many men who chose to stay to defend the baggage train must have been lost and Cadwallon's army weakened. But they were experienced warriors, the victors of many battles, and Cadwallon was the most successful battlefield general in the land. He rallied them, pulling them into some sort of order and began to pull back, leaving the hangers-on and the unfaithful to their fate on the north bank of the Tyne. He must have hoped that, by sacrificing his baggage train, he could also split the army attacking him: many men, faced with a choice between looting a baggage train laden with treasure or pursuing a band of desperate warriors, will naturally choose the former. But Oswald's warband was disciplined and they held together, leaving the baggage train to be dealt with later, and carried on the pursuit, plunging over the bridge after Cadwallon.

Having made it across the bridge, Cadwallon could have

retreated south, down Dere Street. With horses, and a screen of men willing to fight a rearguard, he would have been able to escape. But he did not go down Dere Street. Maybe, in the dark of night, Oswald had sent a party of men across the Tyne to set up an ambush on Dere Street, blocking it off as a path of retreat. Instead, Cadwallon fell back to the south-west, along the Devil's Water. The Devil's Water leads back into the high moors. The southern bank, on which Cadwallon and his men were retreating, becomes steadily steeper and steeper. Perhaps Cadwallon hoped to lose his pursuers in the moors. Maybe he expected to be able to cross the Devil's Water but the water level was too high. Maybe, amid the chaos and confusion, he simply made a mistake.

Whatever the reason, Cadwallon and his troops made a fighting retreat, harried all the way. Cadwallon's warriors were tough men. They fought off their pursuers for three miles, expecting no quarter and giving none. But as the moors loomed higher, and the Devil's Water came to its confluence with Denis Brook, Cadwallon and his remaining men made a stand.

There can't have been many of them left at this point. Caught by surprise, most of the army had been lost in the initial attack, thrown into confusion and split up. Those that Cadwallon had rallied to his support had been cut down as they retreated, the pursuing horsemen sweeping out of the morning to throw spears at backs making haste along the river, bypassing each desperate stand to keep the pressure on Cadwallon and his diminishing band. Oswald led them. That was his task, his appointed duty. *Lamnguin*, the White Blade. Only it would not have been white that morning.

If the Devil's Water had been known by that name when Bede wrote his history, he would surely have found it providential that the man he portrayed in darker hues than anyone else in his book should meet his end beside it. Perhaps the name the river came to be known by was preserved by some dim folk memory of the man who died next to it. On its banks, Cadwallon, king of Gwynedd, victor over Edwin and Osric and Eanfrith, despoiler of Northumbria, the 'furious fiery stag' of the Britons and the last real hope of the Brythonic kingdoms to reverse two centuries of long defeat, died. He died a long way from his home. Even if some survivor of the catastrophe found his body, he could not have taken it the long miles back to Gwynedd. For Cadwallon, there was no stone memorial raised over his grave, only an elegy, the *Moliant Cadwallon*, and the long retreat of his people.

From the plots of strangers and iniquitous monks,
As water flows from the fountain,
Long shall be our weeping for Cadwallon.[3]

15

To the Victor

Stand on the ramparts of Bamburgh Castle today and look north-north-west. Over the sea, blue or grey according to mood, is Lindisfarne. By boat it is less than six miles from castle to island; the journey of an hour or two on a good day. On a bad day, when the wind whips over the wave-tops, it's best to huddle down inside. Lindisfarne is a liminal place, breathing the rhythm of the tides. In summer, in the tourist season, the car park fills on the falling tide, only to empty out again as the tide rises. Indeed, the flow of cars marks the tides as well as any tide table. But in the between times, when the island is an island again, it becomes a quiet place. The remains of the priory, which are under the care of English Heritage, date from the Norman era, when the monastery was re-established as a Benedictine house, remaining active until Henry VIII's suppression of the monasteries. Standing in the ruins of the monastery, and looking south, it's easy to see Bamburgh Castle squatting on a hump of Whin Sill.

Oswald had grown up seeing Lindisfarne from his home

and it held special significance. Lindisfarne is almost the eastern twin of Iona: seaward-facing, mist-covered and insular. It was the place that had given sanctuary to his forefather Theodric when he was besieged there by Urien of Rheged. The special blessings of the island had protected Theodric through the siege, when all had seemed lost for the Idings, and then it had given him victory against all expectations when his enemies had turned upon each other, killing Urien of Rheged and abandoning the siege amid suspicion and mistrust. Lindisfarne had saved his family once – and thus his people, ruling families tending to identify their own well-being with that of their people – and so it was the natural and obvious place upon which to establish the monastery that would be the centre from which he might save his people again, in the spirit, as he had already saved them in the body. Oswald was a man who once set on a course of action did not lack for ambition. After all, now he was sure that he had God on his side.

'Os-wald' is a typical Old English name, combining prefix and suffix. The 'Os' prefix means 'god' or 'divine', the 'wald' suffix 'power'. So 'God's might' or 'Divine power'. Oswald's victory had confirmed God's power; now it was time to demonstrate that power to his people. For his part, Colm Cille had again proven the worth of his intercession. The shining cloak in Oswald's dream vision, the spreading arms of the cross in his rallying call, had embraced the kingdoms of north Britain. It was all Oswald's now. Against expectation, almost against hope, certainly against any reasonable hope, he and his small warband had prevailed. The exile and the exiles were back.

There could not have been any ætheling better qualified to unify the kingdom in the wake of its recent traumas. His father was Æthelfrith of Bernicia, his mother was Acha, Edwin's sister, of Deira. So Oswald united the two kingdoms.

But now that Northumbria was his, what was he going to do with it and with the people who had helped him win the kingdom? With respect to the exiles, it was straightforward. These men had accompanied his family into exile; they had raised their children alongside his younger brother. Oswald knew he could trust them with anything and that no reward was too great. Fortunately, it was relatively easy to reward them with the fundamental marker of status – land. Land was the reward for faithful and exemplary service. The bitterness with which Cadwallon's occupation was still remembered in Northumbria two generations later suggests that, at least among the landed class, the occupation had been brutal, with many people driven from their land. For Oswald, looking to reward his followers and cement his rule, this represented a blessing. There were many estates available for him to settle upon the returning exiles, most of them near the major centres of power.

But what of those men who had joined him from Iona and Dál Riata? The monks and men from Iona returned, praise telling the wondrous advocacy of the saint as they went, and adding another chapter to the monastery's annals of wonders on their return. The same was true for those warriors that King Domnall Brecc had lent to Oswald's cause. When news reached him that the man he had helped claim the throne had become the most powerful king in north Britain, Domnall Brecc must have congratulated himself on the acuity of his political judgement and settled back to enjoy the patronage and power from backing the right warrior. Unfortunately for Domnall Brecc, he seems to have exhausted his political luck after this. The rest of his reign was a tale of reverses and defeats, mostly to do with backing the wrong side in the complicated dynastic quarrels in Ireland, before he finally met his end in December 642 or 643 in a losing battle against the Britons of the kingdom of Strathclyde, who had their capital and stronghold on Dumbarton Rock.

This was awkward for the monks of Iona, as it could have seemed that the power and protection of Colm Cille was failing. Luckily for the saint's reputation, it turned out that Colm Cille had prophesied Domnall Brecc's fall from grace when he had been told by an angel to anoint Áedán as king of Dál Riata. Colm Cille had been initially unwilling to do so, since he judged one of Áedán's brothers to be a more suitable choice. The angel, miffed, whipped Colm Cille for his obtuseness (angelic whips being particularly bitter – he apparently bore that scar for the rest of his life) and appeared three nights running so that Colm Cille really got the message.

But while the rest of Domnall Brecc's warriors probably returned home, the son of Thunder did not. He stayed. Not only did he stay, but he sent for his family to join him. This suggests that ties of loyalty and friendship beyond the usual bonds of men fighting in the same warband existed between Oswald and the warrior. As one of Domnall Brecc's men, he would have had to ask to be released from his oath to the king of Dál Riata, but dispensation must have been given without demur. It suited Domnall Brecc that Oswald should have a living reminder among his personal retinue of the debt he owed to Dál Riata and its king. In thanks for his service, Oswald gave the warrior and his family land somewhere reasonably near Bamburgh. This was prime land for two reasons: the land was rich and fertile, while its location near Bamburgh and Lindisfarne gave the warrior and his family ready access to the king and the monks on Lindisfarne.

For if Oswald gave readily to the men who had fought with him on earth, he gave even more readily to those who had fought for him in heaven. We know that after his victory he made at least one trip back to Iona. Kingship was a peripatetic business, so the travelling was not unusual, but Oswald clearly felt his rule secure enough for him to travel so far outside his own kingdom. According to Adomnán's life of Colm Cille, Oswald gave personal testimony of his dream vision of the saint to his old friend and mentor Abbot Ségéne. We don't know exactly when Oswald went back to Iona, or if he visited more than once, but one of the new king's first acts was to send word to Iona asking Ségéne to send a bishop to teach the new faith to his people.

A measure of the dominance that Oswald had achieved as a result of his victory over Cadwallon is shown by how he went about doing this. When Edwin, who had already been a successful king of Northumbria for nearly a decade, began to think about converting to Christianity, he vacillated about the decision for a long time. Before finally making his decision, Edwin called all his chief men together to sound them out and hear their views. There is no record at all of Oswald doing this. He made the decision without reference to the chief men of Northumbria and imposed it on them; Oswald's prestige and their own diminished state meant that they could not demur.

Bede, though, is too conscientious a historian to pretend that it all went according to plan. After telling of the success of the Ionan mission to Northumbria, he does add the admission that it had, in fact, started badly. For the first representative Iona sent to Northumbria, Bishop Corman, returned to tell his superiors that the Northumbrians were 'an ungovernable people of an obstinate and barbarous temperament . . . who refused to listen to him.'[1]

The saint had given Oswald victory; he would expect Iona to reap the fruits of that victory. Ségéne called a conference of

Irish clerics to ask what they should do. It was at this meeting, according to Bede, that one Aidan offered his critique of
Corman's approach and suggested a better one.

> Brother, it seems to me that you were too hard on your
> ignorant hearers. You should have followed the practice
> of the Apostles, and begun by giving them the milk of
> simpler teaching, and gradually nourished them with
> the word of God until they were capable of greater
> perfection and able to follow the loftier precepts of
> Christ.[2]

Having suggested the solution, Aidan was the obvious
choice to put the plan into action. Ségéne dispatched him to
Northumbria, where he probably arrived either late in 634 or
635. Coming from the Irish monastic tradition, Aidan did what
he knew: he made a monastery on Lindisfarne in the simple
Irish manner, building in wood and thatch rather than stone.
What Aidan didn't know, at least to start with, was the language. He spoke Gaelic and Latin, not Old English.

So when Aidan first began to preach, Oswald, who was flu-
ent in both languages, acted as his interpreter. The word of
God coming from the lips of the king. It must have carried
considerable weight with their listeners. There was also the
magic, the unfathomable power of the written word. For us, an
everyday thing, for a non-literate people, miraculous. Bardic
tradition indicates that it could take a lifetime to master the
king lists or an epic poem, but Aidan could simply read the
words of God from a book, and do it again and again. It was
magic made sound.

Bede presents Aidan as his clerical ideal: austere yet simple,
kind but unafraid to chastise the rich and powerful, efficient in

organisation yet always cognisant that a religious life needed to be grounded in prayer and prayerful retreats from the entanglements of the world. Bede, in the manner of the born teacher he was, illustrates Aidan's priestly virtues by telling stories. In marked contrast to the splendour of the entourage that followed Wilfrid, Aidan walked. He walked everywhere. The ownership and riding of a horse was as much a mark of high social status in seventh-century Britain as owning an expensive car is today. But another effect of Aidan walking the roads and paths of Northumbria was the way it brought him into contact with ordinary people to engage in conversation – once he had learned to speak Old English – telling them stories from scripture. On one occasion, a king, Oswine, with whom Aidan was friendly, gave Aidan a horse for his use, richly caparisoned and highly bred: the equivalent of giving him a top-of-the-range Mercedes-Benz. Aidan accepted the horse, kings being hard to refuse, but, meeting a beggar praying alms, Aidan promptly gave away the horse and all its rich harness. When he heard what had happened, the king remonstrated with Aidan, asking him why he had given away the horse. If Aidan really wanted to give horses to beggars, the king could have provided a less well-bred specimen. To which Aidan replied with a question of his own: 'Is this child of a mare more valuable to you than this child of God?'[3] This was the sort of radical vision of every human equally beloved by God that sat with great difficulty alongside the hierarchies of seventh-century Britain.

Bede presents Aidan as an episcopal ideal: personally austere and ascetic, yet kind to those less able to match his asceticism; unimpressed by wealth as the measure of a man but rather responding to a person's deeds instead of their status and as unafraid to correct the rich and powerful as the poor and weak. Although by necessity frequenting the halls of kings, that were

often scenes of riotous, drunken licence, Aidan would eat spar-
ingly and withdraw before things got too out of hand. And, in
a notable aside to contemporary practices that Bede abhorred,
Aidan made no payments for favour to the rich or powerful,
while any money he received from the rich he either distributed to the poor or used to pay for the manumission of slaves.

Presented as Bede's episcopal model, something of Aidan's
personality still comes through. When Oswine, the king who
had given him the horse, mortified by Aidan's reply, prostrated
himself before the monk, Aidan raised him to his feet and told
him to think no more of the matter. But later, while they were
eating, one of Aidan's companions noticed that he had begun
to weep and asked him, in Gaelic, why he cried? To which
Aidan replied, 'I know that the king will not live very long; for
I have never before seen a humble king.'[4] The comment tells
much about the kings of Aidan's time, and indeed the rulers
of any time, and Aidan's clear-eyed perception of them. This
perception was honed through the practice of solitary prayer,
which followed closely the Irish example. The Farne Islands,
a final upwelling of the Whin Sill through the cold waters of
the North Sea, lie a couple of miles east of Bamburgh Castle,
their guano-streaked cliffs clearly visible from the castle. On
Inner Farne, the island nearest the coast and the largest of the
islands, Aidan built a hermitage where he could withdraw for
solitary prayer, away from the constant press of demands due
to his role as bishop and abbot of the monastery on Lindisfarne.

Aidan succeeded as an evangelist in Northumbria through
these virtues and relentless energy. Bede also holds him up
as an example for the bishops of his own day in the way that
Aidan tramped all quarters of his diocese, personally going and
meeting people in the hamlets and hills, even the notoriously

rough shepherds of the Cheviots. The monastic institutions and churches that Aidan oversaw also created a framework and a training that enabled other young men and women to follow in his footsteps. In a world where the possibilities for young men were limited, the sudden opening up of the monastic world provided a whole new universe of intellectual and prayerful opportunities.

But while Oswald was committed to the new religion in the Ionan form, he was not necessarily opposed to the Roman form that Edwin had espoused. The two differed in a number of ways, most noticeably in the tonsures worn by clerics and the method of calculating the date of Easter. Soon after his victory over Cadwallon, Oswald must have travelled south, into Deira, the heartland of the Yffings and the birthplace of his mother, Acha. If Acha was still alive to see the triumph of her son, he would surely have taken her with him to smooth his acceptance by the Deiran nobility. Oswald appears to have adopted a tactful silence with respect to the apostasy of the Deiran nobility following Edwin's death, but he made a conciliatory but pointed gesture on his arrival in York: he ordered the stone church that had been begun during Edwin's reign as the cathedral church for Paulinus to be completed. Thus it was Oswald, the son of Iona, who finished the first stone church to be built in northern Britain for a century or more. He also allowed the last remaining representative in the north of Paulinus's mission to continue his ministry: James the Deacon, based near Catterick, continued as before, his low-key work enduring when the more high-profile clerics moved on. James would still be there in 664, working away, when the Synod of Whitby was convened and the question of how to date Easter was finally settled for the church in Northumbria.

But in nothing was Oswald's whole-hearted support of the

church more clearly revealed than in the land he gave to it and the way he gave it. Land was the traditional reward for the faithful service of a retainer but the land was effectively leasehold: it reverted to the king on the death of his servant and that servant's heirs could only get it back again as the gift of the king (in effect, a loan) in reward for further service. However, the land Oswald gave to the church was in payment not for military service but for prayers: the necessary prayers that would see him safely into heaven. Even a king as saintly as Oswald would have shed a great deal of blood: many prayers were needed to ensure his safe passage into the next life. Once admitted into God's great hall, there was no suggestion that the deceased king would later be ejected: the welcome was once and for all, the tenure in heaven eternal. The doctrine of purgatory was still only rudimentary at this time, so there was only a nod towards earthly prayers as expiation for purgatorial confinement. However, it did not pay to skimp on prayers where one's eternal soul was concerned: to have monks offer a perpetual round of prayer for one's salvation was as near to an insurance policy as the seventh century offered. But for monks to do this, the land they were given could not revert back to the new king on the death of the old one, nor on the death of one abbot and his succession by another.

We don't know if Oswald realised the implications of what he was doing, but by giving land to Aidan and the monks of Lindisfarne as 'book land', Oswald was creating an institution that could survive his own death and the disintegration of the kingdom that followed. Oswald was giving Aidan and his monks the opportunity to make something that would last.

There was something else at play here too. Oswald and Oswiu had both come of age in Dál Riata. The *Senchus fer n-Alban*, the Dál Riatan document ascribing military obligation to the three kindreds according to a census of households, was in effect an inventory of the riches of the kingdom. Returning to Northumbria, Oswald and Oswiu needed to take stock of what they now had at their disposal. With literate monks available they could record the resources of Northumbria and decide how much land to make over to the church. Transferring ownership of land to the church effectively removes it from normal use but still allows it to provide towards the kingdom as the church paid a healthy tithe on its land to the crown. By the time Oswiu became king, the machinery of government had improved to such an extent that the king could directly tax the population without his nobility administering the tax and taking their cut for doing so. The increase in income allowed the king to redistribute wealth while concentrating power in the crown as never before. It's likely that Oswiu sought to legitimise this accumulation of power by promoting the cult of his brother and empowering the church.

For their part, the monks of Lindisfarne took the opportunity that Oswald had given them. The monastery they built on Lindisfarne was as simple and austere as its model on Iona, but the infrastructure they set about creating was anything but simple. To mark out the monastic compound, the monks dug a surrounding ditch and raised a bank from the spoil; this served as a simple protection for the monastery from raiders and the weather, while helping to keep animals out or in as required. But while the monks of Iona skimped on their own physical comfort, they were committed to producing the best work possible and in the physical realm that work was books. For their spiritual work of prayer, as sung daily in the Office, the monks needed books: psalters, Bibles, Gospels.

With the land settled upon them in perpetuity, the monks of Lindisfarne and the other monasteries and churches that

Aidan established in Northumbria – we only know of two, one at Bamburgh but separate from the stronghold of the Idings, roughly where St Aidan's Church stands today, and another possible church at Yeavering, which Brian Hope-Taylor excavated, although there were almost certainly more – set about clearing land, raising cattle, establishing networks, praying, singing and teaching. Abbot Ségéne, having found a man who could speak the Northumbrians' language (even if he had to use the king to do it), set about supporting Aidan as far as he was able, dispatching further groups of monks to Lindisfarne. The restless nature of Irish monasticism would also have called other religious to venture to the wild new shore where the word of God was being preached.

In the almost completely rural landscape of seventh-century northern Britain, this sudden concentration of people on Lindisfarne was like the eruption of a city in the middle of the Sahara. Being literate, and teachers, the monks were entrusted with the care of many children of the nobility to acquaint them with the strange but undeniably powerful technology that lay at the heart of their learning: reading.

For a non-literate people, the introduction of reading and writing is a revelation. Words, captured and held past the speaking, ready to be spoken again. Books that spoke the words of God and that were themselves as magnificent and beautiful and wondrous as the God of whom they spoke. For surely Aidan came to Lindisfarne from Iona with the necessary books to found the monastery there and while Iona would have kept its very best books for itself, Abbot Ségéne was shrewd enough to give into Aidan's care some books that would convey by their very appearance the majesty and awe of what lay within them.

While the monks could produce what was necessary for a straightforward book, to create a book worthy of its message required things that had to be brought from elsewhere. While the culmination of their art came a generation later with the production of the *Lindisfarne Gospels*, written and illustrated by Eadfrith, bishop of Lindisfarne, the trade contacts and routes needed to acquire some of the dyes and colours used in making the Gospels were already being laid down. The beach in front of Bamburgh Castle was almost certainly used as a beach market, and up and down the north-east coast there are a number of settlements with the 'wic' suffix, indicating that they functioned as markets, not least of which was York (Eoforwic). So there were merchant traders who already travelled up the east coast, putting in at beach markets along the way and selling their wares. With the arrival of the monks, and their requirement for exotic dyes that could not be manufactured locally, there was an incentive for merchants to make the trip, particularly since the trip could be combined with a stop at Bamburgh. The secular and religious markets were both seeking low-volume, high-value items: perfect for a merchant looking to turn a profit and go quickly back south.

By alienating royal land from the loop of royal patronage and settling it upon the Church, Oswald made possible the creation of the first, settled centres of population since the departure of the legions. In partnership with the monks of Lindisfarne, the king of Northumbria and his heirs had embarked upon that most difficult and delicate of operations: the making of a civilisation.

16

A New Home Over the Sea

The warrior wiped the sweat from his forehead and flicked it away. The local men had worked hard all day, sawing and split-ting and joining. The pillars that held up the hall's roof were in place, the thatcher was laying out sheaves of dry grass, and there was a steady procession of families from the area com-ing to greet their new lord. With each greeting, the warrior's pronunciation of English improved, so that by the end of the day people were only smiling, rather than laughing, when he greeted them. The words sounded harsh in his throat; listen-ing to the men work, he missed the sounds of home, the rise and fall of the language of the islands and headlands where he had grown up; a language like the waves of the sea made into words.

When he had first arrived in the district, the king had sent his almoner with the warrior to give succour to the poor of the area. Cadwallon's raiding parties had scoured the stores and houses far and wide, spoiling what they did not take. Many were hungry, some were close to starving. The poor had come shuffling towards them then. When they had seen the wagon that followed behind the almoner, they hurried, pushing the weaker aside in their hurry to get to the wagon. For a mercy, the warrior had his men with him, the five who had accompanied him from Dál Riata and who would stay with him, at least until he had built his hall, and the almoner had brought a dozen stout lads too, armed with staves. They soon sorted the crowd into a queue, doling out the oats and grain and bread – stale and hard now but easily eaten when moistened.

The warrior told the people, with the almoner acting as interpreter, that he was their new lord. He would see them right so long as they stood fair for him. They had shown their fairness by the willingness with which they set to work building his hall and the necessary buildings – storerooms, kitchen, stable, workshops – around it. They had worked hard and the warrior had rewarded them. Now the hall was almost ready.

Anglo-Saxon craftsmen in metal and wood were masters of their trades. The best of them were peripatetic, moving to where their skills would find a market and then moving on. But the basic carpentry skills needed for putting up a hall were widely known and practised in a society where most people had to build, or at least maintain, their own homes. To secure the hall, they put in foundation stones to foot the uprights, blocks removed from the mouldering remains of one of the Roman forts that were slowly subsiding into the landscape north of the Wall. While the Anglo-Saxons were master carpenters, they were poor masons, often recycling Roman stone for their own purposes, as Wilfrid did when he founded Hexham Abbey. Planks were split from logs using wooden wedges. To do this, an incision was made in the top of the log, a wedge hammered in to broaden the crack, and further wedges added as the crack proceeded down the length of the log, with the first wedges hammered in further to help split the wood apart. Once the log was split into planks it was cut to size with axes, and broadaxes were used to shave the wood flat. Planes had not been invented yet, but a good Anglo-Saxon craftsman could achieve a very fine finish to the wood using an axe or an adze. Finishing was done with sandstone. The wood worked was greenwood as it is softer and much easier to work than seasoned timber. Once the planks were ready and the foundation stones in place, the jointing was done with wooden dowels. Very few nails were used in Anglo-Saxon carpentry as the days of industrial-scale nail production ended with the Roman Empire. Wattle and daub was used to finish the walls. Indeed, most of the terms for wattling come from Old English.

The warrior was eager to see his hall finished. So eager that he joined in with the work, sawing and hefting the planks into place. He went to look at the work the men were doing on the door pillars: intricate interwoven patterns of animals and birds and leaping fish racing up the tall wooden poles to the crook. Standing on wooden scaffolds, the two carvers were working above his head, while at ground level two other men were painting the finished carvings red and green and yellow. Usually, the carvers would work on the uprights before they were erected, but the warrior was in a hurry. He wanted the hall finished before his family and household arrived.

When Oswald had asked him to stay the warrior was unsure. The king also wanted to give him land further south, nearer the Wall and more in the Simonside Hills. Each would be enough to support a hall for him and his family and allow them to take advantage of the different crops each location provided. It was a handsome gift but the warrior was still not sure. He had accompanied Oswald on his venture for love and friendship and the duty owed to a man he had fought alongside.

They were as close as brothers and, being nearer in age than Oswald was to Oswiu, could speak of matters that Oswiu was only now beginning to understand.

But his own king, Domnall Brecc, had rewarded him with land. His home was in Dál Riata, on a peninsula looking over the sea – although in truth, that applied to almost everywhere in Dál Riata – and waiting for him there was his wife and son, the boy who brought lightness to his eyes. He would not leave them.

'Bring them,' said Oswald, when the warrior told him of his doubts. 'Bring them here.' The king's arm swept wide, taking in the broad, fertile belt of land that ran down from the hills, and the broader sweep of the sea itself, out of which rose the distant, white-streaked walls of the Farnes. 'There is much room, more good land, than even a son of Dál Riata might want.' Then the king leaned to him, and spoke so that only the warrior could hear. 'I would wish to have you with me, for I shall have need of men I can trust.'

So he had decided to stay. When, not long after his victory, Oswald travelled with the men of Dál Riata and the monks of Iona back to the west, riding fast so that he would not be away from his lands for long and leaving his brother, Oswiu, in his place behind, the warrior rode with him. Oswald went to tell Abbot Ségéne of his dream vision, and to give thanks to the saint in the very place that kept his earthly remains. For the warrior's part, he went to seek release from his oath to King Domnall Brecc and, that being given, to tell his family and household to prepare to move to Northumbria.

Summer had turned to autumn. The leaves were turning on the trees. The warrior, learning the language of the local people, understood that they called this month *winterfylleth* and reckoned winter to begin during it, for during that month the nights become longer than the days; and winter was reckoned to begin on the first full moon of *winterfylleth*. He had started to scan the surrounding tracks and paths more anxiously, for soon the weather would turn to winter storms, and travelling become hard, weary and wet work.

He went into the hall. The building was almost completed. The roof was sound against rain. A fire burned in the centre of the hall. It was still bare though: waiting for the hangings and banners that his household were bringing with them from home. *Home.* This was home now.

One of the local boys came running to him, spilling words so fast that the warrior could not understand them, until at last two stood clear from the torrent: *they're coming.* He ran out with the boy, shading his eyes against the westering sun, and saw them. His steward leading the procession, the rider beside him flying the banner of his house, and behind them a column of men riding and walking and driving wagons.

The warrior ran to meet them, his wife and son . . .

We do not know if this is how it happened. But we do know that sometime shortly after the battle, when Oswald was proclaimed king of Bernicia and Deira, the warrior's son came to join him in the kingdom that his father had helped win for Oswald. The boy was young but past the dangerous years of infancy, when mortality rates were at their highest. He was four. Being so young, the lad must have come to Northumbria with his mother and siblings and other members of the family. It seems likely that they came to stay.

There would be others too. The sword companions and warriors who eighteen years ago had ridden with Acha and her family in their flight were no longer young men; though older men did lead warriors into battle and fight, these men, at least those who had survived the vicissitudes of exile, were now in their forties, even fifties. By such ages, a faithful king's companion would have expected the land to raise a family and regale his children and grandchildren with tales of battles won and narrow escapes. Not unnaturally, these men expected first settlement, and Oswald would have given them the land due for their long service.

Most of the men from Dál Riata had returned to their homeland. But the handful that remained, including the warrior, were among Oswald's most faithful and trusted men. In that respect, they were like the men who came together at the behest of King Mynyddog Mwynfawr of the Gododdin. Warriors from far and wide, the king feasted them for a year until they rode forth to do battle with the king's foes. Their defeat was memorialised in *Y Gododdin*, an elegy that also tells us that warriors from different nationalities and tribes could band together in pursuit of honour, spoil and fame. While many were mercenaries in the literal sense, they were also honour-bound and oath-bound.

For the little boy, the warrior's son, it must have been quite an adventure: they were going beyond the seas and hills of his life, riding east to the rising of the sun. Maybe the boy was the eldest; he was certainly a favourite. We can imagine him importuning his father to let him ride with him, and the warrior reaching down and pulling the boy, laughing, up on to his horse, the two together riding at the front of the column of men, wagons and horses.

The geography of Northumbria is quite different from that of Dál Riata. The inland hills, the Cheviots, were already largely denuded of trees by the early medieval period. The pastoralists of the Neolithic had proved the efficacy of stone axes by chopping down most of the trees while the flocks they pastured on the bare hills ensured they stayed that way, chewing the top off any seedling, whereas the long ridged peninsulas that poked into the Irish Sea were thickly wooded, with agriculture confined to small pockets of level ground, where the trees were cleared and oats and barley sown. So the little boy, perched in front of his father, looked with wonder at the bare ridgeback of The Cheviot, highest of the hills, and the smooth cone of Hedgehope, before they came in sight of the double hump of Yeavering Bell and the salmon-pink necklace of stone that ringed both summits. In the hill's lee, they saw and heard the whirr of work: many men had set to, rebuilding Ad Gefrin, the palace of the kings, which Cadwallon had fired and Oswald had ordered rebuilt.

There is something strange about the age distribution of burials in early Medieval Britain: there are very few infants among the inhumations. If the proportion of infant burials accurately reflects the mortality rate of babies and young children at the time, then early Medieval Britain had a remarkably low infant mortality rate. Though it would have been wonderful for the people of the time if this were true, the paucity of infant burials is not likely to accurately represent infant mortality rates. As it is, inhumations from early Medieval Britain are skewed towards higher-status individuals, as is the case with the Bowl Hole, for example. It seems that the rural, crop-raising population buried their dead either in a more spread out manner, or that the settlements of early medieval farmers have been seldom found and less often excavated.

Still, the relative paucity of infant burials suggests that babies were buried in other places rather than a cemetery such as the Bowl Hole. The most likely possibility is that they were interred near the home of their parents. There is also a preservation bias with respect to the remains of babies. Neonatal skeletons are fragile and the unfused bones and plates do not survive nearly as well as adult bones. When they do survive, they can sometimes be mistaken for rabbit bones or otherwise missed. In the Iron Age, dead babies were often buried in the foundations of the house, presumably to keep the essence of the child with the family.

However, the warrior's son was a baby no longer. Father doted on son, and the son looked up to his father. He wanted to be a brave warrior like his father. But he did not live to be a warrior. The boy was four when he died.

We do not know what the cause of death was but there was no shortage of possibilities: disease, accident, the culmination of a congenital problem. Any of these. It wasn't malnutrition though. The boy had food enough during his short life to grow healthy and strong. Just not strong enough. They buried him. His father and his mother buried him somewhere close, marking the grave, visiting it. Praying for him. He would stay four for ever.

Unlike modern burials, early medieval inhumations were put directly into the ground, without a coffin although they were often buried in shrouds. Even those buried in lintel graves were still open to the decomposition effects of the soil and its organisms. The body of the boy, being small and light, decomposed faster than an adult's body. From twenty-four days after burial the remains of the body enter what is called the dry stage, when all that is left are mainly bones, cartilage and dry skin.

His parents mourned him. They visited the place where they had buried him – most probably it was somewhere near their home – but it was scarely unusual. Life had to go on. But for the warrior, it did not go on for much longer. According to the carbon-14 dating of his remains, he died in AD 635. There is a range of probability about this date: going strictly by the carbon-14 test, it could have been in a range of years either side of that date. But from historical factors, we can probably rule out a burial before 634, when Oswald returned with his warband to reclaim the throne of Northumbria. While it would be conceivable that a Dál Riatan visitor came to Bamburgh during Eanfrith's short reign, or even during the chaotic years after Edwin lost the Battle of Hatfield Chase and Cadwallon ravaged the kingdom, it seems highly unlikely that such a warrior would arrive with a young son, wait around long enough for the boy to die, be buried, then die himself and for the remaining, grieving family members to exhume the body of the beloved son and inter them with his father. Such a scenario requires a much more settled and secure landscape. So we can say with some confidence that the warrior died in 635 or afterwards, but it's very unlikely he died before.

What killed him? We don't know. The warrior's remains are those of a healthy, strong individual. The general morphology of the skeleton showed that he was a warrior. Well-developed muscles require firmer attachment to the bones and this was shown in his remains. He was probably in his late twenties, possibly early thirties, when he died. Unlike the other warrior, the man who was cut diagonally through from collarbone to waist whom Paul excavated nearby there is no indication on the skeleton as to the cause of death. While a sword or axe blow might, as in the case of the other warrior, cause identifiable damage to bones, it was equally possible to die from bleeding out or simply an infection getting into a wound.

There are no records of major battles around Bamburgh in 635, nor indeed of any battles. Given the difficulty of transporting a dead body long distances, it's very likely that the warrior died somewhere close to Bamburgh, with his body being brought to the Bowl Hole cemetery for burial shortly after his death. While he had been a strong and healthy man, disease still killed many strong and, previously, healthy individuals. So in the absence of any signs of physical trauma, the most likely explanation for his death is that he fell ill and died.

Because so many of the burials at the Bowl Hole are of non-local individuals, the cemetery seems to have been specially reserved for the inhumation of strangers: Bamburgh being the chief stronghold of the Idings, it received more visitors than other places. The burial of the warrior in a lintel grave markedly similar to the lintel graves excavated at Whithorn in Dál Riata is further evidence that he was from Dál Riata and, what's more, that there were enough Dál Riatans at Bamburgh to arrange for his burial to be done according to their customs. This also implies that the warrior was not the only Dál Riatan companion of Oswald to remain in Northumbria after the battle. While we know that Aidan set up the mission on Lindisfarne, bringing monks from Iona to help him with that, the warrior's burial indicates the presence of secular Dál Riatan companions to Oswald, and that they remained with him after the battle, perhaps settling in Northumbria.

They buried the warrior in sight of the sea, his feet pointing east. They put with him, into the grave, a seax, the characteristic knife of the Anglo-Saxons. It was an everyday implement, used for almost everything, so perhaps it was simply part of his funeral outfit, his grave clothes. But what is interesting is that this warrior of Dál Riata was buried with the most characteristic of Anglo-Saxon weapons. As a Christian, the warrior was buried simply, without the grave goods that often accompanied pagan burials. But someone put a seax in the grave with him. While this is no more than a supposition, perhaps the seax was a gift to him from Oswald, the Anglo-Saxon ætheling for whom he had fought, for whom he had left his home and settled in a foreign land. Perhaps the king took the seax from his own belt and gave it, a final gift, to the warrior who had given so much for him. Then they covered the body, shovelling the mound of earth and sand that had been dug out earlier back on top of the corpse, mixing it so thoroughly that 1,364 years later the mixture would give the clue to the BRP archaeologists that there was a burial beneath the ground.

Either at the time of the burial or a short time later, some of the burial party returned. They had with them a bag of remains: what was left of the warrior's four-year-old son. They carefully dug down, mixing up the sand and soil even more thoroughly, until they had reached the level where the warrior was buried. There, they put the remains of his son, placing them between his knees. They did that so that when the final day dawned, father and son would stand together, and together they would see the dawn.

Then they covered them, joining father to son in the grave and in death.

They must have loved them both dearly, the people who remained and who did this for them. We don't know their names but even all these centuries later we can still feel their love and their loss, their helplessness before death's blank denial, their helplessness but also their quiet hope.

History is the tale of kings and emperors, warriors and saints. In that tale, particularly in the obscure, barely documented centuries after the legions left, what history we do have is almost all to do with kings and warlords, saints and bishops. But they played out the story against the background of, and with the support of, uncounted numbers of people who are completely lost to us. Oswald, the king from over the sea, the king who came back, could only come back because of the men who came with him. The warrior was one of those men.

Oswald did not reign for long compared with the king before
him and the king after him. Edwin ruled for sixteen years,
from 616 to 632. Oswiu, Oswald's younger brother, ruled from
642 to 670 or 671, a reign of nearly thirty years. In between
them both, Oswald sat upon the throne of Northumbria for a
mere eight years. His reign came to an end in the manner that
was standard at the time: he died on the battlefield, defeated by King Penda of Mercia, Cadwallon's ally in the defeat of
Edwin. King Penda was the last great pagan king in Britain. In
the thirteen years between his defeat of Oswald and the Battle
of the River Winwæd in 655, Penda appeared able to defeat
and depose kings almost at will, disposing of three kings of
East Anglia as well as driving the king of Wessex into exile and
raiding up into Northumbria as far as Bamburgh.

But during this time, what Oswald had put together during
his reign did not fall apart. For the first time in early Medieval
Britain, key parts of a realm survived the death of its leader, its founder, its protector. The fissiparous tendencies of
the two constituent kingdoms of Northumbria did split them
apart again, but Oswiu remained king of Bernicia and eventually regained rule in Deira, through the sort of cold-blooded
ruthlessness that Bede could not approve of but which was,
no doubt, fairly common conduct among kings. But the fledg-
ling institutions that Oswald had helped to create survived his
death – even his death at the hands of a pagan warlord.

The monastic institutions and churches that Aidan had
founded in Northumbria did not waver and their monks and
clergy did not flee. Nor was there the mass apostasy that followed Edwin's death: the converted nobility of Northumbria,
in both Bernicia and Deira, remained Christian despite the

failure of the Christian God to look after his own champion in battle against Penda. The ability of the new religion to absorb this shock was predicated on the continued presence of the monks who preached it and lived it, and the reputation that Oswald's relics swiftly received for being miraculous. Indeed, Bede devotes considerably more space in his history to the miracles wrought by Oswald and his relics than he does to the actions of the man while alive: but then, this is a useful insight into the mindset of the time. Although dead, Oswald was still alive, rendering service and protection to his people.

Oswald died in battle near Oswestry in Shropshire, on the borders between Mercia and the kingdoms of the Britons. Quite what he was doing there we do not know: he was a long way from home in the heart of enemy territory. Penda dismembered his body. Cutting off Oswald's head and arms, he hung them on display on a tree, most probably a tree sacred to Woden. But even in the immediate aftermath of Oswald's defeat and death, stories started circulating of the miraculous powers of the soil where his blood was spilled. People started collecting it, putting it in bags and taking it home to give to sick relatives.

For Aidan and the monks of Lindisfarne, Oswald's death should have been a disaster. But by commending Oswald as a martyr and, now, a heavenly protector, they made over an earthly catastrophe into part of the divine plan: Saint Oswald was more powerful and more protecting than King Oswald. Indeed, so quickly did Oswald's reputation for sanctity spread that one of the first acts of his younger brother, Oswiu, on taking the throne of Bernicia was to lead an extremely risky raid to Mercia in order to recover his brother's remains. He must have moved very fast to go so deep into Mercia and get out again, with Oswald's head and arms, before Penda could catch up with him. Oswiu may have also needed to recover his brother's remains to shore up his own position as king, as well as extinguishing the family disgrace of having his brother on display at a pagan shrine.

The cult of Oswald grew rapidly, spreading to the continent, so that he became one of the most widely revered early medieval saints, his name particularly invoked wherever the next generation of Northumbrian monks, who worked tirelessly towards the conversion of their pagan cousins in Germany, built monasteries and churches. Thus while Penda continued to remove kings from their thrones over the next decade, the spread of Christianity among the royal houses of Britain widened. When, in 655, Penda suffered the same sort of catastrophic reverse that Edwin and Oswald had suffered before him, dying in battle against Oswiu at the Battle of Winwæd, he died as the last great champion of Anglo-Saxon paganism. It turned out that the war of religions was won by the losers. In that victory, in the wresting of a society towards a civilisation that could endure past the death of its leader, the crucial figure was Oswald. But he would never have achieved what he did save for the help of men such as our warrior, who followed him for friendship and love, who fought and died for the return of the king.

17

. . . Known unto God

There are boxes lining the shelves of storerooms in museums and universities throughout Britain. Thousands of boxes. If you should take one down and examine its contents, you would find labelled plastic bags and in those bags: bones. The spoil of hundreds, if not thousands of excavations, lie on shelves tucked away in basements and annexes. Some are waiting for analysis but, more often, they have already been examined, yielding up to the osteoarchaeologists the secrets they had to share. Now, they just wait.

Paul and Graeme and the other archaeologists of the Bamburgh Research Project were determined that this would not happen with the people they had excavated from the Bowl Hole. For they were people, not finds or remains or skeletons. On various occasions, excavating archaeologists have affected a nonchalant disregard for the dignity of the dead they are excavating: there has been more than one photo of a pair of sunglasses perched on a newly exposed skull. As far as Paul and Graeme were concerned, anyone who treated a find like that would be off site faster than a dropped trowel. Soon, this attitude spread through all the staff and was inculcated, by example and speech, to all the many people who came to dig at Bamburgh over the years: they would no more disrespect the dead than they would fail to lay a grid over a trench.

Their original plan was to rebury the warrior, and all the other bodies excavated, back in their original plots in the Bowl Hole cemetery. However, since the ground there was eroding fairly rapidly, they knew they would have to dig the new graves considerably deeper, otherwise the bodies would eventually be exposed to the elements. This plan presented some difficulties, not least the maze of permissions that would have to be navigated in order to bring it about: a burial licence from the Ministry of Justice, authorisation from Natural England, the custodians of the SSSI where the Bowl Hole is located, to dig there again, and agreement from Bamburgh Castle management. Not impossible but time consuming, particularly since there is no recognised system for reburying excavated bodies in the ground.

So when one of the trustees of St Aidan's Church in Bamburgh mentioned to Graeme that they had an unused crypt that could serve as the resting place for the people excavated from the Bowl Hole, it seemed like an ideal solution. While the present church was built between 1170 and 1230, with later additions, it contains a wooden beam over the font that serves no structural purpose. According to local tradition, the beam is a relic from the church that Aidan founded on the same site in the seventh century. It is said to be the beam that Aidan was leaning against when he died. The parish priest of St Aidan's, Canon Reverend Brian Hurst, immediately supported the idea. After all, as he said, they are our people, we'll look after them in our church.

So on Friday 24 June 2016, a slow procession wended its way from Bamburgh Castle through the village to St Aidan's Church. The charnel boxes containing the remains of the 110 people excavated from the Bowl Hole were carried in a horse-drawn hearse with a funeral cortège consisting of villagers, castle workers and almost everybody who had been involved in excavating the bodies. They all came back to Bamburgh to be present as the people were laid to rest. Some came from the other ends of the country; some came from abroad. But they all came. Even though many of the excavators were not religious, they came to share in the religion of the people whom they had brought out of the earth, to join in their reinterment.

At the entrance to the church, the bearers of the bones were met by Canon Reverend Hurst and the Venerable Peter Robinson, archdeacon of Lindisfarne, who together conducted the committal service as the remains of people who lived and died 1,300 years ago were placed in the crypt that would serve as an ossuary for them. Each person's remains had been placed into individual charnel boxes made of zinc; these were then put into the ossuary and, the committal service completed, the remains were made secure by the closing of a knotwork iron grille forged by a local blacksmith, Stephen Lunn. As Canon Reverend Hurst said, 'It seems very fitting that these individuals have found their final resting place in the crypt of St Aidan's Church – they who may have known King Oswald and his gentle bishop, Aidan – they who would have known a church on this site and may have known that here it was that Aidan died. It is almost as if the crypt has been waiting for them to come and offer them this peaceful resting space.'

Seeing the warrior and his son laid to rest in a place where they would be content was, for Paul, the confirmation of the vow he had made when the thunder broke the sky and he had stood alone in a trench with a dead man at his feet. He had vowed then, to the gods of thunder and of archaeology, that he would look after him. Now, as the warrior was placed in the waiting dark of the crypt of Aidan's church, a man the warrior would have known, Paul knew the vow was fulfilled. The warrior, the son of Thunder, might rest in peace, with his boy beside him, until the earth beneath them passes away.

Notes

2 The Sword and the Archaeologist

1   https://thehistoryofengland.co.uk/resource/selected-laws-of-ine-688-695/

3 Iona

1   Adomnán of Iona, *Life of St Columba*, Penguin, London, 1995, p.177.

2   Adomnán of Iona, *Life of St Columba*, Penguin, London, 1995, pp.233–4.

3   Adomnán of Iona, *Life of St Columba*, Penguin, London, 1995, p.234.

4   https://www.e-codices.unifr.ch/en/sbs/0001/

5   Adomnán of Iona, *Life of St Columba*, Penguin, London, 1995, p.106.

4 Italians Abroad

1   Bede, *Ecclesiastical History of the English People*, Penguin, London, 1990, p.108.

2   Bede, *Ecclesiastical History of the English People*, Penguin, London, 1990, p.128.

3   Bede, *Ecclesiastical History of the English People*, Penguin, London, 1990, p.107.

4   Bede, *Ecclesiastical History of the English People*, Penguin, London, 1990, p.128.

6 New Gods

1   Bede, *Ecclesiastical History of the English People*, Penguin, London, 1990, p.127.

2   Bede, *Ecclesiastical History of the English People*, Penguin, London, 1990, p.135.

3   Bede, *Ecclesiastical History of the English People*, Penguin, London, 1990, pp.129–30.

4   Bede, *Ecclesiastical History of the English People*, Penguin, London, 1990, p.92.

5   Bede, *Ecclesiastical History of the English People*, Penguin, London, 1990, p.134.

7 Does it All Mean Anything?

1   Clinger, Janet, *Our Elders: Six Bay Area Life Stories*, Xlibris, Bloomington, 2005.

8 The Sea Kingdom

1   Adomnán of Iona, *Life of St Columba*, Penguin, London, 1995, pp.120–21.

10 To Take Back What is Ours

1   Marsden, John, *Northanhymbre Saga: The History of the Anglo-Saxon kings of Northumbria*, BCA, London, 1992, p.82.

2   Bromwich, Rachel, *Trioedd Ynys Prydein: The Triads of the Island of Britain*, University of Wales Press, Cardiff, 2017, Kindle edition.

3   Bromwich, Rachel, *Trioedd Ynys Prydein: The Triads of the Island of Britain*, University of Wales Press, Cardiff, 2017, Kindle edition.

4   Bromwich, Rachel, *Trioedd Ynys Prydein: The Triads of the Island of Britain*, University of Wales Press, Cardiff, 2017, Kindle edition.

5   Bede, *Ecclesiastical History of the English People*, Penguin, London, 1990, p.140.

6   Bede, *Ecclesiastical History of the English People*, Penguin, Harmondsworth, 1990, p.129. Reproduced by permission of Penguin Books Ltd.

7   O'Brien, Colm, 'The Great Enclosure' in *Yeavering: People, Power & Place*, edited by Frodsham, Paul and O'Brien, Colm, The History Press, Stroud, 2015, p.148.

13 The Return of the King

1   Jackson, K. H., *The Gododdin: The Oldest Scottish Poem*, Edinburgh University Press, Edinburgh, 1969, p.98.

2   Taken from *The Four Books of Ancient Wales*, translated by William Skene; accessed here: https://books.google.co.uk/books?id=DmNlDwAAQBAJ

3   Adomnán of Iona, *Life of St Columba*, Penguin, London, 1995, pp.110–11.

4   Bede, *Ecclesiastical History of the English People*, Penguin, London, 1990, p.144.

5   Bede, *Ecclesiastical History of the English People*, Penguin, London, 1990, p.145.

14 Battle

1   Bede, *Ecclesiastical History of the English People*, Penguin, London, 1990, p.144.

2   Corfe, T., 'The Battle of Heavenfield', *Hexham Historian*, 7, 1997, pp.65–86.

3   https://books.google.co.uk/books?id=EnEBAAAAQAAJ&pg

15 To the Victor

1   Bede, *Ecclesiastical History of the English People*, Penguin, London, 1990, p.151.

2   Bede, *Ecclesiastical History of the English People*, Penguin, London, 1990, p.151.

3   Bede, *Ecclesiastical History of the English People*, Penguin, London, 1995, p.166.

4   Bede, *Ecclesiastical History of the English People*, Penguin, London, 1995, p.167.

Select Bibliography

Abels, Richard P. (1988). *Lordship and Military Obligation in Anglo-Saxon England.* London: British Museum Publications.

Adams, Max (2013). *The King in the North.* London: Head of Zeus.

Adams, Max (2015). *In the Land of Giants: Journeys through the Dark Ages.* London: Head of Zeus.

Adomnán of Iona (1995). *Life of St Columba.* Harmondsworth, Middlesex: Penguin Books.

Alexander, Michael (translator) (1977). *The Earliest English Poems.* Harmondsworth, Middlesex: Penguin Books.

Anonymous (1998). *The Anonymous History of Abbot Ceolfrith.* In Webb, J. F. and Farmer, D. H. (1998). *The Age of Bede.* London: Penguin Books.

Anonymous (1998). *The Voyage of St Brendan.* In Webb, J. F. and Farmer, D. H. (1998). *The Age of Bede.* London: Penguin Books.

Arwidsson, Greta and Berg, Gosta (1983). *The Mästermyr Find: A Viking Age Tool Chest from Gotland.* Lompoc, California: Larson.

Backhouse, Janet (2010). *The Lindisfarne Gospels.* Oxford: Phaidon Press.

Bayley, Justine (1992). *Anglo-Scandinavian Non-Ferrous Metalworking from 16-22 Coppergate.* York: University of York Press.

Bede (1990). *Ecclesiastical History of the English People.* London: Penguin Books.

Bede (1998). *Life of Cuthbert.* In Webb, J. F. and Farmer, D. H. (1998). *The Age of Bede.* London: Penguin Books.

Bede (1998). *Lives of the Abbots of Wearmouth and Jarrow.* In Webb, J. F. and Farmer, D. H. (1998). *The Age of Bede.* London: Penguin Books.

Blair, John (2000). *The Anglo-Saxon Age: A Very Short Introduction.* Oxford: Oxford University Press.

Blair, Peter Hunter (1976). *Northumbria in the Days of Bede.* London: Victor Gollancz.

Blair, Peter Hunter (1977). *An Introduction to Anglo-Saxon England.* Cambridge: Cambridge University Press.

Blair, Peter Hunter (1990). *The World of Bede.* Cambridge: Cambridge University Press.

Brøndsted, Johannes (1965). *The Vikings.* Harmondsworth, Middlesex: Penguin Books.

Bromwich, Rachel (2017). *Trioedd Ynys Prydein: The Triads of the Island of Britain.* Cardiff: University of Wales Press.

Brooks, Nicholas (1984). *The Early History of the Church of Canterbury.* Leicester: Leicester University Press.

Brown, Peter (1989). *The World of Late Antiquity: AD 150–750.* London: Thames & Hudson.

Brown, Peter (2013). *The Rise of Western Christendom: Triumph and Diversity A.D. 200–1000.* London: John Wiley & Sons.

Brown, Terry (2006). *English Martial Arts.* Ely: Anglo-Saxon Books.

Campbell, James (1982). *The Anglo-Saxons.* Oxford: Phaidon Press.

Campbell, James (2000). *The Anglo-Saxon State.* London: Hambledon and London.

Clinger, Janet (2005). *Our Elders: Six Bay Area Life Stories.* Bloomington, Indiana: Xlibris.

Carman, John and Harding, Anthony (1999). *Ancient Warfare.* Stroud: Sutton Publishing.

Carver, Martin (1998). *Sutton Hoo. Burial Ground of Kings?* London: British Museum Press.

Charles-Edwards, T. M. (2013). *Wales and the Britons 350–1064.* Oxford: Oxford University Press.

Clarkson, Tim (2017). *The Picts: A History.* Edinburgh: Birlinn.

Corfe, T. (1997). 'The Battle of Heavenfield', *Hexham Historian,* 7.

Crawford, Sally (2009). *Daily Life in Anglo-Saxon England.* Oxford: Greenwood World Publishing.

Crocker, Richard and Hiley, David (eds) (1990). *The New Oxford History of Music: The Early Middle Ages to 1300*. Oxford: Oxford University Press.

Crumplin, Sally (2004). *Rewriting History in the Cult of St Cuthbert from the Ninth to the Twelfth Centuries*. St Andrew's University thesis.

Davidson, H. E. (1998). *The Sword in Anglo-Saxon England*. Woodbridge: Boydell.

DeGregorio, Scott (ed.) (2010). *The Cambridge Companion to Bede*. Cambridge: Cambridge University Press.

Dickinson, T. and Harke, H. (1992). *Early Anglo-Saxon Shields*. The Society of Antiquities of London.

Dunn, Marilyn (2009). *The Christianization of the Anglo-Saxons c.597–c.700*. London: Continuum.

Eddius Stephanus (1998). *Life of Wilfrid*. In Webb, J. F. and Farmer, D. H. (1998). *The Age of Bede*. London: Penguin Books.

Evans, A. C. (2008). *Sutton Hoo Ship Burial*. London: British Museum Press.

Fletcher, Richard (1998). *The Barbarian Conversion from Paganism to Christianity*. New York: Henry Holt.

Foster, Sally M. (2014). *Picts, Gaels and Scots*. Edinburgh: Birlinn.

Fraser, James E. (2009). *From Caledonia to Pictland: Scotland to 795*. Edinburgh: Edinburgh University Press.

Frodsham, Paul and O'Brien, Colm (eds) (2015). *Yeavering: People, Power & Place*. Stroud: The History Press.

Geoffrey of Monmouth (1966). *The History of the Kings of Britain*. London: Penguin Books.

Gething, Paul and Albert, Edoardo (2012). *Northumbria: The Lost Kingdom*. Stroud: The History Press.

Gildas (2009). *On the Ruin of Britain*. Rockville: Serenity Publishers.

Groves S.E., Roberts C.A., Lucy S., Pearson G., Nowell G., Macpherson C.G., Gröcke D., Young G. (2013). 'Mobility Histories of 7th–9th Century AD People Buried at Early Medieval Bamburgh, Northumberland, England'. *American J Physical Anthropology* 151(3): 462–476.

Groves, S.E. (2010). 'The Bowl Hole Burial Ground; A Late Anglian Cemetery in Northumberland'. In J. Buckberry and A. Cherryson (eds): *Burial in Later Anglo-Saxon England, c.650 to 1100AD.* 114–125. Oxford: Oxbow Books.

Groves, S.E. (2011). 'Social and Biological Status in the Bowl Hole Early Medieval burial ground, Bamburgh, Northumberland'. In D. Petts, S. Turner (eds): *Early Medieval Northumbria.* Turnhout, Belgium: Brepols

Haywood, John (2006). *Dark Age Naval Power: Frankish and Anglo-Saxon Seafaring Activity.* Hockwold-cum-Wilton: Anglo-Saxon Books.

Hawthorne, J. G. and Smith, C. S. (1979). *Theophilus On Divers Arts.* New York: Dover Publications.

Higham, N. J. (1993). *The Kingdom of Northumbria AD 350–1100.* Stroud: Sutton Publishing.

Higham, N. J. (1994). *The English Conquest: Gildas and Britain in the Fifth Century.* Manchester: Manchester University Press.

Higham, N. J. (1995). *An English Empire: Bede, the Britons and the Anglo-Saxon Kings.* Manchester: Manchester University Press.

Higham, N. J. (1997). *The Convert Kings: Power and Religious Affiliation in Early Anglo-Saxon England.* Manchester: Manchester University Press.

Higham, Nicholas J. and Ryan, Martin (2013). *The Anglo-Saxon World.* New Haven: Yale University Press.

Higham, N. J. (2015). *Ecgfrith: King of the Northumbrians, High-King of Britain.* Donnington: Shaun Tyas.

Hill, David (1981). *An Atlas of Anglo-Saxon England.* Oxford: Blackwell.

Hill, Paul (2012). *The Anglo-Saxons at War 800-1066.* Barnsley: Pen & Sword Books.

Hindley, Geoffrey (2006). *A Brief History of the Anglo-Saxons.* London: Robinson.

Hope-Taylor, B. (1977). *Yeavering: An Anglo-British centre of early Northumbria.* London: English Heritage.

Ingram, Rev. James (translator) (1912). *The Anglo-Saxon Chronicle.* London: Everyman Press. Online at http://www.britannia.com/history/docs/asintro2.html (last accessed 27 February 2019).

Jackson, K. H. (1969). *The Gododdin: The Oldest Scottish Poem.* Edinburgh: Edinburgh University Press.

Johnston, Bob (2004). *Dalriada: The Land that Scotland Forgot.* Isle of Gigha: Ardminish Press.

Kirby, D. P. (2000). *The Earliest English Kings*. London: Routledge.

Lang, Janet (2007). *The Rise and Fall of Pattern Welding: An Investigation into the Construction of Pre-Medieval Sword Blades*. University of Reading thesis.

Lapidge, Michael, Blair, John, Keynes, Simon and Scragg, Donald (eds) (2001). *The Blackwell Encyclopaedia of Anglo-Saxon England*. Oxford: Blackwell Publishing.

Leahy, Kevin. (2010). *Anglo-Saxon Crafts*. Stroud: The History Press.

Leahy, Kevin and Bland, Roger (2009). *The Staffordshire Hoard*. London: British Museum Press.

Lucy, Sam (2000). *The Anglo-Saxon Way of Death*. Stroud: Sutton Publishing.

Magennis, Hugh (1999). *Anglo-Saxon Appetites*. Dublin: Four Courts Press.

Marren, Peter (2009). *Battles of the Dark Ages*. Barnsley: Pen & Sword Books.

Marsden, John (1992). *Northanhymbre Saga: The History of the Anglo-Saxon kings of Northumbria*. London: BCA.

Mayr-Harting, Henry (1991). *The Coming of Christianity to Anglo-Saxon England*. London: B. T. Batsford Ltd.

Moffat, Alistair (2001). *The Sea Kingdoms*. London: Harper Collins.

Moffat, Alistair (2013). *The British: A Genetic Journey*. Edinburgh: Birlinn.

MoLAS (2004). *The Prittlewell Prince*. London: Museum of London.

Nennius (2008). *History of the Britons*. USA: Book Jungle.

O'Brien, Colm (2015). 'The Great Enclosure' in *Yeavering: People, Power & Place*, edited by Frodsham, Paul and O'Brien, Colm. Stroud: The History Press.

Oswald, Al, Ainsworth, Stewart and Pearson, Trevor (2006). *Hillforts: Prehistoric Strongholds of Northumberland National Park*. Swindon: English Heritage.

Ottaway, Patrick (1992). *Anglo-Scandinavian Iron Work from 16–22 Coppergate, York: c.850–1100 A.D.* York: University of York Press.

Pierce, Ian (2005). *Swords of the Viking Age*. Woodbridge: Boydell.

Pirie, Elizabeth, J. E. (2000). *Thrymsas, Sceattas and Stycas of Northumbria*. Llanfyllin: Galata Print.

Pollington, Stephen (1996). *The English Warrior from Earliest Times to 1066*. Ely: Anglo-Saxon Books.

Renfrew, Colin and Bahn, Paul (1996). *Archaeology: Theories, Methods and Practice*. London: Thames & Hudson.

Reynolds, Andrew (2009). *Anglo-Saxon Deviant Burial Customs*. Oxford: Oxford University Press.

Robertson, A.J. (1956). *Anglo-Saxon Charters*. Cambridge: Cambridge University Press.

Rollason, David (2003). *Northumbria, 500–1100: Creation and Destruction of a Kingdom*. Cambridge: Cambridge University Press.

Rowland, T. H. (1987). *Medieval Castles, Towers, Peles and Bastles of Northumberland*. Warkworth: Sandhill Press.

Rushton, Sara et al. (eds) (n.d.) *Bamburgh: Archaeology in Northumberland: Discovery Series 1*. Northumberland: Northumberland County Council.

Sawyer, Peter (2013). *The Wealth of Anglo-Saxon England*. Oxford: Oxford University Press.

Siddorn, Kim J. (2000). *Viking Weapons and Warfare*. Stroud: Tempus Publishing.

Smith, Scott Thompson (2007). *Writing Land in Anglo-Saxon England*. University of Notre Dame, Indiana, thesis.

Stancliffe, Clare and Cambridge, Eric (eds) (1995). *Oswald: Northumbrian King to European Saint*. Stamford: Paul Watkins.

Stenton, Frank (2001). *Anglo-Saxon England*. Oxford: Oxford University Press.

Stephenson, I. P. (2002). *The Anglo-Saxon Shield*. Stroud: Tempus Publishing.

Theophilus (1980). *On Divers Arts*. New York: Dover Publications.

Tweddle, Dominic (1992). *The Anglian Helmet from Coppergate*. York Archaeological Trust.

Underwood, Richard (1999). *Anglo-Saxon Weapons and Warfare*. Stroud: Tempus Publishing.

Waddington, Clive (1999). *Land of Legend: Discovering ancient Northumberland*. Milfield, Wooler: Country Store Publishing.

Waddington, Clive (2001). *Maelmin: An Archaeological Guide*. Milfield, Wooler: Country Store Publishing.

Ward-Perkins, Bryan (2005). *The Fall of Rome and the End of Civilization*. Oxford: Oxford University Press.

Watkins, Ann E. (translator) (n.d.) *Aelfric's Colloquy*. http://www.

kentarchaeology.ac/authors/016.pdf. (Last accessed 27 February 2019.)

Webb, J. F. and Farmer, D. H. (1998). *The Age of Bede*. London: Penguin Books.

Welch, Martin (1992). *English Heritage Book of Anglo-Saxon England*. London: BCA.

Whitelock, Dorothy (1979). *English Historical Documents; volume 1, 500–1041*. London: Eyre & Spottiswoode.

Wickham, Chris (2009). *The Inheritance of Rome*. London: Penguin Books.

Williams, Allan (2011). *Estudio Metalurgic De Algunas Espadas Vikingas*. Gladius PDF.

Wood, Michael (2003). *In Search of the Dark Ages*. London: BBC Worldwide Ltd.

Young, Graeme (2003). *Bamburgh Castle: The Archaeology of the Fortress of Bamburgh AD 500 to AD 1500*. Bamburgh: Bamburgh Research Project.

Acknowledgements

No book is written alone. Since this one was written by two of us, we're making no secret of that fact, but the writing and the research and the help required to turn an idea into this book extended far beyond the people credited on the cover.

In the beginning was the dig. Without all the people who have dug with the Bamburgh Research Project in the twenty plus years that it has been excavating in and around Bamburgh the Warrior would still be lying in the Bowl Hole and we would know much less about the kingdom of Northumbria. Graeme Young, whose idea to dig at Bamburgh it was in the first place, has been there from the start, co-director of the Project with Paul. Rosie Whitbread and Phil Wood were the other members of the original quadrivium: without their work, inspiration and trowels the BRP would never have been anything more than an unrealised idea. David and Margaret Whitbread provided invaluable financial, moral and culinary support in the early years of the dig.

The Armstrong family, initially Lady Armstrong and more recently Francis Armstrong, have been unfailingly generous and kind in allowing a bunch of archaeologists to dig holes in their property. The staff at the Castle have put up with twenty years of disruption with good cheer and genuine interest at what's been discovered beneath their feet.

At Granta, we have been blessed with two contrasting but wonderful editors: Max Porter, whose enthusiasm for the project swept it past every obstacle and whose editing skills guided the book unerringly towards its proper end; and Bella Lacey, whose calm and thoughtful support has ensured we have steered through the nervous shoals that surround publication. All the staff at Granta have been great: we were delighted to be the occasion for the first works' outing, when we took everyone (yes, everyone) around the extraordinary Anglo-Saxon Kingdoms exhibition at the British Library.

Our agent, Robert Dudley, is the epitome of what anyone might hope for from an agent: supportive, insightful and a really good negotiator. Thank you, Robert.

Our families have put up with us disappearing into the past for extended periods of time with good grace and more support. I (Edoardo) must extend my particular thanks to my wife, Harriet, first reader and best critic, who stopped me cold when I was heading full steam down the wrong siding with the book and put me back on track. My sons, Theo, Matthew and Isaac, have all been willing participants in re-enactments of the tactics of the shield wall. My parents, Victor and Paola, came themselves from far away to settle in this country on the edge of the world: strangers here, they made a home for me and my brother, Steven, and inculcated my love of reading. Thank you all.

For my part (Paul) I owe a huge debt of gratitude to my wife, Rosie. She is my inspiration, my motivation and my equilibrium. I need to thank my kids, Freya, Alexander and Cuthbert for their forbearance and grounding mockery. And finally, my mother, Jean. Without her initial bravery I would be just another mote, floating on the ocean of what might have been.

Index